MAKE MONEY,
Not Excuses

MAKE MONEY,
Not Excuses

Wake Up, Take Charge,

and Overcome Your Financial Fears Forever

JEAN CHATZKY

CROWN
BUSINESS
NEW YORK

Library of Congress Cataloging-in-Publication Data
Chatzky, Jean Sherman, 1964–
Make money, not excuses : wake up, take charge, and overcome your financial fears forever /
Jean Chatzky.—1st ed.
1. Women—Finance, Personal.   I. Title.
HG179.C5357   2006
332.024'01082–dc22   2006015158

ISBN-13: 978-0-307-34152-5
ISBN-10: 0-307-34152-6

Printed in the United States of America

Design by Robert Bull

10 9 8 7 6 5 4 3 2 1

First Edition

This book is for my mother, with love and admiration.

$$$$$$$$$$$$ CONTENTS $$$$$$$$$$$$

Why Aren't You Richer?

I t took me only fifteen years reporting on money and how people should be using it to have the following epiphany: If you want to get rich, if you want to be wealthier than you are today, you really need to do only four things. That's right, just *four* things:

- *You need to make a decent living.*
- *You need to spend less than you make.*
- *You need to invest the money you don't spend so that it can work as hard for you as you're working for yourself.*
- *And you need to protect yourself and this financial world you've built so that a disaster–big or small–doesn't take it all away from you.*

Everything else is just window dressing. The fees—and how to avoid them. The advisers—and how to hire them. The deals. The scams. The ins. The outs. They are all interesting. Some of them are even quite important. But until you have conquered the heart of the matter, they are all minutia.

The four cornerstones, by contrast, are the meat and potatoes of your financial life. If you do those things today, you'll start getting rich tomorrow. And once you feel set financially, you'll be able to start focusing on the truly important things in life.

After I had my epiphany, I stood there for a little while. (Okay, I'll let you in on a little secret: I had my epiphany where I often have my best thoughts . . . in the shower.) As I let the hot water run out, I had little doubt that every woman, every person, in America wants a little more financial security and the independence it would bring. So the real question is, If it's so simple, why aren't we all richer?

And that's where, for women in particular, the answer is more complicated than the question. Most women in the country are far from rich. We've all heard the dismal statistics:

- *At retirement, a woman's average payout will be 56 percent less than a man's her age.*
- *Women lose roughly $650,000 in earnings, missed promotions, raises, and benefits as a result of caregiving to children and aging parents.*
- *For one in four women, Social Security is the only source of income.*
- *One-third more women than men live below the poverty level.*

You hear these numbers cited so often (yes, sometimes by me) that you'd be perfectly reasonable in thinking these are the *reasons* women aren't richer. But these are not *reasons*; these are *results*. These are examples of the things that happen because you and other women aren't as wealthy as you'd like to be.

The *reason* most women aren't richer—and the *reason* you aren't as rich as you'd like to be—is that you can't get out of your own way. That's right, *you* are a big part of the problem. You set up roadblocks that stop you on the way to wealth. You have a million excuses that prevent you from earning as much as you'd like, saving as much as you'd like, keeping as much as you'd like for the future. Have you, for instance, ever heard yourself or the other women in your life say . . .

"I'm just not good with money."

"I can't get up the nerve to ask for a raise."

"My husband (or partner) takes care of our finances."

"My husband doesn't want me managing our money."

"I'm going to buy those shoes. After all, you only live once."

"I can't find a financial adviser (or planner or broker or lawyer or accountant or insurance salesman) I trust."

"I don't have time to deal with my money."

"I'm not a numbers person."

"Organization isn't my strong suit."

"I hate paperwork."

"I shop. He saves."

"I'm afraid if I manage my money I'll lose it!"

"I don't know where to start."

"I can't talk about money."

"I can handle money, but investing is over my head."

"Managing money is too depressing (or intimidating or over-whelming or scary)."

"I'm single. I'll think about money when I get married."

"I'm young. I'll think about money when I get older."

"I'm too old to make a difference."

"I don't have enough money to make a difference."

"Managing money is boring."

"I'm not materialistic. I just don't care about money."

If you're sitting there rolling your eyes, cringing, or shaking your head because these excuses sound sooooo familiar, then you've come to the right place. Maybe you don't say them in exactly that way. Maybe you prefer to think them silently rather than saying them out loud. But you know exactly what I'm talking about. And the fact is, these words—these harmful, negative, demoralizing words and phrases—have to go.

Why?

Because these excuses allow us to believe it's okay that we don't know where to start. They give us the leeway to set off on what might very well be the right path, then get sidetracked. They let us off the hook when something big, even monumental, rocks our world and sends us all the way back to "Go."

I understand all of these reasons. I understand the excuses, too. In fact, for many years if they didn't come out of my mouth, they definitely wrapped their ugly little tentacles around my brain and prevented me from taking action. And I know—reading that—you probably think: No way.

But I also know that somewhere in San Francisco, a woman named Liz is nodding her head. She was my good friend in college and my roommate in Brooklyn when we were in our twenties. And she's the one who suffered when I didn't pay the phone bill or the cable bill and our service (on both) got turned off.

Liz knows. But I'm sure that those of you who see me on television and read me in magazines telling you what to do with your money think that I emerged from the womb this way, that my umbilical cord was a ticker tape, that my nursery was wallpapered with dollar bills. I wish that were the case. Nothing could be farther from the truth.

I went to college figuring I'd be a systems analyst or an engineer. I got a C in a programming class my freshman year and immediately became an English major. In my first job out of school, as an editorial assistant at *Working Woman* magazine, I earned all of $11,000 a year. That certainly wasn't much, but I earned a little extra writing freelance stories and tutoring kids for their SATs. My rent was only $400 a month. I should have been able to manage.

Instead, I did a terrible job. Not only did I neglect to pay my bills, but I racked up credit card debt equal to half a year's salary. I didn't understand the benefit of paying down my debt on that 18 percent credit card with money sitting in a savings account where it was earning an anemic 3 percent. (Liz, who worked at Citibank, explained that as well.)

I made other mistakes. I completely botched my first foray into a retirement account. I knew that I had this thing called a 401(k) into which my company and I made contributions that slowly added up to about $2,000. But I didn't understand very much else about how it worked. I let all the money sit in money market funds when the stock market was making its mid-1980s surge, for example. And I certainly didn't understand that when I left my job I had to roll the money into another retirement account—an IRA—or I'd be penalized and taxed. I wasn't even savvy enough to be dismayed when the rollover period lapsed and I got a check for the balance. I paid the taxes and bought a few new outfits with the rest.

Not surprisingly, I lived paycheck to paycheck. I had no desire to think about my money, much less *talk* about my money. Money was a nuisance, a problem, a worry, a strain.

So you won't be surprised to hear that when I got married a few years later, I was delighted to give up every bit of financial control. I had become a little better at earning money—doubling, then tripling my small salary—but I wanted nothing to do with it. I signed up to have my paychecks direct-deposited into our joint checking account and let my husband do the rest.

I told myself that because he earned substantially more than I did, he had the right to make all the decisions. I convinced myself that because he'd made one brilliant move—buying Microsoft when it was in its infancy—he had a better shot at building our wealth than I did. I assured myself that because I was reporting on money and finances all day at work, I knew plenty about both—so there was no need for me to *actually* deal with them at home. I even had myself believing that he *liked* paying the bills. (In retrospect, I realize it always made him cranky.) And I rationalized that I did other things—shopping, cooking—that were equally important to our growing family. We were on the health insurance policy from *my* employer. Wasn't it a fair trade that *he* fill out all the forms?

Eventually, though—and this took years—it started to bother me that I had no idea where the money was going. I had no idea how much we were spending. I had no idea how much we were saving. With the exception of my own 401(k), I had no idea how our investments were doing. I didn't know the online passwords that enabled my husband to pay our bills over the Internet. I'd never met the accountant who prepared our joint tax return.

Part of the reason it started to bother me, and I'm ashamed to admit that it took this to get me there (and because I'm ashamed to admit it, we'll explore this notion in greater detail in Chapter 3), is that my salary had grown to a point where it equaled his. I started to feel as if I deserved to know what was happening with our money. I started to feel that he needed to be as accountable to me as I was to him.

But by this point, it was a little late. Because I had ceased to pay attention, I was constantly worrying about money. Did we have enough? Enough to go on vacation? Enough to retire? Enough to send the kids to summer camp? Enough to eat out a few times a week? He said we did. But that didn't stop me from waking up in the middle of the night wondering if I'd put too much on the MasterCard or if we could really afford the bathroom renovation that was starting—gulp—tomorrow. Plus, by that time, my marriage was on its way to being over. I'm sure that realization played into my sleepless nights as well.

So I decided to grow up. I did it slowly, starting with the money-related decisions that were closest to my comfort zone: the spending ones. I started saving all my receipts to figure out what I was spending—and found I was spending much more than I had ever suspected. I took on the role of chief negotiator. I started getting us on the best phone plans, haggling over rental car and hotel rates. Eventually, I bought a car (demanding to talk to a second salesman after the first one—the one who took me on a test drive—told me he didn't think we should negotiate because my husband wasn't there). I fought the health insurer when the claim for our son's surgery was denied. And I took pictures for the Northwestern Mutual representative when Hurricane Floyd did a number on our house. Then I moved on to saving tasks. I opened separate savings and checking accounts and started paying some bills myself online. I took a more active role in rebalancing the investments in my 401(k) and IRAs. And eventually I had a face-to-face with an accountant.

The change wasn't instantaneous. Developing systems that actually worked for me took a while. (Sticking receipts in my vast wasteland of a tote bag was an initial disaster; putting them in my wallet was much better.) And it took a while to get over the feeling that I was about to make a big mistake at any moment. But guess what? I definitely made some small gaffes, but I didn't make any from which there was no recovery. The more information I had, the better I felt. The more in control I was of my money, the more in control I felt of my life. That control wasn't absolute, of course; it wasn't unshakable. Life being life never allows you to control everything. And life often sends you down some bumpy roads. But I know that a good foundation makes dealing with even the roughest of them easier.

The upshot? For the first time in many, many years not only did my wealth start to grow but I had the ability to track that growth. And the fact that my savings account and 401(k) were getting fatter inspired me to make them fatter still. I found my money confidence. And money confidence breeds more money.

So now—just as I've helped you climb small money mountains (finding the right mortgage, getting the right credit card, deciding if you want a 529 plan or UGMA to save for college)—I am going to help you climb the biggest one. I am going to help you have a safe, secure financial future. I am going to help you get rich.

It was time for me. It is time for you. In fact, it is time for *all* women. It is my theory that we, as women, are at a turning point with wealth. It is a change that has come in three stages.

- **We started earning more.** On average, it is true that men working full-time still outearn women working full-time. But it is also true that since the 1970s, almost all the income growth in this country has come from women's income. Men's income growth has stagnated. Women's income growth continues to rise. That's why today 30 to 40 percent of women (depending on whose numbers you believe) earn as much as or more than their husbands. One lauded researcher now predicts that by 2030 the average woman in America will outearn the average man.

- **We started wanting control.** Many women—like me—started feeling for the first time that they deserved to take an active role in making money decisions. That's why today in marriages, the number of separate checking accounts has skyrocketed. Women on their own started taking more control, too—buying cars, buying houses, saving for retirement. No more waiting for the right husband or partner to come along. Anyone who wanted to share her life could share her three-bedroom Colonial as well.

- **We started wanting wealth.** It's okay to admit that. For decades many women believed that it wasn't. Wanting a fat bank account wasn't feminine. It wasn't attractive. It meant you didn't need a man in your life to support you—and what man was going to want a woman who didn't need him? That is changing. It is finally starting to be okay to want to have enough money to live comfortably, to afford a nice lifestyle for yourself and your family. It is finally okay for women (it has always been okay for men) to want to be wealthy. Today, we call it "our money" rather than "his money." Someday soon, even the words "my money" won't sound all that bad.

It's time. Just as it was time for me—it is time for you. It is time for you to stop standing in your own way, and to stop sabotaging yourself. I don't want to hear anymore why you're not meant to be rich, why society doesn't want you to be rich, why the world is structured in a way that prevents you from getting rich. I don't want to hear anymore that it's not your fault, that it's the way you were raised, the way you were taught, the hand you were dealt, that the deck is stacked against you.

It's time to stop making excuses—stop bitching, stop moaning, stop griping, and stop fussing. It's time to put an end to this whopper of a pity party—and to start taking action. It's time to start making moves that will improve your financial position, make you feel better, and make you some money.

To that end, each chapter in this book contains three distinct elements:

- **Don't Bitch** examines the reasons you use for avoiding financial responsibility. Where did this logic (confounded though it may be) come from? How can you get rid of it?

- **Get Rich** provides you with practical steps for building a healthy and wealthy financial life now that you've blown past the emotional roadblocks.

- **Maps to a Million** show you precisely how much money you should be able to sock away and how to use it in the best way possible to help you achieve a better life.

In the movie *Miracle*, Kurt Russell as Herb Brooks, coach of the 1980 U.S. Olympic hockey team, gives his young players a pep talk before they head out to face the heavily favored (and much older) Russians. "This is your time," he tells them. "Their time is over. This is your time. Now go out there and take it." And of course they do, beating the Soviets 5–3 and bringing the country to its feet.

Well, this is *your* time. It's *your* turn to do the taking. And I will be your coach.

You probably suspect that actually doing something about your money is much tougher than just complaining about it. That's true. Doing anything is tougher than simply talking about doing it. You'll need a helping hand in this endeavor.

That'll be my job. I know not only what you need to do but also *why* you're not already doing it. Chapter after chapter, I will line up the excuses you're using, and not only will I knock them down, but also I'll help you find the easiest, quickest, most painless ways to incorporate in your life the financial changes you need to make. I will explain your financial life to you in words and terms that you'll understand—whether you're a beginner or are already on the road to wealth.

Together, we will deal with the tactical changes you need to make to accomplish the four essential wealth-building habits I described above. We also will deal with the emotional reasons that for so many years have prevented you from making these changes. I call them the "ations"—and they include organization, procrastination, participation, motivation, and communication.

Look, managing your money is just one part of managing your life. It may not be your favorite part. But like getting dressed every morning, taking out the garbage a few times a week, and visiting the gynecologist once a year, it has to be done. It's irresponsible to do otherwise. If you're not managing your money, then you're not taking care of yourself. And if you're not taking care of yourself, you can forget about taking care of your kids, your spouse or significant other, your aging parents, your employees, or your friends—in fact, any of the people you love.

I've watched a lot of women go through this sort of financial awakening, and I've gone through it myself. And what I've learned is that the very best thing about stepping up and starting to deal with your money—despite the title of this book—is not that you'll make money (although you will). It's that you'll feel *so much better*. That's right. Taking steps to get yourself on the right financial track will enable you to take your mind off your money and will free your mind to focus on other, more important things in your life (many of which are things that having money will allow you to pursue). And that will make you rich in an entirely different—but completely significant and earth-shattering—way.

WELCOME TO MY MONEY GROUP

One of the big problems women have with money is that it's a tough subject to talk about. We used to have that problem with sex. Then prime-time shows like *Friends* and *Will and Grace* (that purported to be about life but were in fact *all* about sex) hit it big, and all of a sudden, talking about sex was much, much easier. If Jennifer Aniston and Debra Messing could do it with a straight face, then, by gosh, so could you.

Money never got that sort of introduction into everyday conversation. "How much do you make?" is still a question that's whispered. "How much did they pay for that house?" is asked under the breath. That's why I started a Money Group. Because it's easier to have these conversations when that's the purpose for meeting.

A Money Group is like a book group but with no books. It's a bunch of friends who get together on a regular basis to talk about financial matters. At one meeting you might talk about getting the right life insurance, at another about paying for college for your kids, at another about figuring out how to quit quibbling with your betrothed over his spending (or yours).

Money Groups are different from the investment clubs of the 1980s made famous by the Beardstown Ladies. In investment clubs (which still exist), members pool assets. Everybody chips in $50 or $100 each meeting, and you use that money to buy stocks, which you hope will go up. The point of an investment club is to research and pick good stocks. The point of a Money Group is to learn about—and discuss—your financial life.

Of course, as in good book groups, you'll discuss other things as well. You'll discuss your kids. Your vacation plans. That new stoplight going up at the corner. You'll probably (if your money group is made up of good friends) even get around to talking about sex. But mostly you'll talk about money. Think of your Money Group as that part of every *Sex in the City* episode where Carrie, Charlotte, Miranda, and Samantha gathered for brunch and discussed the topic of the week. You get down to business, say what you have to say, feel as if you made some progress, and get back to the rest of your life.

I'm not the only person in America starting a Money Group these days. There aren't nearly as many Money Groups as there are investment clubs (of those there are about twenty thousand), but the number is on the rise. The appeal is understandable. You get rid of a certain amount of anxiety about money simply by realizing you're not the only one who has it.

One of the benefits of having a Money Group—at least for me—has been that members were able to read the manuscript for this book as I wrote it. I asked them not to correct my spelling and grammar (though some of them did anyway—thanks, guys) but to shoot me lists of questions they came up with as they were going through the text. Each chapter begins with the questions. Following these questions are my answers. I hope you'll find comfort in learning that you are not the only person to not know what a Roth IRA is or what a P/E ratio means.

Starting A Money Group

If you're interested in starting a Money Group, how do you go about doing it?

- **Pick your members.** Try to include people who do different things and have different life experiences. Mix working women with stay-at-home moms, singles with marrieds, moms with grandmoms, women who don't have kids with those who do, entrepreneurs with corporate types, younger with older. Why? Because they'll bring different life—and money—experiences from which everyone else will be able to learn. The members of my Money Group range in age from 29 to 65. The 29-year-old is a single young reporter in New York. The 65-year-old is my mother, recently widowed. The rest of us are suburban moms, some divorced, some married, some with kids close to college, others with infants at home. I think you're best aiming for ten to twelve members. You want to have about eight at each meeting, so you need some leeway for people's schedules.

- **Decide if you want a leader.** If one person is clearly an expert— I am the leader of my Money Group—then it makes sense for that person to lead. If everyone is on a level playing field, it works well to rotate leadership duties.

- **Pick some topics.** Gather everyone together for your first meeting, serve some food and drink, and start brainstorming about what everyone wants to get out of this experience. You'll find some people are most concerned about retirement, others college, others real estate, and still others the more emotional sides of money. Come up with a list of the subjects you'll focus on and in which order. Appoint one member to be in charge of each of the upcoming topics. And remember: You want this to be easy, not cumbersome, so the member-in-charge should circulate articles (not books) on the topic and come prepared with a book-group-like list of questions to get the conversation started.

- **Invite experts.** There are probably plenty of brokerage firms and financial planners in town that would love, love, love your business. If you're about to discuss something that none of you feels qualified to talk about, invite in someone who knows her stuff so she can lead the discussion. Tell her you're looking for someone to educate the group on a particular issue and to answer members' questions. Who knows? You may end up finding a financial pro you'd like to work with.

- **Check my website for more resources.** With the launch of this book, I'll be putting Money Group materials up on my website, JeanChatzky.com. Come for a visit and check them out.

"I Don't Know Where to Begin"

DON'T BITCH

Getting Over the Unknown

I am one of the fortunate people who really like what they do for a living. One of the main reasons I enjoy my work is that it takes me out into the world. About once a month I travel to far-flung places such as Phoenix (Arizona), Pasadena (California), Fort Worth (Texas), or Fort Wayne (Indiana) to talk to groups of people—often groups of women—about money.

My favorite part of these journeys isn't the half-hour or so prepared speech I get to give. It's the question-and-answer session that comes after.

Some of the questions are always regional ("Is now a good time to buy a house in this market?" or "What do you think of the future of the big national corporate conglomerate that just happens to be based three miles down the road?"). But others are so wide-ranging I can count on them being raised whether I'm holding court in Detroit, Duluth, or Des Moines. Someone generally wants to know: "What's the best way to choose a financial adviser?" Someone else typically asks: "Should I be buying long-term-care insurance for me or my parents?"

But the question I get asked more than any other—the one I get asked every single time—is the following. It's never first. In fact, it's often last . . . as if the person speaking waited until the moderator said, "We have time for only three more." It usually comes out of the mouth of someone who feels a little silly asking it—who prefaces her question with an apology to me and the rest of the audience for being "so basic." And it goes like this:

> *I don't even know where to start. I mean, really. I feel like I know so little about my money that I don't even know where to begin. Can you point me to a book or a magazine or a website or something that can get me going?*

Sometimes, the floodgates really open, and the questioner ends with the complete truth, confession-style: *"I'm tired of feeling like a total idiot about my money."*

I have to admit, the person who asks this question immediately becomes my favorite person in any crowd. Not just because she dug deep and was honest about wanting help. But because now that she's revealed that she's looking for help, I can do something for her.

As I collected—via e-mail—letters and excuses from women around the country about why they don't take a more active role managing their money, this feeling of total inadequacy popped up again and again. From young women, older women, women with college and graduate degrees, women in the workforce, stay-at-home moms . . . in other words, from all types of women, in all parts of the country.

This one, from Rebecca, a stay-at-home mom, is typical:

> *For anything else in my life, I would get on the Internet, read some articles, talk to some people I know, and make a decision. But I'm paralyzed when it comes to money. I don't even know where to start.*

Jennifer, a publicist, put it even more succinctly:

> *I don't know where to begin.*

This Is Where You Begin

You're in the right place: This is where you start. In this chapter, I'm going to give you a set of tools you can rely on to make any financial decision, to sound brilliant defending why you're making it, and to quickly get on the road to a richer life.

But first, let's explore why you can't get started with your money.

Rebecca put it really well when she said: *"For anything else in my life, I would get on the Internet, read some articles, talk to some people I know, and make a decision."* That, in a nutshell, is how women make nearly every large, important decision. We do our homework using the resources at our fingertips—the Internet, newspapers, and magazines. We tend to be consensus builders so we gather the opinions of the people we trust most: our mothers, sisters, and girlfriends. We take our time readying a case we could defend in the toughest of courts, and then (only then) do we pull the trigger.

Most of the time, as we've learned through experience, that sort of decision making works fine. Say you're an East Coaster trying to plan a vacation for your family of five. You know you want to go to the beach in December. So you hop on the Internet and go to a site like weather.com. You learn that at that time of year Florida's weather is inconsistent but the Caribbean can be counted on for sun. Your spouse wants a direct flight, so that eliminates a few of the smaller islands. You both want a short flight, so you focus in on Puerto Rico. Next you surf to tripadvisor.com to see what people are recommending as kid-friendly places to stay. You narrow your search to a Westin and a Hyatt. Finally, you talk to your friends who have been to Puerto Rico, settle on a hotel, book flights, and emerge confident you'll have a great vacation.

And that's, as I said, a fairly large, important, *expensive* decision. You make smaller decisions with confidence every single day. Paper or plastic? *Grey's Anatomy* or *Law and Order*? Coke, Pepsi, or—what the heck—Fresca? You blow through them as though they're absolutely nothing. If, occasionally, you hit a stumbling block—heels or flats? pants or a skirt?—a little trial and error (or a call to a close friend) does the trick.

Why are you able to make these decisions—large and small—with such aplomb? Because you've learned, over the course of your life, that for you there are right and wrong answers. Fresca gets drunk in your house; Pepsi sits in the pantry. *Grey's* Dr. McDreamy does more for you then *Law's* not-so-dreamy detectives. Unless you're fighting a spouse over the remote, there's no argument. One is better. One is right.

Yet in the world of money—particularly in the world of investing—there are few right answers. Which stock is the best one to buy? Which mutual fund will rise the fastest? People may claim to know (just turn on CNBC and you'll see a dozen of them within an hour), but no one really does. That makes it tough to get to the starting line, particularly for women.

We like to know the outcome before we make any decision. That's why we not only cook from recipes but prefer that those recipes come from Julia or Martha or Rachael because we've learned that we can trust them. We may *loooove* Tom Hanks as much as we love our spouses, but we're willing to spend $10.50 for a ticket to his latest picture only after we've read a handful of uncontested reviews. Everything from the books we select for our book clubs to the doctors we see for our children gets sliced and diced and picked apart and commented on before we step up to the plate.

And women not only need more information but need it to be broken down into small, digestible pieces. Along the way, if we're not convinced of a particular piece, we stop and ask for help—we'd prefer it from trusted sources. (Figuring out how to get good help is such a conundrum for women that I deal with that matter specifically in Chapter 9.) Not surprisingly, it takes women longer than men to make most decisions. Not just about money, about everything. Men don't need to know the answer before they tackle the question. They tend to say, "Gimme the facts, gimme the figures, gimme the logic and the rationale, and let me build a machine." It's very much a left-brain approach. They work from start to finish, from left to right, from point A to point B. If they like Denzel Washington, knowing that Denzel Washington is *in* a new movie is enough to make them buy a ticket. If the end result isn't totally to their liking, they either fiddle with the decision to make it more acceptable or—more likely—figure out a way to defend it, convincing everyone around them (and themselves in the process) that the outcome was precisely the result they had in mind all along.

And there are other complicating factors:

- **The world of money has its own vocabulary.** Don't worry, I define terms—in *English*—beginning on page 251.)

- **The world of money is shrouded in secrecy.** Some progress has been made, but talking about financial things—how much credit card debt you're carrying, the size of your student loans— just isn't polite. If the number is too high, friends will think you're bragging. If it's too low, they'll think you're asking for a handout. Nobody wins.

- **The world of money involves higher stakes than picking a movie to see on date night.** When you're deciding whether to contribute to a 401(k) and how to invest the money you're contributing, whether to refinance the mortgage, whether to accept a new job, whether to buy life insurance, or whom to name as guardian for your kids in your will, money decisions tend to be important, potentially life-changing decisions.

And there are no right answers. Of course you're stuck.

The Power of "Good Enough"

The logical next question is: How do you get unstuck? Step one is getting yourself to acknowledge—no, more than that—to really *believe*, that in this particular area of your life, you do not have to be right. Yes, you heard me correctly. *You don't have to be right.* Not only that:

You don't have to be perfect.
You don't have to be the best.
You don't have to be at the top of some class.
You don't have to be the smartest.
You don't have to be the winner.
You don't have to prove yourself.
You don't have to do better than your neighbors or your parents or your siblings or your friends.

Instead:

You have to be good enough.
And *you have to believe that good enough is just fine.*

What does that mean in real terms? It means your investments don't have to do better than the market as a whole or better than other people's investments. They simply have to do well enough to meet your goals. It means you don't have to save more or spend more or make more than anyone else. It means you have to negotiate these areas of your life well enough to secure your happiness and make *yourself* comfortable.

You do not have to justify your financial life. Not to the markets. Not to your friends. Not to your relatives. And, most certainly, not to the men in your life who may not understand how you can sit there, perfectly satisfied with your "good enough" portfolio, without reaching for the stars. (Try not to blame them. It's in their DNA, just as not taking so many risks that you can't sleep at night is in yours.)

I know this sounds foreign. We live in a world where relativity is key to our sense of inner peace. It's not enough to be thin or smart or funny. You have to be thin*er* or smart*er* or funni*er* than someone else. The problem is, in the world of money this kind of measuring up won't make you rich. It will make you poor. Why? Because it will entice you to behave in one of two ways, neither of them any good for your wallet. Either you will go over-board in your quest for wealth, taking risks that are both unnecessary and unwise (Amazon at $400, anyone?). Or you will become so convinced of your inability to be richer than the next guy or gal that, once again, you will become stuck.

The truly great thing about "good enough"—and the reason it is so powerful—is that it allows you to get to the starting line in a way that wait-ing for the ultimate, best possible result does not. Take an example that you may have faced dozens of times in the past several years: refinancing your mortgage. Say you're sitting with a $200,000 30-year fixed-rate home loan at 6 3/4 percent. Rates have fallen to 6 percent. Refinancing now would save you $98 a month—the difference in your $1,297 monthly payment and the $1,199 new one. But some "experts" have been quoted in the paper saying they see rates falling to 5 percent, maybe even lower. Do you refinance now? Or do you wait?

If you're expecting the best possible ultimate result, you are stuck. What if tomorrow rates fall farther? Then you'll be kicking yourself, won't you?

But if you're a believer in the power of "good enough," you forge ahead. And then—guess what? Starting tomorrow, you pay nearly $100 less a month. Over the life of your loan, that means you'll save $35,314 in inter-est alone. If you put the money you're saving into an IRA or other account where it can grow tax-free, at the end of those thirty years you'll have a fat $147,126 in addition to your paid-off house.

MAP TO A MILLION

How much more money could you save if you made the little changes I'm going to suggest to you throughout this book? How much richer could you be? I want you to see the answers in straightforward numerical terms. I want you to see the actual dollars—and in some cases cents. So throughout the chapter I've sprinkled lots of little *Maps to a Million*. Unless otherwise noted, I've calculated returns at 8 percent and assumed that the savings invested were tax-deferred. Follow the actual steps and you'll see the wealth start to add up. Then, starting on page 241, you can see exactly how fast incorporating a few of these steps into your life really does add up to a million—or more!

REFINANCE A $275,000 MORTGAGE

Prior rate:	6 3/4 *percent*
Monthly payment:	$1,783
New rate:	6 *percent*
Monthly payment:	$1,648
Annual savings:	$1,620
10-year savings:	$24,997
20-year savings:	$80,182
30-year savings:	$202,674

If the rates fall to 5 percent—or lower—as the "expert" predicted, you can always refinance again. But what if rates don't fall that far? What if the "expert"—because in this world of no right answers even "experts" can be off-base—got it wrong? In the world of ultimate perfection, you would lose. But in the world of "good enough," you still would come out a winner.

Who Are You Doing This For? You!

My aim is to make you feel like a winner. I want to make you feel better about yourself and your life. But in order to do that, I need your help. The unfortunate truth is that taking control of your financial life won't work until, like a good diet, you are doing it for yourself. You may be able to lose five pounds for your husband or your doctor. But you'll keep them off only if you're doing it for yourself. You can buy a book on money management because it makes your partner happy to see you walking into the business section of your local bookstore. But you'll read it and follow its advice only if you're doing it for yourself.

Sound selfish? It's the furthest thing from selfish. Becoming financially self-sufficient is like giving a huge gift to the people you love. It means you will not be a burden to your parents or your children. If you are in a committed relationship, having a handle on your own money makes you a full partner rather than an associate. (And no, having more than enough money to live on doesn't mean you don't have to take the reins. Do you think your grown children relish the thought of taking over your checkbook because you never learned how to pay bills during your long marriage? Think again.)

You are taking control of your money because doing so will make you feel happier and smarter, more confident, more content, and more useful. Having a little extra money in your wallet will not make you feel more satisfied with your life. What you *do* with the extra money will do that. Having better control of that money, however, will make a huge difference in how you view yourself and your place in the world.

The folks at *Real Simple* magazine did a study in which they asked women to describe in a word or two what they'd need to feel successful. Here is what the respondents said:

Happiness	80%
Peace of mind	75%
Fulfillment	71%
Self-confidence	71%
Freedom	70%
Balance	70%

Learning to manage your own money can help you achieve about every one of those line items. For JoAnn, who is 68 and retired, it did precisely that. Here is her story:

During my growing-up years, there was very little money to manage. At the age of 10, I asked my parents to give me the money that they would have spent on my clothes and allow me to do my own purchasing. I was unhappy with the things my mother bought for me in a very low-end department store in Detroit. I felt that I could do a better job. I found I could buy three semi-attractive outfits instead of the six cheaper ones that my mother purchased. Each year, I added a few better things and even managed to snag a much-lusted-after cashmere sweater on sale. I was very proud.

Lack of money continued into my married years, this time accompanied by bill collectors. It was a time of minimum payments on credit cards and trying to meet the needs of the children. And it was very depressing and stressful for the whole family.

I took a minimum-wage job when the youngest child went to kindergarten. The job had health benefits and a pension to make up for the low salary. My husband felt that every cent I earned was needed to reduce our debt and run our family. I made a decision on my own, however, and signed up at work to purchase a $25.00 U.S. Savings Bond every two weeks.

Each time I was promoted or received a raise, I invested most of that money in more and higher-denomination bonds. Over the years, I quietly accumulated the unimaginable (to me) sum of $100,000. My husband and I managed, through both of our jobs, to resolve our money problems and shortages. Today, the bonds are untouched in a safety deposit box for use in case of an unexpected major expense or a future big surprise for the kids! It was a difficult time for me, and I never want to be poor again.

In recent years, I have left most of the money management to my husband. I am knowledgeable about my life-time pension, I know when the Social Security checks are direct-deposited, and I know where our money is invested. And I also know I could carry on financially in the future if I had to.

Can you imagine: $100,000-plus on $25 twice a month. Yet JoAnn did it. How? By taking control of her life. By taking control and starting to save even when her husband thought the money would be better spent in other ways. By doing what she knew was the right thing for herself, her future, and her kids. And how did managing her own money make JoAnn feel? "Very proud," she said.

JoAnn had every right to feel proud. And you can feel that way, too.

GET RICH

Eight Ways to Begin

For women, mastering money is a challenge for a number of reasons. First, some of us have trouble actually doing it. Second, we have trouble acknowledging the fact that we're doing it. Why? In part because it feels as though we're wresting control from the men in our lives (we'll deal with this issue in Chapter 3). But also because, when we were growing up, many of us were taught how to put together an outfit in the morning, set the table for dinner, write a book report, or parallel park, but nobody taught us how to save or spend or invest. Nobody sat us down and said: "Honey, if you save some of that money you made babysitting, it will grow to be a lot more ten years from now." And even in cases where somebody (usually a parent) tried to teach us those lessons, the teacher didn't do a particularly good job. Instead of telling us "Tough luck" when we ran out of babysitting money right before we wanted to go to the movies with friends, our parents bailed us out. They gave us $5 or $10 and told us to be more careful the next time. But we'd already learned that oh-so-powerful financial lesson: There's plenty of money where that came from. If you need more, ask Mom and Dad.

The New Lesson: Get Started Now

Here are eight quick-and-easy fixes you can make in your own financial lives today. None of them will take more than a few minutes. But I don't want you only to do these things. I want you to understand why you're doing them. So along with the fixes are explanations that get to the heart of what you're up to. Feel free to repeat them to anyone who asks what you're doing these days.

_Do it:_ Sign up for an automatic savings plan at your bank or brokerage firm. Have $100 a month diverted into a separate money market account that you promise yourself you won't touch. (Don't get an ATM card for this account to be sure.) As soon as you find you don't miss $100 a month, up your contribution to $200. Eventually, you'll invest that money so it can grow even faster.

Say it and sound smart: *"I put away a little money every month so that if I have an emergency, I won't have to float my life on my credit card."*

MAP TO A MILLION

Saving $100 a month every month for 30 years: $150,129
Saving $200 a month every month for 30 years: $300,259
Saving $300 a month every month for 30 years: $450,388

Do it: Call a local lawyer and tell him or her that you need a will. The lawyer will suggest that you get a living will, a healthcare proxy, and a durable power of attorney to go with it. Those are good ideas, too. For the whole package, expect to be charged between $500 and $1,000. If you can't afford it, you can create your own will using software available online. These are perfectly valid documents and will stand up in court.

Say it and sound smart: *"I think it would be insane not to have a will and not to name guardians for the kids. Do you know what could happen if we die without one? A huge, ugly court battle over the money and the children. That's not how I want to be remembered."*

Do it: Pause before you purchase. Think twice before buying anything you didn't go to a store or onto a website to buy. If you're in a store, put the item on hold and wait twenty-four hours before you go back and buy. If you're online, put the item in your cart and leave the site. If you surf your way back the next day, the site is likely to remember you. Impulse buying really adds up, but so does the money you'll save if you push the pause button before you buy unneccesarily.

Say it and sound smart: *"I'm sure I have another just like it at home."*

MAP TO A MILLION

Money you'll save *not* making one $79 impulse purchase a month:

Over 1 year: $948   *Over 20 years: $46,921*
Over 10 years: $14,628   *Over 30 years: $118,602*

Do it: Start protecting your credit score. Your credit score is the number by which financial institutions—insurers, lenders, even employers these days—gauge your responsibility. You want it to be as close to 800 as possible. Here are two things you can do right away to improve your credit score: (1) Pay your bills on time. (2) Pay down the balances on your credit cards, particularly the cards that are nearly maxed out.

Say it and sound smart: *"Well, I pulled my credit report for free from www.annualcreditreport.com. Good thing, too, there were a couple of mistakes I had to fix. That should make my credit score go up."*

Do it: Use a debit card, not a credit card. That way you don't risk getting in over your head in credit card debt—a problem that plagues more than half of adult Americans these days.

Say it and sound smart: *"Oh, I use a debit card most of the time these days. That way I never have to worry about being surprised by bills."*

Do it: Take money out of your savings or money market account to pay off high-rate credit card debt. This makes sense as you're likely only earning 3 or 4 percent (max) on your savings, while you're paying 16, 18, even 24 percent on your credit card. By eliminating the debt, you gain an instantaneous 12 or 14 or 20 percent. Why? Because you're no longer spending the money on interest.

Say it and sound smart: *"I used to think having money in savings was safer. But I'm so far ahead by paying off my credit cards. And if I have an emergency and don't have the cash, that's the time it's smart to charge."*

MAP TO A MILLION

Take $4,000 out of your savings account to pay off your credit card bill.

Annual savings on interest: $720   *20-year total: $37,611*
10-year total: $12,178   *30-year total: $94,063*

Do it: Call your benefits department at work and talk to a benefits manager about signing up for the 401(k) (if you haven't already), contributing more to your 401(k) (if you're not maxing out), opening a flexible spending account to use pretax dollars for health care, daycare, and transportation to and from work, and making sure you're in the right health plan for you. You may not be able to make any changes immediately, but let the manager know that these are your goals. And ask her to give you a call to make sure you're doing everything correctly when the time you're allowed to make changes rolls around.

Say it and sound smart: *"Thank goodness for my 401(k). The money comes out of my paycheck before I can spend it. So every time I get a raise I kick in a little more."*

MAP TO A MILLION

Pay for $2,000 in health care, child or elder care, and transportation with pretax dollars (28 percent tax bracket).

Annual savings: $560   *20-year savings: $29,253*
10-year-savings: $9,471   *30-year savings: $73,160*

Do it: Save some money on auto, homeowners, and life insurance. How? Call your carriers and ask if you're getting all the discounts (for safety precautions, proximity to water and fire stations, good driving records, etc.) to which you're entitled. Take their best quotes; then shop three other carriers. If your health has improved—maybe you've quit smoking or lost weight—use that as a rationale to buy a new term-life insurance policy (you could save thousands). Use the money you save to buy insurance that you need—renters, disability, more life—but aren't buying now.

Say it and sound smart: *"What do you mean you don't have renters (or life or disability) insurance? I'd never take that kind of a risk."*

LOOK HOW FAR YOU'VE COME!

Congratulations! I know this is only the end of the first chapter, but by making your way through it, you've overcome one of the biggest financial hurdles: You've started. Now you have in your arsenal a number of small moves you can make—from using a debit card instead of a credit card to thinking twice before you make a purchase. Used together, these and the other strategies I've taught you will make a big difference in your financial life, and there are many more to come. Stick with me . . .

What if I make a mistake?

You will make a mistake. Let's get that out on the table right now. You will make more than one. You will take out a mortgage and then find one—right after you've closed—that's a quarter point cheaper. You will sell a house and watch prices continue to rise. And you know what I want you to do about all of these things? Absolutely nothing. Do your best. Do your homework. Then make a decision—pull the trigger and put your decision into action—then move on. That's right. Because the mistakes that you make locking into a mortgage at a rate that's not bottom-of-the-barrel, or selling a house while the prices are still headed up, are nothing compared to the mistakes you make by not acting at all. That's when you miss opportunities. That's when your financial life passes you by. So act. Deal. Move on. And if you need to reconnoiter and take a different course in the future, that will be okay, too.

When I set up an automatic savings plan or investment account, where do I put the money?

If you're just beginning to save, the money should go directly into a savings account. Your goal there is to accumulate an emergency cushion—three months of living expenses if you're part of a two-income household

and six months of living expenses if you're a single-income household. Once you've got that money together, you can start to invest the additional money that comes in by putting it into the stock market, where there's a greater risk you'll lose it but also a greater chance you'll earn a higher return. (In Chapter 8, I lay out a plan for you to invest your money. If you can't wait until you get to Chapter 8 to get started, put 60 percent in a total stock market index fund and 40 percent in a total bond market index fund. Once you get to Chapter 8, you can tweak accordingly.)

Does it look stupid or silly to go into negotiations with the things you want in writing? I might get so nervous that I could forget some important item.

No! Going into a negotiation with a written list is a fabulous idea. It makes you look the opposite of silly. It makes you look prepared, as if you've put some serious thought and effort into what you are proposing. Feel free to put it that way, by the way. Say to your boss, "Here's what I'm proposing. Here's what I suggest." That sounds a lot less confrontational than, "Here's what I want. Here's what I'm asking for." And realistically, a negotiation is a tense situation. It's one in which you might forget important items unless they're on a handwritten list. Forgetting would be much worse than taking along notes.

CHAPTER 2

"I Like Money— It's Numbers I Can't Stand"

DON'T BITCH

When I set out to write this book, the very first thing I did was some fieldwork. I sent an e-mail to friends, colleagues, associates, and my mother, and I asked them: What reasons do you give for not managing your money? What excuses rank highest at the top of the list?

This e-mail gathered some steam. And soon I was getting letters back from Chicago, California, Charlotte, and Des Moines. I was getting e-mails from women I'd never met, women I never would meet, women of all ages—the older ones to whom my mother and aunt had forwarded the e-mail and their friends, the younger ones the college chums of my twenty-something assistant.

I got hundreds of e-mails and hundreds of excuses. But not *just* excuses. These wonderful women wrote me e-mails that ran on for pages. They opened up about why they don't manage their money, how inadequate and small and "stupid" that makes them feel—even though they know they are not inadequate or small or "stupid." Some of these e-mails and explanations I had anticipated. I fully expected, for example, to hear women complain that their husbands or significant others didn't want them managing the money in the family. And I expected women to tell me that they don't deal with certain aspects of their finances—like wills and life insurance—because doing so reminds them that someday they're going to die. And they'd rather not think about that, thank you very much.

But I did not expect to hear women say—in a variety of ways, using an assortment of different words—that they simply don't like money.

Some were as blunt as Jeannette, an administrative assistant:

I think of money as the necessary evil. I hate every aspect of my finances. I can't figure out why that is the case, but I wish I could.

Others couched their dislike in the sort of excuses kids use when they don't want to go to religious school or do their science homework:

Money is so dull!
Ellen, divorce mediator

Money is so boring!
Jane, social worker

I have to say, their words left me scratching my head. I know for a fact (I've done the research) that there are plenty of things you like about money:

- **You like having money.** Having enough money to live not lavishly but comfortably gives you a feeling of safety. (What's enough depends on where and how you live. On average it takes a minimum of $50,000 to $60,000 in annual household income to reach that threshold of comfort each year.) Once you know there's enough in the bank or the brokerage firm or the mattress to pay the rent or mortgage, put gas in the car, and outfit the kids for school, you can sleep at night.

- **You like the security money gives you.** Having enough of an extra stash—to replace the dishwasher if it hits the skids, to go out for a nice dinner if you want to, or to get on a plane to see a sick parent in a pinch—makes you feel even more secure.

- **You like the choices money gives you.** Having money allows you to explore the things you want to explore, see the places you want to see, do the things you want to do. Money allows you to support the people who are important to you—to help your children get involved in a range of extracurricular activities, for instance, or your elderly parents get the help they need at home. Money allows you to go back to school when your career is on its last legs (or you just don't like it anymore). It lets you get out of uncomfortable situations—to fly home when your choice of travel companions leaves a lot to be desired or to leave a marriage in which you don't feel respected or loved. It's true that in many of these situations an all-important ingredient is having the courage to act in your own best interests or in the best interests of the people you love. Once your courage is readied, though, money gives you the keys to the car.

- **You like spending money.** C'mon, admit it. You *do*. At least most people do. Recent academic research has shown that the act of shopping brings on a rush of the same chemical that comes flowing into our brains when we jump out of an airplane or fall in love. In other words, buying something—particularly something you really want—actually makes you a little high. Women have always made about 80 percent of the purchasing decisions. In prior generations, though, the male/female buying breakdown was big vs. small, important vs. mundane, long-term vs. everyday. No more. Today, women are either purchasing or playing a bigger role in the purchases of cars (66 percent of car purchases are made by women), homes (single women represent 22 percent of new-home purchasers), and technology. The shift is significant enough that all of these things are now being designed with women in mind.

- **You like spending money—on yourself.** It's always been acceptable to provide for the other members of your family. These days, though, particularly as you earn a bigger share of the household pie, you like spending money on yourself. It's okay to admit that as well. Once you realize that there is enough money to take care of yourself as well as the rest of your obligations and family, you understand that a little self-indulgence from time to time is perfectly fine. That's why personal services have become the fifth largest category that Americans spend money on (following homes, cars, food, and travel). And it's why day spas (you can't get more woman-centered than the concept of a day spa) have become a $15 billion annual business.

- **You like giving money away.** I know that charitable organizations base their frequent pitches on all the good that you can do for their particular mission or cause. And most of the time they're absolutely right. But my research has shown that the act of giving—particularly the act of giving money away—actually makes you happier. It is, to borrow a phrase, chicken soup for the financial soul.

- **You like earning money.** It's okay to admit this, too. When someone gives you money to do a job, it means, in the simplest of terms, that someone believes you're worth that money. It makes you feel good because it's validation, which provides an automatic, instantaneous boost to your self-esteem. Please don't misunderstand me. I am not advocating that every woman (or every person) be in the paycheck-earning world. What I am telling you is that it's not unfeminine or aggressive or overly ambitious to want a paycheck. It's also not unfeminine or aggressive or overly ambitious to want that paycheck to be a true reflection of your qualifications and good work. (P.S. If you want to see the size of that paycheck increase, turn to page 48.)

If It's Not Money You Hate, What Is It?

If you agree with me—and I know that deep down, you do—that you like all of those things about money, what is it, specifically, that you dislike?

It could be the effect money sometimes has on people. Perhaps you had a very close friend who came into a load of money. She got a huge promotion, sold her small company for a bundle of cash, married into wealth, won the lottery—whatever. And all of a sudden, she had a slew of new friends, took up golf, spent her free time at "the club," and had no time for you. It would be perfectly understandable for you to say you "hate money," because only after the money arrived did this person stop having time for you. (And let me borrow a page from my mother's "real friends" lecture here and tell you: This person was never a real friend. Real friends don't let things like economic status come between them. When one person can't afford to do the same things as the other person, real friends take a no-cost walk in the park or foot the bill themselves.)

Perhaps you're afraid if you come into too much money you won't like how your inner circle starts to treat you. I ride the train with a lawyer who specializes in asbestos lawsuits. She told me of one of her clients who won a multi-million-dollar judgment and then—with his wife—decided to pretend that it never happened. They stayed in their same modest house, drove the same old cars, took the same vacations, went to dinner with their same friends in the same local restaurants, and never told a soul. Why? They were afraid their friends would start to view and treat them differently, and they were happy with life as it was. (But, she said, they were happy to be able to pay in full the college tuition bills for their kids.)

Maybe you're fearful of the difficulties and hardships lack of money can cause. If you grew up in a household without enough money to pay for life's basic needs—food, shelter, transportation, and an occasional bout of relaxation—this is certainly possible. Not having enough money for life's basic comforts can certainly cause unhappiness.

Maybe you're all wound up about the frequent fights that are caused by, or revolve around, money. Perhaps your parents argued about money—even divorced over money. Or maybe you've been in a relationship where finances were a big cause of strife. That's not unlikely. We know that money is the number-one cause of divorce as well as the number-one cause of fights in a marriage. If you bore the brunt of money squabbles, it's understandable that the word *money* itself would cause the short hairs on your neck to stand at attention.

Or maybe—more likely than all of those reasons—maybe what you hate is the work involved in managing money and how inadequate or pressured or stressed-out trying to perform those tasks makes you feel. Maybe you feel as Sally, a real estate broker, does, when she says: *"Dealing with money is overwhelming."*

Like Sally, many of us feel intimidated, overwhelmed, and infantile when facing the prospect of coming up with a game plan for our money that will get us from point A to point B. Even going through our credit card statements to see if all the charges detailed are actually ours can send us over the edge. It makes us feel out of control.

For 73 percent of all Americans, money is the number-one cause of stress. So, like Sue, a writer in California, we say things like this:

I can't deal with it right now. . . . Dealing with my money always makes me feel like I'm having a fat day—when you feel like a horse, regardless of whether it's founded in reality, and you feel like your life is down the tubes and you can't make rational decisions about anything.

What Is It with Women and Math?

When we say we can't deal with *it*, or we can't handle *it*, or *it's* overwhelming, the "it" is more specific than money. The "it" in that sentence is math. Generally, we are saying that we don't like numbers, can't deal with numbers, can't handle numbers. The numbers overwhelm us.

Before I started researching this book, I didn't know that fear of math, or math phobia or math anxiety (it's called all of those things), is a very real and very common problem. It even has a diagnosis code from the American Psychological Association: 315.1.

What is math anxiety? It's a fear, like fear of flying or fear of spiders or fear of heights. It typically shows up in adults, but it's rooted in childhood—in math class, to be precise. If you suffer from fear of math, you may remember being sent to the blackboard to work out a problem. When you couldn't figure it out, you stood there (for what seemed like *forever*) wishing you could crawl under a rock. Or maybe you studied your head off for a particular exam yet scored really poorly and were never able to figure out why. Or perhaps you ended up being called on again and again by a particularly insensitive teacher—despite the fact that your hand wasn't raised.

Experts say all it takes to bring on math anxiety is a single bad experience. But it can also be the result of feeling, time and time again, that you are *slow* in math and that being slow means you're *stupid*. Remember that in Chapter 1 we talked about women not liking questions when they're not sure of the answer. Well, many girls are the same way. We—more than boys—pondered our answers in math class to be sure we were correct before raising our hands high. For boys, it's more of a race to be first. They care less about having the perfect answer (although, of course, they'd prefer to be right) than they do about being called on and getting the teacher's attention. If they're wrong, they laugh and move on to the next question. Girls, by contrast, think twice about raising their hands the next time.

However math anxiety comes upon you, the result tends to be that you shut down—physically, mentally, emotionally, completely—whenever you face the particular aspect of math that first set you off (fractions, percentages, solving for x). At other times, the phobia is more inclusive: Math of any type is enough to start your heart racing, your palms sweating, your brain fogging up.

Experts estimate that math anxiety effects some 50 percent of Americans to at least some degree, women more than men. That means more than half of all women in this country are afraid of numbers. They don't "do math," and that means, unfortunately, that many of them don't "do money," either.

It's Not Nature, It's Nurture

Why is this? In January 2005, Lawrence Summers, then president of Harvard University, speculated—to the disappointment of many people in the audience he was addressing and, later, to the disappointment of a great many around the world—that innate differences between men and women might provide one reason why fewer women than men succeed in science and math careers. In fact, the jury is still out. Quite a bit of academic research says Summers was completely off base, and he acknowledged that he was mistaken in the multiple apologies that followed his talk. But there is other information suggesting that the paths of boys and girls split much earlier than most people previously thought.

As young children, boys and girls have equal natural abilities in math and science. But by the time they're 4 or 5, studies show, their parents' expectations of what they can accomplish have diverged. In one study, parents of boys said their sons would be able to solve math-related problems faster than parents of girls said their daughters would be able to do so. As a result of those lower expectations, I believe, it's not long before girls start to doubt their own math and science abilities and to express preferences for careers that don't require those skills.

One University of Denver psychologist surveyed middle schoolers about their career aspirations. Girls said they did not want to have science-related careers. Those who aspired to be doctors or veterinarians said they hadn't known that math and science were a big part of the curriculums. Boys, by and large, said just the opposite. As boys and girls enter high school, the gap between what they believe they can (and therefore want to) accomplish and what they actually can accomplish gets even wider.

And there's more. The problem isn't merely the fact that girls, then women, are avoiding math. It's that we feel that's an okay thing to do. We feel it's *acceptable*. Once you head down this road, you start telling yourself that you'll do enough work through the rest of your schooling to get by in math, you'll fake it when you can, and all will be fine because you'll never need any of this information in the "real world." That's precisely the logic Carolyn, a real estate agent, used on herself.

> *Remember when you were in school in math class and you thought "When am I ever possibly going to need this information in the future?" Well, that's me! I am horrible with numbers and math and feel the results of that not only in handling my personal finances, but in my job.*

Unfortunately, you feel it's okay not only to avoid math but to admit that's what you are doing. Would a man feel comfortable doing that? Not likely.

Sheila Tobias, a leading expert on math anxiety, told me this story about a remedial math class at Harvard. Math at Harvard was a requirement. At the beginning of each semester, this low-level class consisted of 80 percent women, 20 percent men. Then the first exam period rolled around, and men who couldn't handle the math in the upper-level classes they'd enrolled in were forced to admit their shortcomings and find their way to the remedial course, making the gender divide fifty-fifty.

That cycle repeats again and again and again. Boys and girls are born with equally matched abilities. But because parents and teachers expect less from girls, girls start to expect less of themselves. These lowered expectations mutate into fears that we could never do math in the first place. So as we age, we find ways to avoid math-related challenges—like managing money—and we allow other people—like husbands—to handle our money for us. We model that behavior for our daughters, and the cycle begins again.

I find the whole thing pretty depressing. But I'm holding out hope because over the past few generations we have taken small steps forward. Today, 50 percent of college chemistry majors are women, 40 percent of med school students are women, 25 percent of physics majors are women. That's positive. But it is not enough, not nearly enough.

If you are a woman who "hates numbers," it's time to understand this is a learned response. There is no reason that you should feel less able than your father or brother or uncle or husband or best male friend to do math, to handle numbers, or to deal with your money. You are a victim of low expectations. You not only *can* learn to handle numbers and handle your own money but *must* learn to handle numbers and handle your own money.

So we're going to break this cycle, right here and right now. I'm going to tell you which numbers you need to know—and how to deal with them. Because dealing with numbers is a very big step on the road to getting rich.

GET RICH

Learning How to Deal

As you began this chapter, certain feelings, certain behaviors, probably rang a bell. Find yourself again in the following descriptions, and then follow the fixes that make sense for you.

If you have an overall feeling of not liking money—what it has done to people you know, to society, even to you—it's time for you to do some things with your money that make you feel good.

Do it: Save some. Savers are, in general, happier people. They feel more secure because they not only have enough money to bail themselves out of a jam but are also doing something positive for their future. Financial advisers, unfortunately, often draw a random line in the sand and advocate saving 10 percent of whatever it is you make. Problem is, it's much too difficult for most people to start there, particularly if they're saving for the very first time.

The bar is set too high. So, set it lower. Try 3 percent. If that's easy enough, try 5 percent. In Chapter 7, I'll tell you more about where to put this money. **Say it and sound smart:** *"I've been trying to save a little money every week. I'm amazed at how quickly it's adding up."*

MAP TO A MILLION

The average American earns $44,389 a year. Here's what saving 3, 5, and 10 percent of that will do for your future. Keep in mind, this assumes *no* raises. If you think you'll get even modest raises through your career and if you boost your savings to keep up with those raises, the numbers will be *much* higher.

SAVE 3 PERCENT

1-year savings:	*$1,332*
5-year savings:	*$9,845*
10-year savings:	*$22,529*
20-year savings:	*$69,580*
30-year savings:	*$174,017*

Note: Clearly, saving 3 percent of whatever it is you earn is a start. But it's not enough to retire on. Think of it as a building block instead.

SAVE 5 PERCENT

1-year savings:	*$2,219*
5-year savings:	*$16,402*
10-year savings:	*$37,532*
20-year savings:	*$115,916*
30-year savings:	*$289,899*

Note: At 5 percent, your retirement nest egg could spill off income of around $25,000 a year. Add Social Security to that and you're starting to get somewhere.

SAVE 10 PERCENT

1-year savings:	*$4,439*
5-year savings:	*$32,811*
10-year savings:	*$75,072*
20-year savings:	*$231,884*
30-year savings:	*$579,938*

Do it: Spend some. Buying things you can't afford isn't going to make you happy. But setting a goal for yourself—a dream vacation, membership at a great new yoga center, whatever you're pining for—and then taking the necessary steps to achieve that goal will produce a feeling of satisfaction. One thought: Research shows that spending money on experiences makes you happier than spending money on things. Why? Things tend to get a little worn with age. In contrast, we embellish experiences, and they become even better in the retelling.

Say it and sound smart: *"I think the fact that it took me a while to pull together the money for this vacation will make me appreciate it even more."*

Do it: Invest in something you feel good about. We are a society of multitaskers, so it makes sense that you'd be able simultaneously to invest and support a way of life you believe in. There are now nearly 250 mutual funds that screen their holdings to weed out investments in tobacco, alcohol, or companies with labor or equitable pay problems. One caveat: Just because an investment is well meaning doesn't mean it's well managed. If your goal is to do something good for a cause and for yourself at the same time, you need to make sure you don't get the short end of the stick. So if you're pouring your dollars into a mutual fund, do some homework. Go online to Morningstar.com, and make sure that the fund in question has performed in the top one-third of funds in its class over the last one-, three-, and five-year periods. Then read through the report on the fund to be sure Morningstar's independent analyst believes it's sticking to its mission.

Say it and sound smart: *"This social index fund not only invests in things I believe in, its expenses are really, really low."*

Do it: Give some away. Giving to charity feels great. Really, it's as good for your heart as it is for the literally one million charitable institutions in this country that would like a piece of your pie. And Americans are great at opening their wallets. We typically give away about 2 percent of our disposable income—on average—each year, more when disasters such as tsunamis and hurricanes strike. The key: Before you donate, be sure that you will be giving wisely.

You may not have time to research your charity as if it were a term paper. If you're dealing with a name brand organization like the American Heart Association or Save the Children, you may feel research isn't necessary. But let me just say that countless charities throw the word *heart* or *children* or *humanity* into their names to throw you off. So take the time to do at least cursory research. Use the website Guidestar.org to make sure at least 70 percent of the money donated to an organization goes to achieve its underlying mission. Use Give.org to make sure a group has the Better Business Bureau's seal of approval. And, at the very least, go to the website IRS.gov and call up Publication 78. That's a list of all groups with charitable status. You don't want to give money to a charity that turns out not to be a charity after all.

Say it and sound smart: *"I'm planning my giving in advance from now on. This way I'll know I won't forget organizations that really mean something to me."*

Do it: Spend some and give some simultaneously. If your budget is a little squeezed (whose isn't?), you can give by purchasing something for which a portion of the price will be donated to charity. Don't expect that more than 10 percent of the purchase price will go to the underlying cause. That's the norm. And watch out for situations where you can't tell how much of the purchase price will go to the underlying cause.

Say it and sound smart: *"I like to know how much of 'sales' are going to the cause rather than proceeds or profits. Why? It's impossible to know, after all expenses are computed, how much 'proceeds' or 'profits' will actually be."*

Money Math 101

Bottom line: If you're afraid of money because of the math or numbers involved, it's time to attack those fears. Okay, don't panic. The math involved is easy, really, and calculators and other tools are encouraged. You may think using them is "cheating." I don't. They're fine with me.

Find your motivation

Whether you're trying to lose ten pounds, learn a foreign language, or train your new puppy to come when called, having a good incentive really helps. Perhaps it's your impending class reunion, a second honeymoon in Paris (where you've heard the locals are much friendlier if you can parlez-vous a little français), or the fact that you're simply sick of waiting until Fido is ready to do as you ask. When it comes to your money, your motivation may be a personal goal. You may wish you were able to help your children with their math homework—rather than telling them (day after day) that they'll have to wait until their father gets home. Maybe *you'd* like to be the one who calculates the tip in a restaurant. Or maybe—as is likely if you picked up this book—you'd like to get a grip on your financial life and build some real wealth. That's a very, very smart goal.

In other cases, you don't have to find your motivation. Sometimes the motivation finds you, as it did Cyndi, 45. Here's how she conquered her math malaise:

I grew up in the conservative South. My father was the "head of the household," and my mother was the "caretaker" of our home. My father was the "breadwinner," and my mother was the "nurturer." My father taught my brother all about being a smart investor and businessman, like him. My mother taught me how to love and care for a family, like her. My brother always had aspirations of making money and being a businessman. I always had aspirations of marrying someone who would continue the role of my father. Some of my favorite classes in college were Women's Studies. Yet I never even partially considered the mantra of those classes, which was, "A woman can do everything a man can do." Instead, I married a businessman and let my husband handle our finances.

During my marriage, I had an idea of what we had in the bank, but I never really made conscious efforts to be a part of the financial process. I was busy making sure our home was being nurtured. And I had my "breadwinner" husband to take care of our financial decisions so I didn't have to worry.

Four years ago I found out that I was not so good at nurturing our home. My husband found someone else to nurture him, and I no longer had someone to take care of my finances. I was faced with the reality that I actually had no real comprehension of what we had financially or any substantial knowledge of what the difference was between IRAs, mutual funds, or term- or whole-life insurance. There were no files for me to even comb through to see exactly what we had amassed together. At the age of 40, I was going to have to begin to be a financially savvy woman.

I was quickly put into a crash course when my divorce attorney required me to itemize everything we had together. Drawers were haphazardly stuffed with monthly statements, many still in their envelopes, unopened. I began my first financial lesson by spreading out the statements all over the floor so that I could figure out what everything was. Next, I had to find out what everything meant.

Since then, I have read several books on money matters, I have subscribed to financial magazines, and I love to watch TV shows and listen to talk-radio investment segments. I no longer toss unopened envelopes with financial matters into drawers. As a single parent, I know I cannot sit passively waiting for someone to handle my financial decisions for me. I am sad that it took this huge change in my life to get me to pay attention to my money. But I take pride in what I have been able to accomplish. I am constantly planning and tweaking my financial picture for me and my children and our future. And I know that, in the end, I will be just fine.

Cyndi is very honest about the fact that she still has down days as well as up. She doesn't know that the checking account will ever be quite as flush as it once was. She went back to work full-time and scaled back her lifestyle—selling jewelry *and* a flashy car—to keep her kids in the family home and her son in private school. And she understands more downsizing may be in the offing.

But she's feeling great about her accomplishments. She's feeling great about the fact that she took control, that she *could* take control. But as she said in her e-mail to me—and as I know from talking to her at different times—she really came from nowhere. She was at the starting line. She felt as if she were ten yards behind it. Yet step by step she did what she had to do to make the world a safer place financially for herself and her kids. She's proud of herself. And she deserves to be.

Learn the basics

You do not need algebra and calculus. You don't need geometry or trigonometry. You don't even need long division (or if you do need it, you certainly don't need to do it by hand). You need addition, subtraction, multiplication, and simple division. You can use a calculator. But it's also helpful to have some of these sums and products at your fingertips so that if you're in a store, for instance, and you want to know what it'll cost you to buy 7 turtlenecks for your kids at $12 apiece, you can do the math in your head. You also need a basic grasp of percentages, decimals, and fractions. If you feel you need some help boning up on these skills, I've provided a basic primer below. If this is not an issue for you, skip ahead to the next section on negotiating.

PERCENTAGES

What are they? The word *percent* means "parts of 100." If someone says you scored a 70 on a 100-item math test, that means you got 70 out of 100 correct and achieved a 70 percent success rate.

REAL-LIFE/REAL-MONEY USE

Interest rates, inflation rates, tips in restaurants, and how much interest you're earning on your money are expressed as percentages. You can use them to compare the deals you get on money market accounts from various banks. If one bank is offering 2 percent annually and another is offering 3 or 4 percent, you can easily tell where you'll be getting the better deal.

DECIMALS

Decimals are also parts of 100, but they are expressed as "points" rather than "percent." Think of taking a child's temperature: 98.6—"ninety-eight point six"—is really 98 and six-tenths (a fraction—we'll get to those in a moment) or 98 and 60 percent.

REAL-LIFE/REAL-MONEY USE

To use decimals in real life, you need to be able to convert decimals to percentages. When you shop the sales, for instance, you'll see signs (particularly after the holidays) that say items are selling for 40 percent off the original price. Suppose the original price of an item is $120. How can you find out how much 40 percent of $120 is? First, convert 40 percent into a decimal. To do that, start at the right-hand side of the number and put a period two digits to the left: 40 percent becomes the decimal .40 (7 percent would become the decimal .07). Then multiply the decimal by the original price to get the discount: $120 × .40 = $48). Finally, subtract the discount from the original price to get the new selling price: $120 − $48 = $72. If you get in the habit of carrying a calculator, you can figure out what sort of prices you'll pay *before* you get to the checkout counter.

FRACTIONS

Fractions are numbers expressed in parts as well—a numerator over a denominator. A percentage can be stated as a fraction in which the denominator is 100: 50% = $^{50}/_{100}$. With fractions, your goal is to reduce the denominator to the smallest possible number so that the fraction becomes easier to deal with. Thus, $^{50}/_{100}$ is the same as ½, and 25 percent or $^{25}/_{100}$ is the same as ¼. Often, thinking of these amounts as parts of a dollar—coins—can be very helpful. For example, $^{50}/_{100}$ is equivalent to a half-dollar (50 cents), and $^{25}/_{100}$ is equivalent to a quarter (25 cents).

REAL-LIFE/REAL-MONEY USE

Fractions, like percentages, show up all the time when stores put things on sale. You often see things marked "½ price" or "½ off." Fractions also are common in recipes.

Once you get good at percentages, decimals, and fractions you'll be able to use them interchangeably. Here are the ones you'll see most often whether you're perusing the stock tables, clearance sales, or a recipe book.

Percentage	Decimal	Fraction
10%	.10	⅒
12.5%	.125	⅛
25%	.25	¼
33%	.33	⅓
37.5%	.375	⅜
50%	.5	½
62.5%	.625	⅝

Percentage	Decimal	Fraction
66%	.66	⅔
75%	.75	¾
87.5%	.875	⅞
100%	1	1

PERCENTAGE CHANGES

This is the last concept you need to grasp for now. Percentage changes show you how much more or less something is worth this year than last year—how much money you've made in your 401(k), for example, or how much you've earned on your house.

Often, when you deal with brokerage firms and read the stock pages, the percentage changes are computed for you. But knowing how to do it yourself can be helpful—and it's easy.

Figuring out a percentage change is a two-step process.

1. *Take today's value and from it subtract the prior value.*
2. *Divide that answer by the prior value.*

Suppose the following: Your house is worth $300,000 now, you bought it for $220,000, and you want to know how much money you made in percentage terms. First, subtract the prior value from today's value: $300,000 − $220,000 = $80,000. Then divide that answer by the prior value: $80,000 ÷ $220,000 = .363636.

You made slightly over 36 percent. In other words, you made a killing.

MAP TO A MILLION

Make a simple math move that's guaranteed to improve your financial situation. Move $2,000 a year from a savings account earning 1.5 percent to a money market account earning 4 percent:

	1.5%	4%	EARNINGS DIFFERENCE
10 years	$23,738	$27,076	$3,338
20 years	$48,993	$64,461	$15,468
30 years	$78,332	$120,196	$41,864

Move $2,000 a year from a savings account earning 1.5 percent to an index fund earning 8 percent:

	1.5%	4%	EARNINGS DIFFERENCE
10 years	$23,738	$33,828	$10,090
20 years	$48,993	$104,475	$55,482
30 years	$78,332	$261,288	$182,956

Learn shortcuts

Let's get one thing straight: When it comes to doing math in the adult world, there will not be any final exams. You don't need to have the answers precisely right. You don't need to use particular formulas. And you don't need to show your work. So by all means, use whatever shortcuts you find helpful.

ROUNDING

When you are rounding, you bump a number up, or you knock a number down, to the closest big (or round) number. If you think in terms of tens, then 77 becomes 80, and 72 becomes 70. If you think in terms of hundreds, then 267 becomes 300, and 234 becomes 200.

REAL-LIFE/REAL-MONEY USE

It is absolutely fine to round cents off to the nearest dollar when figuring tips or approximate costs. It's even fine to do this if you're trying to balance your checkbook. As long as you have enough money in your checking account to cover the checks you're writing, no financial police are going to rat you out.

ESTIMATING

When you estimate, you do enough of a calculation to come up with a ballpark answer to a numerical or financial question.

REAL-LIFE/REAL-MONEY USE

Suppose you need to buy three pair of panty hose and they cost $8.50 a pair. You know you're looking at spending roughly $26. Estimating is a perfectly fine—in fact, time-saving—thing to do. Just be sure to estimate up, not down, to be sure you have enough of a cushion in your credit line or sufficient cash in your wallet to complete the transaction without penalty or embarrassment.

Use technology to your advantage

CALCULATORS

I've already mentioned pulling out a calculator, so you already know that I'm all for taking advantage of that technology. There's no reason for you to feel as if you need to run heavy-duty numbers in your head when your cell phone, BlackBerry, or even your wristwatch have perfectly good calculators built in. Use them and stop stressing.

ONLINE BANKING OR PERSONAL FINANCE SOFTWARE

I am a huge fan of banking online and personal finance software programs such as Quicken and Money from Microsoft. Either can take a person who doesn't like to watch her money coming in and going out and turn her into someone who can't wait to see what percentage of her spending each month went to eating out and what percentage to entertainment. How? The software makes it easy to input your financial information by asking you questions in plain English. The setup may seem tedious, but once you're up and running, using finance software is a piece of cake. And you'll actually save time in the long run—particularly if you start paying your bills online.

A study from Javelin Strategies showed that it takes the average American family about two hours a month to pay bills by handwriting checks. If you do it online (once you get past the hour or so needed to start up), it takes fifteen minutes a month. Consider the extra hour-forty-five a freebie.

Asking for More

A few pages ago, I promised you some advice on improving your earning power—on increasing the size of your paycheck. This involves fine-tuning skills that have less to do with math (*or* money) and more to do with negotiating (*for* money). If you're like many women, one of the things you "hate" most about money is asking for it. That has to change.

Recently, a study came out from UC Irvine. Professor Lisa Barron put MBA students through a series of mock job interviews. Barron set it up so that every student did well enough in the interview to merit not only *a* job offer—but *the same* job offer. She offered each person the same position for an annual salary of $61,000. Then she sat back and waited to see what sorts of counteroffers ensued. On average, the men Barron interviewed asked for $68,500; the women, $67,000.

Now remember, these were students in the same program who had learned the same things and were graduating the same year. Why the discrepancy? Why did the men feel they were entitled to $1,500 more than the women?

Barron learned by interviewing her subjects after the fact that two things were going on. The men said they believed they deserved to earn *more* money than all the others in their class. So to them it was natural to ask for a higher salary. The women said they felt they deserved to earn the *same* money as all the others. So they didn't want to overshoot. The other big difference: Four out of five men had studied the market enough to have a decent sense of their true value. Only one out of five women had done the same.

You don't have to turn a lot of pages in books on women and money before you come upon the wage gap: the fact that even today, more than sixty years after Rosie the Riveter went to work and nearly thirty-five years after Gloria Steinem founded *Ms.*, women still earn just 77 cents for every dollar earned by men. But here's the thing—and it's a point that I make in many chapters of this book: These averages, like all averages, are talking about all women as a group. They are not describing particular women. And they do not have to describe you.

So, let's take a step back and focus on why you're not earning as much as you could be earning. Why do you get the smaller office—the one without a window? Why do you get an assistant with fewer years of seasoning or—yikes!—no assistant at all? Step away from the workplace and look at other areas of your life and ask yourself: Why do I pay more for certain things—cars are the most prominent example—than do those on the planet with a little more testosterone? What is going on?

Part of the problem is probably historical. There are likely longstanding biases in your own corporate hierarchy just as there are in the world at large. You may earn less than the men in your office who do similar work because the women who came before you earned less. You may pay more on a new car than a man pays because the women who came before you paid more. Biases like these can be fought. But you have to be willing to fight them. And doing so takes a set of skills you probably don't have. Not yet, anyway.

That's precisely how Connie feels. She admits quite candidly (as do Lisa and Susan and many other women): *"I'm a terrible negotiator."*

I want to pull that statement apart. What Connie and Lisa and Susan are saying when they say *"I'm a terrible negotiator"* is *"I am terrible at negotiating . . . for money . . . for me."*

Connie, for one, is a consultant and an attorney. She has absolutely no problem negotiating brilliant business deals on someone else's behalf. But when her own money is on the line, Connie falls apart. You probably have little difficulty negotiating for things other than money. Your teenager wants a later curfew? Your babysitter wants to borrow the car? You want your town to institute a system of policing the parks at night? You have absolutely no difficulty in presenting a coherent argument, in making your case, in being sure that you are heard, and in laying down the law. But when the subject is money and the beneficiary is you, somehow it all falls apart.

There are four emotionally charged reasons that this happens:

- **You don't believe you deserve it.** Sometimes financial success is very difficult to stomach. Perhaps you grew up in a family that looked down on wealth or on wealthy people. Perhaps you grew up with a father who worked incredibly hard at a job (teacher, clergyman, government employee) that brought a lot of respect but not a lot of wealth. A large paycheck may bring with it considerable baggage. You may feel guilty for working less hard (and earning more money) than your father. You may feel guilty for earning more than colleagues who have families to support when you do not.

- **You don't believe other people think you deserve it.** I've had this problem from time to time. I am very efficient at work. I get in at a decent hour (after I put my children on the bus), and I get out at a decent hour (so that if I can't get home in time for dinner, I can at least put them to bed). Over the years, I've feared that the people who come in much earlier than I do or stay much later than I do think that I don't deserve a paycheck that is larger than some of theirs. I would tell myself that they don't see the fact that some mornings I get up and work from 5 a.m. to 7 a.m. I would rationalize I had more years of experience under my belt. Finally, I just had to get over it. There is only one person—besides you—who needs to believe that you deserve your wage, and that's your boss. As long as your existence makes his or her existence easier and makes the company more profitable, chances are that's precisely the logic that boss will follow.

- **You know you deserve more, but not how much more.** This problem is easy to solve thanks to the Internet. Jump online and head to Monster.com, Salary.com, or one of the other large résumé sites. Peruse the job listings to see how much people with your qualifications are fetching on the open market. If you don't find enough information to convince you, start networking with people at other companies until you know one or two of them well enough to ask, "What would I earn if I jumped ship and came to your place?" Of course, the ultimate signal of your worth is another job offer. But don't take it to your current employer unless you're actually willing to make the shift. More on that momentarily.

- **You know precisely how much more you deserve, but you don't know how to get it.** Aha. In other words, you know you're underpaid and overworked; you just can't find the vocabulary to help yourself out of this particular jam. Now we're getting somewhere!

You need to stand up for yourself—and your money

This is a crucial skill to add to your workplace toolbox. There are a number of reasons. When you start out receiving a smaller-than-necessary raise, whatever subsequent raises you get build on that smaller base. That means you end up more behind down the road. Add in the fact that women's raises—because women take breaks from the workforce to care for kids or for elderly parents—tend to be sporadic, and that when women reenter the workforce, they do so for less money, and well, you get the picture.

One thing that's very likely standing in your way are some ingrained misconceptions about negotiating. You need to acknowledge that negotiating does not mean being pushy.

I have children and nieces and nephews. So I believe I have a pretty good sense of how today's children play. And guess what? Once you get beyond the computers and gizmos and gadgets, it's pretty similar to the way you and I played. Girls like to play lady. And ladies—for better or worse (and often, I think, for worse)—don't always say what's on their minds. Ladies—think Glenn Close in the remake of *The Stepford Wives*—speak in measured tones. A lady might believe that negotiating is pushy. A woman needs to understand that it is not.

Getting what you're worth, as long as you have the conversation appropriately, is the polite thing to do. Harboring resentment because you're not being paid what you're worth is far more dangerous. It's then that the whistle on your teakettle is going to blow.

Negotiating is also not personal. What do you think the person across the table is thinking as you throw numbers back and forth? Do you think he or she is sizing you up, thinking: *"Hmmmm, Suzie or Charlotte or Lily or Gail, she isn't really worth another $175 a week. I don't like the outfit she's wearing today. Besides, she can't even roast a decent chicken. She can't do the crossword puzzle in ink"*? Not even close. That person is thinking about himself or herself. His needs. Her budget. What will make his or her life easier? And how can that be accomplished for as little money as possible so that there will be enough in the till to give a raise to the next person who asks? It's not about being your friend. It's about getting the job done. If you keep that in mind throughout the process, you'll have an easier time getting through it. And remember: Negotiating is productive. If you do not negotiate—if you do not ask—the answer will always be no.

Let me repeat that: If you do not negotiate—if you do not ask for what you want—then the answer will always be no.

So whether your aim is a raise or a better price on your next new car or house, here are the rules you need to follow to get the very best deal:

- **Gather all the information.** When you are negotiating for anything, you have to think of yourself as a lawyer. You're Angie Harmon from *Law & Order*. You're Kinsey Millhone from Sue Grafton's novels. And that means before you say word one, before you form your hypothesis or make your case, you get the goods. If it's a salary you're negotiating for, then you've been online to see what similar jobs are offering, you're talking to headhunters to see what sort of offer you might expect, and you know how that compensation is structured in terms of wages, commissions, and bonuses if it isn't paid as straight salary.

Sometimes the best nuggets of information come from people who hold similar jobs. I recommend posing the question like this: "I'm thinking of getting a job doing x, y, or z. How much do people with experience like mine typically get paid?" That gives those on the receiving end of the question the liberty to reveal all the information without saying that they're revealing their own salaries (which, generally, they will be). That's very helpful. In the same vein, if it's a car you're buying, you know how much the dealer paid for it and how much of a markup it's typically fetching. You know what the best financing rates are today, and you've secured financing before you even walk into the dealership. You need to be prepared; otherwise you won't have answers to the questions you're inevitably going to face.

- **Visualize the result.** Wanting a raise or a new car isn't specific enough. You need to know how much of a raise (in actual dollars) you want to get out of this conversation. When your boss asks what your number is, suggest one that is 10 percent higher than your actual number. That gives your employer room to negotiate. (Neither side wants to seem to give in too easily.) Also, enter this negotiation with a list of things you might be willing to accept other than money: more vacation time, a title bump, the flexibility to spend part of your time working from home. Even if a particular employer does not have enough wiggle room to give you a bump in salary, having a list of backup options means you don't have to walk away empty-handed.

- **Be prepared to walk.** I once had an employer suggest to me that I get another offer before I ask for a raise. That way, as he put it, he'd have ammunition to take to his boss that could be used to get me more money. It worked. But it could have backfired. If you go to your employer with another offer in your back pocket (or, for that matter, to a car dealer, or to anyone else you're negotiating with), you have to be willing to walk if you don't get what you're asking for. If you're not willing to walk, don't play that card. You might find yourself headed out the door before you're fully ready to leave.

- **Know what you are contributing to the bottom line.** If you're asking for money, point out to the boss how you've made money for the company, saved money for the company, or contributed something that has led to the advancement of everybody around you. If you're buying something, point out to the salesman how much of a profit he stands to make on this car or this house. And do both without one drop of apology in your voice. Do not start with "I know the company has had a tough year" or "You may not be able to do this, but I thought I'd ask." That's not how men do it. They believe they deserve more money (or a better deal), so they walk in the door assuming they'll get what they're asking for. Not surprisingly, they often do.

- **Give a little to get a little.** I have received the best deals—on both purchases and salaries—when I stopped behaving like a bulldog and started listening to what the person on the other side of the transaction needed to make a deal happen for me. In the case of the car, I had a number in my head—a monthly payment—I wanted to hit. The salesman couldn't do it on a new car coming off the lot. He tried. We ran the numbers several different ways, with his financing choices and the financing I brought in my back pocket. Finally, I just opened the window and asked: Is there any way you could make this work? He left the room. He came back. And when he did he said, "How about a demo? I have a six-month-old demo. I can give you the full warranty, and I can come in below your number." I took a look. It had six thousand miles on it and was in perfect condition. Done deal. Likewise, in previous job negotiations, I've promised employers things I knew they could take to the bank in exchange for a greater salary up front or for other things I valued, such as an options package and more flexibility to work from home.

- **Be willing to do things others are not.** Take traveling for business as an example. It's a considerable strain so it's not something that everyone is willing to do. But it is something that can get you paid more handsomely. The same is true of working evenings, weekends, early mornings, or at far-flung locales. And the same is true of buying a car in a particular color that isn't moving quickly off the lot or with a package of options that hasn't proven to be especially popular.

Lastly, and this has everything to do with job choice and selection rather than negotiation, if you want to be paid more, it's time to stop making lateral moves. You may be unhappy for a whole host of reasons, but you have to understand that men don't leave a job simply to get out, as women tend to do. When men get out, they move up. You need to do the same.

LOOK HOW FAR YOU'VE COME!

When you have a fear or phobia—whether you're scared of crowds or heights or snakes or numbers—it takes a lot of courage to acknowledge it and attempt to face it down. For those of you whose math anxiety has prevented you from dealing head on with your money, I applaud you for taking a huge step in the right direction. You don't need calculus to get rich in this lifetime, but you do need basic money math. And you need to know how to ask for what you need and want. Armed with the knowledge in this chapter you can move forward on the path to wealth. In the next chapter we'll look at another one of the emotional blocks that may be standing in your way: Your relationship with your partner or spouse.

How can I slowly start to manage my money? What is easy to do so I can first get some confidence in my ability?

It's all about small steps. If you can incorporate one small step into your financial life each week (or even each month), you can slowly start to turn your life around. Here are the two changes I'd make first: (1) Tackle the bills. Pay them as soon as they come in. (2) Incorporate saving into that bill payment system. Pay yourself each month by opening a savings account and automatically transferring a small amount of money into savings each month and telling yourself that money is *hands off*! You'll gain a huge amount of confidence just from these two maneuvers. Paying your bills as they come in means that you'll have more in savings, less in credit card debt, and you'll be happier. It also ensures that you'll have few if any late payments, which means your credit score will start to increase. And you'll see your savings start to rise. In other words: It'll be win-win-win all around.

I just read the section on giving to charity. How do I manage to save and give money away, also?

You manage to give money while simultaneously saving if you plan in advance to do both. If you know that this year your goal is to put $2,400 in savings and to give $600 to the American Heart Association, then you'll be able to break your goal down into manageable bites. You know that saving $2,400 this year means saving $200 a month and that giving $600 this year means giving $50 a month. Those smaller chunks are much easier to wrap your brain around and actually accomplish. I do want to tell

you one other thing: There may be a time or two in your life when you are too strapped to give to charity. You may not be able to swing it. That's okay. Find another way to give. Give of your time. Or donate your old belongings to charity. You'll feel almost as good as if you wrote a big, fat check. You may get a tax deduction, too.

How long will it take until I stop feeling so lost?

Not as long as you think. I've believed for a really long time that beginning to exercise is a good metaphor for beginning to manage your money. The first time you pull on your sneakers and head out to the high school track prepared to run—gasp—a mile, you're not halfway around before you start to lose your breath. But if you keep at it, running then walking, then running a little more and walking a little less, it won't be long before you can circle the perimeter a full four times. That mile is under your belt; then you're working on five laps. Managing your money is similar. The first time you read the financial pages of your newspaper, try to explain to the counter agent that you want to open an IRA, or interview a financial planner, you will feel lost. You will feel as if you're speaking in a foreign language. But a week or two into your newspaper experiment, and a conversation or two later with those financial pros, you'll find you feel significantly better. But promise me something right here and right now: No matter how fish-out-of-water you feel, if you don't understand something, I want you to ask question after question after question until you really do understand it. This is *your* money we're talking about. The financial pros make a piece of it for convincing you to put it with them. It's fine to make them earn their fee.

CHAPTER 3

"But My Husband Does That . . ."

DON'T BITCH

In my twenties, before I was married, I managed to balance my check-book and keep track of what was coming in and what was going out. As long as I made sure there was more of the former than the latter, I was okay. I maintained a simple checking and saving account, and I never thought about investing beyond signing up for a 401(k) with my company.

When I got married, I kept my own account as long as I continued to hold down my full-time job. When I switched jobs, I knew so little about how 401(k) money was taxed that I chose to receive the money in a lump sum rather than reinvesting it! (Alas, I found the words lump sum *more appealing than actually focusing on what I should do with the money to avoid the hefty penalty.)*

Sometime after my second child was born and I left my job to go free-lance, my husband and I merged our money into a joint account. That was the last time I had anything to do with managing it. That was six years ago. The money I make freelancing gets deposited into the account, but I don't even bother to record it (other than get receipts from the cash machine, which I promptly crumple up and shove into my purse).

Likewise, though I diligently record every check I write, I make no attempt to "balance" the checkbook because my husband takes care of paying the major bills (mortgage, car payments, insurance, utilities, credit card). I'm never aware of how much money is going out and, consequently, how much is in the checking account at any given time. It's complicated by the fact that my husband runs his own business and pays himself at somewhat erratic intervals. So every time I write a check greater than $20, I feel like I have to check with him to make sure there are sufficient funds in the account. What's more, though the statements from our accounts with investment banks are slipped through the mail slot every day, I simply collect them into neat piles and leave them on my husband's chair, glad to clear them off the kitchen island and be done with them.

How did I become this person??!!

Kelly, freelance writer

Sound familiar? You don't have to feel bad about that. But it is something you ought to think about, and after thinking about it, you may want to change. Here's the deal: There are two big reasons (and a host of little ones) why you let your husband or partner take control of your financial life.

Reason 1: He wants control. He wants it because his father had it before him, because he trusts himself more than he trusts you, because he thinks it's easier if only one set of hands messes with the money, or because he's earning more of it so he feels entitled to say where it goes. He also wants control because it makes him feel like a man—a traditional man, but a man nonetheless.

Filling the traditional roles that our parents and grandparents filled before us feels safe. It feels secure. That's why you want (or at least don't want to let go of) to make the beds and pack the school lunches and do the laundry and cook dinner. You may complain about doing all these things. But give them up? That's surprisingly tough as well. Doing these traditional tasks makes you feel needed. Being asked to stop doing them feels like an affront. Not just to you—to him as well.

That's what Kate, a physician, found every time she asked her husband about taking on some of the money management tasks:

When I have approached my husband about our money and have tried to get more involved (like insisting we go see a financial adviser), he gets very defensive. With all the strains that our busy family lives put on a marriage, it can be easier to cede this territory.

A man may want to maintain control even though dealing with the money makes him cranky or irritable and he believes he is not particularly good at it. That's what Ellen experienced:

My husband and I had a fight just yesterday morning when he was sitting down to do the bills. He was not happy. So I told him I would take over the bills. I said, "I already have two jobs (the kids and my work). What's the difference if I take on a third?" But of course, that would never happen. He doesn't want me to, because he doesn't think I can handle it.

These arguments come from fear. In some deep-seated and fundamental way, your husband believes that if you can manage the household money, then you'll stop needing him. And that if you stop needing him, then you'll stop wanting him. In other words, he believes that if you don't need him to do the "traditional man" things, then your participation in the marriage will no longer be a necessity (it will be a choice), and he fears that if the relationship hits a rough patch, you'll be out of there.

He has a point. It's no coincidence that as more women have started earning more money, more women have started initiating divorces. High-earning women *are* more likely to leave their husbands than women who don't work outside the house. But wanting your spouse to feel needed is no excuse for not taking responsibility for your money. In the best relationships, both partners have a hand in running the money—no matter who's bringing home the more sizable paycheck. More on that, momentarily. First let's explore the other reason men tend to manage the household finances.

Reason 2: You want him to have control. Having a husband or partner who controls the money makes you feel taken care of, coddled, indulged. It makes you feel loved. It brings out your inner princess. And that—as many, many women noted to me—is a very appealing notion.

We all—admit it—we all want someone to take care of us and do the icky stuff that we don't like such as deal with money, numbers, spiders, and plumbing.

Karen, publicist

I am somewhat ashamed to admit it, but I believe there is that '50s housewife lurking somewhere beneath most women's Ivy League degrees, wanting to be taken care of, to trust completely in her man. I think a lot of us keep her well hidden beneath our independent mannerisms, feminist sensibilities, and smarts.

Abby, dentist

Interestingly, even some women who earn the lion's share of the family money feel that a fair division of labor is for him to take over inside the house. Amanda, a communications director for a large corporation notes, *"I probably have some expectation that if I'm going to make all the money, then I think my husband should manage it."*

Trouble is, indulging that inner princess—allowing her to sit primly on her throne and have all of the "icky" stuff taken care of for her—is a dangerous thing to do. If you don't understand why, reread Chapter 1. It will remind you with lots of facts and figures that you will in all likelihood be forced to handle your own money at some point in your life. You want to know how to do that before some event—some life emergency—puts you in a position where you don't have any choice.

This Is What You Were Taught

I understand there may be an awful lot of history here to erase—or at least to plow through—before you'll feel comfortable asking for or insisting on (and you may *have* to insist) equal ownership. Ilene wasn't the only one to say, *"My mother always told me that the man should handle the money."* Lauren, a corporate trainer, says:

"I guess I could get Freudian about it and say that it's because it was always my dad who made the financial decisions in our household."

Have you ever stopped to think about why your mother taught you as she did? Sure, in part, she did it because her mother taught her in the same way. It worked well once, she figured, and would work well again. But she also kept you out of the financial matters at home in order to maintain peace.

Observant Jews have a concept known as *Shalom Bayit*, or "peace in the home." (Many other religions and cultures have a similar concept, just as most cultures have a version of the egg roll.) According to Shalom Bayit, the world is cold; it is a place in which you have to fight for what is yours and what is right, a place in which people are just as likely to give you an icy stare as a warm smile. In contrast, the home is to be a place of peace and harmony, where human interaction is *non*confrontational.

Money can be a very confrontational subject. So you may have grown up watching your mother get along—no matter what the cost—rather than confront, rather than even try to cooperate. When it came to the household finances, that meant ceding control. You modeled your behavior on hers. And as a result, it feels natural to you to do what she did.

Marriage Changes Everything

The interesting thing is, unlike your mother—but like Kelly, the freelance writer whose story starts this chapter—you may have run your own finances quite successfully before you got married or settled into a permanent relationship. You may have done it for quite a long time—years, decades. You may even have found, as Lauren, the corporate trainer, did, that you have a knack for managing money. (*"It's funny,"* Lauren remarks, *"everything I've tried to invest in has actually done really well."*)

Yet after a walk down the aisle, the urge is to get those money management jobs off your plate, to give them up. Researchers have even seen a marked difference between people who live together and people who are married. When people are "just" living together, they still operate as two independent souls who happen to reside under one roof. They both wash the dishes. They both pay the bills. Women feel little pressure to give up a career or job that is meaningful to them. But when they marry, they start carrying the cultural weight that for generations has come along with being husbands or wives, and their behavior changes accordingly. Not in every case, of course, but generally: Husbands no longer do the laundry. Wives no longer take out the garbage. Husbands hand over the social calendar. And wives, who are now more likely to stop working (especially when children come along, even if they have jobs they like), hand over the finances.

Interestingly, the more financial independence a woman has, the less eager she is to get married. Working women are 50 percent more likely to move in with a partner and 15 percent less likely to marry than women who don't work steadily, according to research from Cornell University. By contrast, the more financially independent men are, the *more* likely they are to want to put a ring on some woman's finger. Men who earn an above-average salary are 26 percent more likely to get married than those who earn an average one. Again, that's tradition talking. Once men get to the point where they can comfortably support themselves, it's second nature for them to want to provide for others, first a spouse and then a family. Doing so makes them feel like men.

As Earnings Shift, We Enter a New Era

Trouble is, all traditions—and the way we feel about them—are on very shaky ground these days. That's because the world of earnings is changing. And it's doing so very quickly. Consider:

In 1981, 16 percent of women earned more than their spouses.

By 2000—nearly two decades later—that number had climbed to 22 percent.

Today, it's 30 percent (some researchers say it's even higher), which means the needle moved by 8 percentage points in only six years.

Experts who look at educational trends—the fact that more women than men are now applying to college and to many graduate schools—believe that by 2030 the average woman will earn more than the average man.

Those changes may signal a big problem for American family life. Research completed in the past few years shows that men *and* women prefer the traditional model. Men *and* women are happier in marriages in which the husband earns more than the wife. Men *and* women are happier in marriages in which the woman does most of the housework. These days, however, that model is not always possible to achieve. When a woman marries a man who is younger than she is (according to the AARP, one-third of women ages 40 to 60 are dating younger men) and has less experience in the workforce, she is likely to earn more than he. Male-dominated industries like manufacturing have been among those shaken hardest by outsourcing, which means the women in those families may be on firmer ground. And the simple fact that women traditionally have earned less makes them more attractive employees to keep in times of downsizing.

So women compensate. If you are a woman who outearns her spouse or partner, you know exactly what I mean. Some families hide the fact that the woman is the breadwinner by putting complete financial control in the hands of the man or by earmarking the woman's income to pay the big bills (such as the mortgage and car payments) so there's no money left for her to spend as she sees fit. Other times, the woman feels so guilty about outearning her partner that she takes on more and more of the housework. Rarely will either spouse admit that the woman is the breadwinner to their families or friends. And if and when those superficial fixes fail to work, more of these families split up than the average.

That's right, in situations where women earn more, the likelihood of divorce rises. We know that it's more often the women who want out. However, we do not know which comes first: Does the fact that women are earning more make them think they can find a better life outside their marriage? Or do unhappy women seek to earn more as a way to escape a bad situation? This is a very important distinction. But either way, the paradigm shift raises a crucial question: How do you find a safe place that allows you to get rich and stay married? Or, if you're single, a place that allows you to build a secure and loving relationship with a partner in the future?

Here are my suggestions, based on current research, my conversations with women in this situation, and my own life experience as a woman who has been in the position of earning more—and earning less—than her spouse. These are some ways to think about the work you're doing and the money you're bringing in. I'm asking you to change your attitudes, not necessarily your habits. (In the next section, we'll get to specific tactics that allow you to build wealth.)

Do it: Talk—and listen—to each other. Paychecks and housework aside, a new study from the University of Virginia shows that the factor that contributes *most* to whether you are happy in your marriage is whether your husband or partner is engaged *emotionally*. If he listens to you, is concerned about what's important to you, stops and focuses when it is clear that you are happy or unhappy about something and want to share, you are likely to want to stick around for more. How do you get him to this point? Start by doing the same for him. If he doesn't get it, then ask—outright—for him to pay attention.

Say it and sound smart: *"I really want to know what happened during your day—and how you feel about it. And then I want to tell you about mine."*

Do it: Date. You may have to get each other out of the house, out of the busyness of everyday life, in order to pay attention to each other's needs. So date. Once a week is a must. Twice a week is a plus. And at least a few times a year (even if you have to bribe a sibling or a friend or pay a sitter) leave the kids at home or ship them out so you can have a quiet overnight or weekend. Being in your own house in front of a fire, reading books and rubbing each other's feet, or eating popcorn and watching a video you've chosen together without little ones begging for attention is *necessary* for the preservation of a romantic relationship.

Say it and sound smart: *"I made a dinner reservation for 8:00, the sitter is coming at 7:30. You can thank me later."*

Do it: Be his biggest cheerleader. Make the effort to understand why your husband gets such a kick out of his career, say, teaching middle-school Social Studies or, if he doesn't work outside the house, why he enjoys staying home with the kids. What does it do for his psyche? How does it feel to him to be the teacher all the kids *want* to have or the dad who gets to see the smiles coming off the school bus? Tell him how much you admire what he's doing. Tell him how you feel about the fact that he can be home after school to help your kids with their homework and how it's helping them pull better grades. Here's the key: You have to believe, deep down, that what your partner is bringing to the relationship is just as valuable as what you are bringing to the relationship. Otherwise, you are destined to fail.

Say it and sound smart: *"I am so grateful for the great job you're doing for our family. You're a great role model for the kids."*

Do it: Let him be your biggest cheerleader. Share enough about your day to allow him to get the same sense from you. What's it like working in that big hospital? Do you get a rush having all those people report to you? Share with him when you get a raise or promotion or kudos for a job well done. Don't bury it because you're afraid to overshadow him. Allow him to be proud of you in the same way that you are of him. Concentrate on what's good for your family, not the perceptions of the outside world. It will help immensely if you can shut out the noise. As women have risen in the working world, we have seen instances where they turn down jobs involving travel or promotions—even if they would enjoy those opportunities—because they think they'll be perceived to be bad wives or bad mothers. You'll be a lot less likely to make choices that matter to others (others who are largely irrelevant) if you and your spouse are working as a team.

Say it and sound smart: *"As long as it works for our family, who cares what anyone else thinks?"*

Do it: Focus on the endgame. Discuss your paychecks—both of them. But try to do so in the context of getting somewhere as a family. Talk about what you want your money to do for you. What are your shared goals as a couple? As parents? Do you want to pay off the house? Travel to Greece? Put the kids through college with as few loans as possible? Retire promptly at 65? Well, okay then. And if you disagree about the goals, compromise. Even agreeing to disagree about certain things is part of the process. These are the important things, not the size of your individual paychecks. The size of your paychecks is relevant only to whether there's enough there—combined—in order to make those things possible. And if there's not, then you both modify the goals, or modify your jobs, to make them possible. But you do it working together. You keep the lines of communication open.

Say it and sound smart: *"That raise you got will really help us pay off the car this year. Then we can focus on stockpiling for college."*

The Bitch Factor

Let's get this out on the table: There's one big fear with taking financial control in a family situation, even if you're not taking over but are asserting an equal position or even are just getting up to speed with where your family is with its money. As one woman (who asked me not to print even her first name) wrote: "I'm afraid my husband—and everyone else—is going to think I'm a bitch."

Ahhhh.

Remember that old Enjoli commercial? If you're near 40, you probably do. (If not, ask your mother to sing it.) It featured a sexy woman in her skivvies warbling about how she could "bring home the bacon" while never letting her husband "forget he's a man." Many women hated it. But they never forgot it, either.

The harsh reality is, despite the decades that have rolled by, in many households it seems necessary to do precisely that. That's why in most two-income households—even those where the woman is outearning the man—of the 28 hours of housework that needs to be done, the man is doing an average of 8. That's why, even in households where a husband is *unemployed,* the wife often actively denies that she is the primary provider. Admitting otherwise would be wearing the pants. And by wearing the pants, she might come off—you got it—as a bitch.

The solution—the only one that works—is to close ranks. The secret that couples in happy marriages have always understood is that if it works for the two of you, inside the house and inside your heads, the outside world can't touch you. As long as you both feel good about your situation, secure in your devotion to each other, supported by one another emotionally and tactically (some sharing of those household chores has to occur; if neither one of you is up for it, try hiring out), then it really doesn't matter who thinks you're a bitch, does it? The only opinion you really care about is that of the husband or partner who loves you and the happy, well-adjusted kids you raise together. The outside world suddenly matters much less.

Getting a Grip on What's Yours, Mine, and Ours

Once you get past the emotional barriers that are causing you to give up control of your money, you have to understand the tactical advantage of keeping at least partial control. I want you to think, for a second, about a Little League baseball game. Picture a bunch of ten-year-olds trekking around the bases on a spring day. Some of them can hit. Most of them can't. It's a comedy of errors. And it's deadly boring and slow unless . . . that's right, unless your child is playing. Then it's dramatic. It's exciting. You keep stats with the other parents. And you don't want to be anywhere else.

Money is exactly like that. It's boring and uninteresting unless you have a personal stake in the game. If you give up control of your paycheck or control of the household accounts—even to a spouse—you lose that personal interest. But, as Karen the publicist notes, that's what many women do:

> *Most women I know have no idea what's in the bank account or where the money is—and it's actually a double-edged sword. Because as angry as it makes men, I have come to realize that they like it that way because it keeps us dependent on them. Let's face it, they can't find anything, don't know where anything is, don't know who's who and what's what, yet they want us to depend on them. And truth be told, it's scary to be fully independent. But as Mom told me as a little girl, if you want freedom and independence, you have to embrace re-sponsibility. That's why I truly believe taking responsibility for our money is our red sports car, our "affair," so to speak.*

And it really can be that exciting. Witness the power you feel the first time one of your investments—one you picked on your own—experiences stellar growth. Think about how smug you feel when you read the real es-tate section of the Sunday paper and realize the house you insisted on buy-ing, four years ago, is now worth twice what it was worth back then. (You wanted a retirement account? You're living in it!) And consider how smart you look now that your mortgage rate, the one *you* shopped for, locked into, and decided was the right one to take, is a total steal. New mortgages are three percentage points higher! You did that!!

Or maybe you didn't, just yet. But you have the potential. You *can*. Here is the only key you need to get started.

A Bank Account of Your Own

I used to believe that as long as both members of a couple agreed on joint or separate checking accounts, that was all that was necessary to make the money in a marriage work. I would point to my parents, who merged everything and stayed married forever.

It took me a while to realize that my parents were an anomaly. My mother (who spent only a few years out of the workforce) managed the money. Paying the bills made my father irritable, so my mother took over. She wrote the checks. She picked the bond funds. She allocated the retirement funds. As far as money was concerned, my mother was an equal partner. And she was quite concerned for her friends and relatives who were not. She didn't like the status quo. She was one of few women who would openly discuss that.

Over the years, I have come to believe that *everyone*—man, woman, and child (if children are to grow to be financially independent adults)—needs some financial autonomy, some independence. You need some money that is yours to do with as you want without having to answer questions about it. You need it to feel like a grownup. You need it because without it you might choose to abstain from money management (and that's not good for your financial health). You need it because you need to be able to buy a cup of coffee without discussing the purchase with your significant other.

That's precisely how Mindy, a stay-at-home mom who only recently left the workforce, is feeling. She says:

> *I do not regret my decision to stop working, and in so many ways I love it. But I do miss feeling worthy in society and at times feel fairly vulnerable. I absolutely hate the idea of having to ask for more money in my account for basic household necessities. But I know that what I am providing for my children is worth something, and I try to remind myself of this when I question my lack of bringing money into the house.*

The best way to go in any relationship is a combination of joint and separate accounts. One for you, one for your partner, and a household account for both of you—in other words: yours, mine, and ours accounts. If you both work and earn a paycheck, you can set up this system in one of two ways. (If only one of you earns a paycheck, you'll need to use the second system.) Don't worry, both systems work. They just have slightly different psychological implications.

System 1: Divide, then conquer

- **What to do:** Have your paychecks direct-deposited into separate checking accounts. Then have a preset percentage of your income funneled (put this on automatic pilot with your bank) into joint checking.

- **How much to contribute:** The percentage of earnings each of you kicks in should be the same. Let your guide be the amount of money you need in that joint account to (a) pay your monthly expenses (mortgage, utilities, dinners out for the two of you, day care) and (b) reach for your family goals (saving for retirement and college long-term, paying for your annual holiday party short-term).

- **An example:** Say you earn $50,000 a year. You get paid twice a month, and your pretax (preretirement plan and benefit plan) earnings are $2,083. After taxes (and all those contributions), you bring home $1,458 per pay period, or $2,916 a month. Say your spouse earns $75,000 a year. He gets paid twice a month, and his pretax (preretirement plan and benefit plan) earnings are $3,125. After taxes (and all those contributions), he brings home $2,002 per pay period, or $4,004 a month. Your total combined earnings are $6,920 per month, or $3,460 per pay period.

Your household budget each month amounts to $5,250:

Your mortgage and utilities cost $2,200 a month.
Your car payments are $500.
Insurance for both is $200.
Gasoline another $200.

Groceries are $400.

After-school care is $600.

Clothing and other expenses for your son are $300.

You spend $75 on date nights twice a month, or $150.

Every month you put $300 into long-term savings.

You like to give yourselves $400 wiggle room for emergencies.

Because $5,250 represents about 76 percent of your combined monthly earnings, each of you agrees to kick in 76 percent of your take-home pay to the joint account—$2,216 for you and $3,013 for your spouse. The rest of the money—$710 per month for you and $991 for him—is yours to do with as each of you pleases.

System 2: Conquer, then divide

- **What to do:** Have your paychecks direct-deposited into a joint checking account. Then have a preset amount of money (in dollars) funneled into separate checking or money market accounts.

- **How much to move to your own stash:** Work backward from your household budget. It identifies your fixed costs, the money that you have to spend to keep your family running. Whatever is left over can be divided. But because the money is in the same pot to begin with, it's a little easier to discuss your needs and your spouse's in actual dollar terms. If one of you works in a corporate job that demands corporate (i.e., more costly) clothing, that person should likely get more of the leftover dollars. Hobbies, too, can come into play. If your spouse has a gym membership and it keeps him sane and happy, you want to make sure there's enough money in his account to make those payments as well. In other words, negotiation is necessary. And if the first plan doesn't work well for a month or two, go back and discuss it again. Do not let your anxiety or your anger fester.

- **An example:** Let's start with the same earnings and budget as in the previous example. You earn $50,000 a year. You get paid twice a month and bring home $1,458 per pay period. Your spouse earns $75,000 and brings home $2,002 per pay period. During the month, $6,920 is deposited into the joint account. Your household budget is $5,250 a month. That leaves $1,670 to play with. Who gets that money? Some couples split it fifty-fifty. Smarter couples base the split on their individual needs and negotiate. (If you take a spa weekend with the girls once a year or he takes a ski weekend with the guys—or vice versa—the money shouldn't come from joint funds.)

MAP TO A MILLION: AN IRA OF YOUR OWN

Once you've discovered the allure, the freedom, the feeling of self-worth that goes along with having a bank account of your own, you're going to want to take the next step. You're going to want a retirement account of your own. If you're in the workforce, you may already have one. As I've said time and time again, if you're not participating in a 401(k) where matching dollars are being offered by your employer, you're leaving *free* money on the table. If you're not in the workforce and believe you're not entitled to a retirement account of your own, you are mistaken. There is, in the tax code, a provision for something called a Spousal IRA. This is essentially an IRA just like the IRA a working person has. You can fund it every year, and you can take a deduction on your income taxes for doing so.

There are a few limitations. Your spouse has to earn enough to cover both his own and your retirement contributions. You and he have to file your taxes jointly. And your ability to make contributions phases out once you reach an adjusted gross income of $160,000. But—as you'll see below—a spousal IRA can add up very quickly and go a long way toward securing your retirement.

Let's say you decide you're going to stay home and raise your children from the time they're born to the time they go to college. You have two kids, two years apart, so that's a twenty-year time frame. In every one of those years you contribute the maximum (currently $4,000, $5,000 if you're 50 or over) to a spousal IRA. Afterward, you don't make additional contributions (because you're back at work and into a 401(k)), but you don't touch the money until you retire. Here's what that picture looks like:

WHILE YOU'RE MAKING CONTRIBUTIONS
($4,000 A YEAR, 8 PERCENT GROWTH)

After 5 years:	*$29,566*
After 10 years:	*$67,656*
After 20 years:	*$208,951*

CONTRIBUTIONS STOP; GROWTH CONTINUES

After 30 years:	*$463,796*
After 40 years:	*$1,029,460*

Getting Over Money Battles

All of these tactics, however, are fairly useless if you can't have a conversation about money without it deteriorating into an argument. Or if you're indulging in a cycle of passive aggressive behavior that has one or both of you secretly overriding each other's wishes, squirreling money away, lying about how much things cost, how much debt you really have, or where the money actually went.

You have to understand that money fights usually are not about money at all. They are about who wields power in the family. They are about controlling the actions of your partner or spouse. If assets are unequally divided (or short due to one or the other person's lack of earning power), money fights are about self-esteem. If you regard money as a direct expression of love, you are likely to feel unloved if your partner doesn't have money to give to you or spend on you. It's really important for you to try to understand what's driving your anger, what's at the root of your money squabbles. Then you can turn your attention to solving them.

And yes, that means talking about money—the subject Freud once called the last taboo. Here's the secret: Once you start to talk about money, doing so gets easier.

Here's a look at some of the most common money fights and how to get through them.

The fight: *"You spend/charge too much."*
The fix: A line in the sand.

The last thing that couples should do is micromanage each other's expenditures. That's a sure road to disaster. But if you're trying to stick to a budget, it's really important that you discuss *big* expenses. The best way to do this is to draw a line in the sand. Pick a number that makes sense given your financial situation—$300, $500, $1,000—and agree with your partner that you're not going to spend more than that without *talking about it first.* That doesn't mean that he can't buy a great new digital camera or that you can't buy an incredible new suit. It simply means that you have to talk about the purchase first to make sure it's not going to throw a monkey wrench into the rest of your finances for that month or year.

The goal here, I want to remind you, is a level playing field. Research has shown that from one-quarter to one-third of men believe they have the right to have the final say about big financial decisions. Your spouse will exercise that "right" only if you acquiesce when he tries to exert final control. If your spouse believes that he really can say no and it will stick without an argument, he will need some retraining. So be firm, be patient, don't lose your cool, but hold your ground.

The fight: *"You're too cheap."*
The fix: Separate bank accounts.

If your spouse or partner refuses to spend money on just about anything—if he's inclined to hoard money to the detriment of you and your family—you have to realize that what he's really saying is "I don't feel safe." (And that's what you're doing too, if you're the hoarder in the family.) This sort of compulsive saving generally traces back to childhood. The saver likely grew up in an environment where there wasn't enough money to provide for basic needs and as a result has become somewhat anal about saving as an adult.

It's generally not possible to make a compulsive saver feel safe with words. Telling someone that you earn plenty, that you have enough to cover the mortgage and the car payments and still have money left for retirement, will go in one ear and out the other. Instead, a compulsive saver needs to see a stash of money and needs that money to be under his or her control. Separate savings accounts can solve that problem.

If your partner's cheapness is getting in the way of your family's safety or happiness—if your partner doesn't believe a babysitter should be paid more than $5 an hour, for example, and in your neighborhood all the good babysitters get $10 an hour—you can handle it in one of two ways. Plan A is to try to build a case. Show him a list of all the good babysitters and what they charge. Explain that you need a night out for your sanity and that you can afford the expense and still pay all your bills and save x amount each month. Then ask him to trust you on this one. Plan B is to do an end run. Calculate how much additional money you'll need to put in your separate savings/checking account in order to pay for "extras" without a battle. Then load up the account, clue him in about what you intend to do just once, and get on with your life.

The fight: *"You're too controlling."*
The fix: Taking turns paying the bills.

Generally, both parties in a relationship have strengths. Your frugality may help you shop smartly and get out of debt; his investment savvy may help you set up a portfolio that will help you retire in style. But if one of you feels that the other one is being too parental—telling you how much you're allowed to spend and on what—there are two solutions. First, separate accounts (as described earlier). Second, take turns paying the bills. This allows both partners to see funds moving. The fact that there's not as much as you thought left over after each paycheck may give you a window into why your partner is so intent that you spend only so much on eating out, so much on clothing, so much on the cars. It may allow you to see why your spouse is so cranky. Also, bill paying is a crucial skill to have in case something happens that prevents your spouse from managing the family money. You don't want this to be a skill you're lacking. (You may also want to take turns doing the shopping. Until he understands how much it costs to outfit the kids for a season, to put food in the pantry for a week, to buy a reasonable gift for his mother's birthday, you may not be able to stem the tide of complaints. He needs to understand what it means to take a walk in your shoes, as well.)

The fight: *"You don't tell me anything."*
The fix: A scheduled conversation.

If you or your partner is feeling out of the financial loop, you need to schedule a financial conversation once a week. Decide that Wednesdays at dinner or Fridays right before you go to sleep you're going to spend ten minutes talking about financial matters. Have any expenses popped up that you're going to have to deal with? How are you going to handle the fact that camp costs $1,000 more this year or that property taxes went up or that the babysitter wants a raise.

Start with the positive: your shared goals. You both have to learn to think of money as a means to an end. It's not just green stuff; it's what the green stuff does for you that matters. If you and your spouse can agree on what you want your money to do for you—put a down payment on a house, pay for a great vacation, get through the holidays next year with no debt—then you'll find you're both working toward the same endgame, not against each other.

In the beginning, jot down a brief agenda of the things you want to raise with your partner so that you don't veer offtrack. Small issues can wait from week to week. But if a big problem comes up before your next scheduled conversation, try to deal with it immediately. If you let it fester, you'll end up fighting about something else instead. The other fix for feeling out of the loop: online banking. People in the military with a deployed spouse find that this works well because it allows both partners to keep tabs on how the money is moving—ATM withdrawals, checks written, bills scheduled—without talking about it.

Finally, if you are at an impasse, it's time to get help. A mediator may be necessary to get you through. These days there are plenty of couples therapists specializing in money issues and plenty of compassionate financial planners who can talk you through family issues.

LOOK HOW FAR YOU'VE COME!

Now that you've finished Chapter 3, you've made your way through all of the *emotional* roadblocks that may have been preventing you from grabbing hold of your money and making it into more. You now understand what was holding you back from regaining control of your money from (or even sharing control with) the man in your life. As we move forward, we'll look at some more *tactical* roadblocks: time management and organization. Then we'll get down to the building blocks you'll need to make your nest egg grow, grow, grow.

It's not my husband who is critical of my working and my earning power. It's our parents (both his and mine). What's the best way to handle other cynics?

When I mentioned closing ranks earlier, I meant it. When it comes to your finances and your marriage, you and your husband need to know everything. The rest of the world—and that includes your in-laws and your friends—gets information on a need-to-know basis. Your goal is to protect each other, your kids, and your relationship. If his mother or father starts giving you a hard time about how hard you work, or if they mention that they think your working represents a blow to their son's ego, divulge nothing. Instead, change the subject and sweetly say: "Did I tell you Ben and I are planning a trip to St. John this fall? We can't wait." Or: "Did you see the fantastic report card Sophia brought home this quarter?" In other words: We're fine with our relationship. We're fine with our kids. Butt out and we'll be fine with you as well.

I know the woman in a relationship always gets the bad rap for spending all the money, but in my house it's different. My husband can't help buying any new (and of course ridiculously expensive) gadget he finds. What do I do?

I know women take all the heat in this area, and it irks me as well. Some new research shows that men are just as prone to overshop as women are. When women spend too much money, they have a "problem." When men do it, we call them "collectors." In other words, men get better spin. The first thing you need to do is figure out whether your husband has a problem. Is he a compulsive spender, as about 2 to 5 percent of the population is thought to be? Or does he simply spend too much from time to time? Compulsive shoppers are a lot like alcoholics. They get excited in anticipation of their next purchase. They get a little high when they're making it. And they feel a huge letdown when it's over. Compulsive shoppers also put their own or their family's future at risk by racking up bills they often cannot pay. If your spouse is a compulsive shopper, he needs *professional* help. If he's simply overshopping, he needs *your* help. Offer to be his shopping buddy, which may help curtail his urge to splurge. And help him figure out ways to avoid falling into that new-tech trap by getting off the e-mail or mailing lists that are tempting him or by finding a new hobby to occupy his free time.

CHAPTER 4

"I'm Too Disorganized to Deal with My Money"

DON'T BITCH

"According to modern astronomers, space is finite. This is a very comforting thought, particularly for people who can never remember where they have left things."

Woody Allen said that, and it's funny—unless you happen to *be* one of those people who can never remember where you left things. If you're among them, I guarantee, the reaction Allen's comment elicits isn't a giggle or chuckle but a roll of the eyes, a hefty sigh, a nod.

As a former clutter queen, I can attest that being disorganized in any aspect of your life is a problem. When your closets are disorganized, it costs you time because you end up spending twice as long getting dressed in the morning as you might otherwise spend. When your CDs are disorganized, it costs you headaches because you end up wracking your brain to find Tony Bennett in time for your romantic dinner. When your calendar is disorganized, it costs you friends because even the people who like you best get sick of being stood up. When your pantry is disorganized, it costs you money because you end up buying 24-ounce bottles of soy sauce and vinegar even though you already have half-full bottles at home.

But when your finances are disorganized? It costs you time (where, in heaven's name, did you stash the health insurance forms?), it costs you headaches (if you can't find where you put those 1099s in the next fifteen minutes you're going to scream), it costs you friends (no one wants to hang with a mooch), *and* it costs you money. Sometimes it costs you a dollar here and a dollar there when you lose currency in a variety of purses and pockets. But other times, disorganization costs you hundreds or even thousands of dollars. That's what happens when you don't keep good enough records to know that you have $800 left in your flexible spending account as the year comes to an end (if you don't use that money, you lose it).

Unfortunately, many people don't believe they have the skills to organize their finances themselves. They can do their own closets, their own pantries, their own wallets and pocketbooks and drawers. But finances are just too . . . overwhelming.

That's how Josie, who writes grants for a living (a profession for which you have to be organized), says she feels: *"I'm organized with everything else, but not thinking about and keeping track of what I spend and how I spend it."*

Others, like Jennifer, who works as a publicist, have an even bigger problem. They feel as though they have to clean up all their surrounding messes before even approaching their money. Jennifer says: *"The rest of my life is unorganized. I can't possibly get to the bills until everything else is organized. So first I have to clean the apartment, do the dishes, do the laundry . . ."* As a result, though, her financial life is a huge mess. Late fees are piling up. Her credit score is headed down. And she says: *"I can't afford to pay all my bills at once, and I don't know which are the priorities. Do I pay the credit card or Con Edison? Or do I pay the medical bills?"*

Because her finances are a mess, Jennifer, like so many people, feels out of control. She doesn't know where her money is, how much she has on any given day, how much is coming in, and when or how much she owes and to whom. She doesn't know if she's swimming along nicely, treading water, or starting to sink. And her ignorance makes her nervous, anxious, worried, even on occasion physically ill. Not organizing your financial life can get in the way of even the best relationship (try explaining to your husband that you didn't pay the heating bill because you lost it). And it can get in the way of your life.

It doesn't have to be that way.

You can—I mean it, you can!—conquer the financial clutter. But first you have to understand it. And that means examining the problem. Have you ever stopped to think about why you have these messy piles in the middle of your otherwise calm and organized existence? Or, if you're more like Jennifer, why your entire life seems like a messy pile? Understanding what's driving you to surround yourself with clutter is the first step toward eliminating it forever.

The Comfort of Clutter

Whether your clutter takes the form of books, piles of paper, gadgets, clothing, or all of the above, when you strip it down to its essence, what it is doing is surrounding you. It's enveloping you. It's providing you with a warm, cozy wrapper, a form of shelter from the cold, critical, difficult outside world.

It is perfectly natural for you to like the feeling of being covered and protected. Before you were born, you were covered and protected in your mother's womb. As an infant, you were swaddled in receiving blankets, tucked into a bassinet and then into a crib. As a child, you very likely had an entire community of stuffed animals on or around your bed. They were your friends, your company. They were *starter* clutter, and they taught you a lesson that, as an adult, you're having a great deal of trouble escaping from: More is better. Just as more stuffed animals were better than a few stuffed animals, more sweaters became better than a few sweaters, more books better than a few books, more papers better than a few papers.

As you grew up, you became addicted (sometimes slightly, sometimes greatly) to all this clutter, to all this *stuff*. Without it, you fear, you might feel empty or lonely or helpless. With it, you feel full, satisfied, safe. Without it, you fear, you might feel small and meaningless. With it, you feel busy and important. Without it, you might feel poor for lack of things. With all this stuff surrounding you, how could you feel anything but rich? Without it, you'd have limited choices. With it, naturally, you are the one in control.

The problem is—and it's a problem shared by people with every type of addiction—that this clutter doesn't bring the feelings of safety and security or control that you're looking for. So you pick up some more, and then some more. Then all of a sudden you're surrounded with so much stuff that you can't think straight anymore.

How do I know? I know because you and I live in America, and because in America, more is better. In America the person who dies with the most stuff wins. Except really, she loses.

Find Your Urge to Purge

Let's tackle the financial clutter in your life by first tackling clutter in general. We'll start by attacking the arguments you use to keep it around. There's a nugget of emotional truth and fear buried in each one.

You say: *"I might need it someday."*
You mean: *"I'm afraid to give this up."*
You think: *"What if I want to wear this particular camisole on New Year's Eve? If I don't wear it, the man across the room, the one I'm meant to fall madly in love with, may never notice me. Then I won't get married, I won't have lots of sex and babies. I'll end up alone and miserable. All of which wouldn't have happened if I'd worn my camisole. So, I better keep it."*

You say: *"It might come in handy someday."*
You mean: *"This will bail me out of a really big jam."*
You think: *"If I get rid of this credit card statement from 1997, next year I'm going to get audited by the IRS. And there is going to be something in this statement that is going to get me off the hook. If I throw it out, I will owe thousands of dollars. But it wouldn't happen if l had this particular Visa bill. So, I better keep it.*

You say: *"But it's supposed to be a really good issue."*
You mean: *"There might be something in this magazine that I need to know, so I better read it before I throw it out."*
You think: *"I'm going to be on a job interview, and the boss is going to refer to this* New York Times Magazine *from three years back. If I read the story, I will be brilliant and be offered the job at twice the salary I'm earning now. If I don't, I will sound like a complete and total idiot. So, I better keep it."*

You say: *"But it still works."*
You mean: *"It's useful to somebody; it's just not useful to me."*

You think: *"What are my neighbors going to think if they see me putting this perfectly adequate computer out on the curb for trash pickup? They'll think I'm wasteful or stupid because I made a bad decision about an important piece of technology. So even though I'm going to upgrade, I better keep this one, too."*

You say: *"But it cost a lot of money."*

You mean: *"I wish I hadn't bought it in the first place, but I did, so I better use it."*

You think: *"At this point, it doesn't matter how much it cost. I've had it for three years, I've never used it (or worn it), and I'm pretty sure that I won't be using it (or wearing it) in the future. But getting rid of it is admitting I flushed $500 down the drain. So I better keep it."*

These are not unreasonable arguments. Who hasn't let go of a piece of clothing, a pair of shoes, a newspaper or magazine article, then wished she'd held on to it? Who hasn't replaced old technology with new before the old technology is truly on the fritz? Who hasn't bought something pricey, then wished she hadn't?

You'll start to win the clutter wars, however, when you focus on the flip side of these very same arguments:

Instead of thinking: *"I might need it someday."*

Think: *"How many other things do I have that I can use instead?"*

Instead of thinking: *"But it might come in handy."*

Think: *"How easy would it be to get another copy of this if I really did need it?"*

Instead of thinking: *"But it still works."*

Think: *"What else could I do with this extra space?"*

Instead of thinking: *"But it was so expensive. Isn't getting rid of it throwing money away?"*

Think: *"Buying it in the first place was like throwing money away. Next time I'm going to make smarter spending decisions."*

MAP TO A MILLION: HAVE A MOTHER OF A GARAGE SALE

There's nothing like a good garage sale to give your house a breath of fresh air. By clearing out the old and the dusty, you give yourself the space to bring in new elements, you help yourself get *really* organized, and you make money. A good single-family garage sale can easily net from $1,000 to $2,000. The key to bringing in big bucks is to approach the sale like a business. (And, oh yes, have plenty of change.) How?

- **Stock your shelves.** It's important to look as though you have a lot of merchandise to sell; otherwise potential buyers will simply cruise on past. If you don't feel you have enough to look voluminous, consider a multifamily sale. Then as the sale progresses through the day, rearrange the merchandise that's left into piles that look plentiful. And keep moving the best stuff to the front.

- **Spread the word.** As long as you're putting in the effort, you most certainly want to draw a crowd. Advertise in local papers and circulars. Post signs around your neighborhood. Make sure the way to your house is clearly marked. Use arrows, neon poster board, balloons if you have to. And include the words "No early birds." That way you'll be sure to have a line at the gate.

- **Divide and conquer.** Make one person—your best salesperson—the chief haggler. Put another in charge of collecting the money. Have others roaming the grounds answering questions and directing people who want "a deal" to the haggler-in-charge.

- **Have a game plan.** Price everything the night before; then cover the merchandise with tarps and move it back into the garage. That way, the next morning you simply have to move the tables out. Decide ahead of time how much wiggle room you'll give on particular items. And pick a time—perhaps an hour or so before the sale is to end—at which you'll mark everything down by 50 percent.

Have another sale next year. Yes, your first garage sale will likely be your most lucrative. But once you've started looking at your clutter with an eye toward what it will net on the open market, you'll soon find you can put a price on many other things in your life. How much can having an annual garage sale contribute to your future? More than you'd think.

SAVINGS FROM AN ANNUAL GARAGE SALE: $1,000

10 years of garage sale proceeds (invested at 8 percent): $16,914

20 years of garage sale proceeds (invested at 8 percent): $52,237

30 years of garage sale proceeds (invested at 8 percent): $130,644

So, how much does this disorganized state cost you? Consider . . .

- *Women spend an average of 55 minutes every day searching for stuff, including 8.2 minutes searching for a receipt.*
- *Getting rid of excess clutter could eliminate 40 percent of the housework in the average American household.*
- *People with messy desks spend an average of 7 1/2 hours per week being distracted by pieces of paper, folders, and stationery supplies.*

Can't you think of about a hundred other things you'd rather do with that time? Sleep might be good. Or exercise. You could play Scrabble with your kids. Cook a meal. See two movies over the course of a week. Have a meaningful conversation with a girlfriend or a spouse. Heck, in an hour, you could even have some pretty good sex. And you could make some meaningful money by working one—yes, one—extra hour per day.

MAP TO A MILLION: WORK ONE EXTRA HOUR FIVE DAYS A WEEK

$8/HOUR $2,080

Over 5 years:	*$10,400*
Over 10 years:	*$20,800*

If you do this for 10 years, put the money in an IRA, and let it grow for 30 years to use for your retirement (and never contribute another dime after those 10 years), you will have **$173,335.**

$10/HOUR $2,600

Over 5 years:	*$13,000*
Over 10 years	*$26,000*

If you do this for 10 years, put the money in an IRA, and let it grow for 30 years for your retirement (and never contribute another dime after those 10 years), you will have **$216,666.**

$20/HOUR $5,200

Over 5 years:	*$26,000*
Over 10 years:	*$52,000*

If you do this for 10 years, put the money in an IRA, and let it grow for 30 years for your retirement (and never contribute another dime after those 10 years), you will have **$433,333.**

GET RICH

Tame the Paper Tiger

Before I get too far into the business of organizing your financial life, let me take a minute to tell you that I pay my bills online—and I love it. It is largely responsible for the fact that I'm organized. It saves me time. It saves me money. Managing my money online has changed my life. It takes a little bit of time to set up your accounts—it took me about an hour—and you're going to be a little slow while you get used to the interface, go through the process of memorizing your passwords, and so forth. But once you're up and running, paying your bills online is the way to go.

You can schedule certain bills to be paid every month (this works nicely for those like the car payment and the mortgage that are the same amount due on the same day each month). When you get variable bills in the mail, you sit down at your computer, and just as quickly as you'd respond to an e-mail, you type in an amount and write a check. No need to go to the post office. No need to stamp envelopes. Banks are so eager to get you to do this that many offer the service for free, which means you save $5 to $6 a month on stamps.

MAP TO A MILLION

Saving a few bucks a month on stamps doesn't sound like much, but it can quickly become thousands. If you pay 15 bills a month, you spend $5.85 on stamps (at today's 39-cent first-class rate). Over a year, that's $70.20. Online bill payment is widely available for free. What if you take your bank up on its generous free online offer, and invest the money saved on stamps at 8 percent?

Saving over 10 years:	*$1,187*
Saving over 20 years:	*$3,667*
Saving over 30 years:	*$9,171*
Cost of not going to the post office:	*Priceless*

A Strategy for the Rest of Your Papers

Someone very smart once said to me: "If you can't find it, you don't have it." She was probably talking about my sock drawer, but I've long considered these words to live by. It's no coincidence that people who are pretty well organized—you don't have to be neat as a pin—live happier lives. They don't feel as though they're wasting time and money searching for socks or financial paperwork. They know where things are, deal with them, and move on.

We'll get down to the nitty-gritty in a moment. First, here are a few thoughts I want you to hold on to as you go through this process of organization.

1. Be selective in what you keep in your office and doubly selective in what you bring home

It's much tougher to get rid of something than it is to decide never to own it in the first place. So don't buy books, magazines, or newspapers unless you're sure you want to read them. Don't save catalogs you *might* want to order from someday. Before you bring anything into your precious space, think: Do I really need this? What am I going to do with it? And when? Once you do bring an item into your space, understand there are only three things to do with it: (1) Deal with it (if it's a bill, pay it). (2) Put it away (after you pay that bill, file it). (3) Toss it (if it turns out you don't need it, put it in the trash). If you do anything else—leave it on the kitchen counter, put it in a basket or pile or inbox—it eventually becomes clutter. The more things you can keep from becoming clutter, the better. If you're loath to toss things in the trash, consider selling them or giving them away.

2. Consolidate, consolidate, consolidate

One of the problems we as a society have with our financial papers is that there are just too many of them. Take retirement accounts as an example. Every time we leave a job, we're offered the chance to roll our 401(k)s into IRAs. However, most people these days leave jobs an average of twelve times over the course of their careers. That's a dozen different accounts. Your best bet: Consolidate. Merge your IRAs into one. Do the same with those fourteen different credit card accounts you have open. Pay them off, one by one; then pull the cards from your wallet and stick them in a drawer or in your freezer. As you pay them off, call the card companies, close the accounts, and ask the companies to be sure it says on your credit report that the accounts were "closed by customer."

(Don't close accounts six month or less before you apply for a mortgage or a car loan. I know it sounds counterintuitive, but closing accounts will lower your credit score.) Finally, move all your brokerage activity (including IRAs) to one brokerage firm, and all your banking activity to one bank. Result: Rather than getting fourteen different brokerage statements a month, you'll get one. Rather than getting several bank statements a month, you'll get one. Rather than getting fourteen different credit card statements a month, you'll get two or three. Less clutter coming in means less clutter to deal with.

3. Less mail is better than more

On the same principle, make sure you're off the junk mail lists. If you haven't done so already, sign up for the mail preference service of the Direct Marketing Association by sending a letter or postcard including your name, home address, and signature to

Mail Preference Service
Direct Marketing Association
PO Box 643
Carmel, NY 10512

Some mail—including items addressed to "homeowner" or "recipient"—will slip through the cracks. Toss it. Same with solicitations and catalogs you didn't request. When companies ask if they can pitch you with other lines of business, say no. And when cashiers ask if they may have personal information such as your address, phone number, or e-mail address, say no as well. They'll be astonished at your brazen disregard for the big corporate machine. You, however, will feel powerful.

4. Create a place for receipts

Make a compartment in your wallet the holding pen for receipts you need for expense records or tax purposes (or because you may, someday, want to return things). Your wallet works because once it gets to the soon-to-explode stage, you'll have no choice but to go through these annoying pieces of paper to reconcile them with your bank and credit card statements or file your expenses (before the deadline has passed).

5. Make lists

What do Martha Stewart, Lee Iacocca, Benjamin Franklin, and Aristotle have in common besides fame, power, and incredible success? They make (or made) lists. So do many successful women. Lists help keep you organized because they allow you to stop trying so hard to remember things. Once an item is down on your list, your mind is free to try to deal with other challenges of the day. Usually, lists work best if you keep one master list (probably within your calendar, which, by the way, you also should have only one of) and one list for each day. Every day, move no more than ten items from your master list to your daily list, and let those be the things you try to accomplish. Note: Huge long-term goals, such as running a marathon, don't belong on your daily list. Modest goals, such as running three miles today, do. Once you finish a particular task, cross it off with a flourish, and allow yourself to enjoy the satisfaction that comes with getting something done.

6. Organize your electronic desktop

We tend to think of the messes we make in our physical space. Don't forget about the mess you've made in cyberspace. Taking an hour or so to organize your computer files and desktop can help you work more effectively in the months and years to come.

Bills in a Box

You probably think you have no idea how to sort and organize your finances. But in fact, you have a very good model. You know how to clean a closet. And you are going to use the very same skills to get your financial paperwork in tip-top shape. In this exercise, a file box with a carry-handle becomes your closet. If you don't have one, you can pick one up at any office supply store and many drugstores. If you'd prefer not to spend the money, that's okay. You can use a filing cabinet or a drawer that can accept hanging folders. My preference is for the box, though, because it's portable. If you want to pay bills on your wireless laptop while sitting outside on your back porch, you can tote the box with you. If you need to visit your accountant, you can take it along so that you'll be able to answer any of his or her questions. Once you have the box, here's what you need to do.

1. Get the right stuff

When you clean your closet, you need to have the right hangers for pants, sweaters, suits, and so forth. When you organize your finances, you need office supplies:

Hanging folders (Note: If you are married, get hanging folders in three different colors so that you can see quickly what's yours, what's mine, and what's ours.)

Sharpie markers (if you have neat handwriting), a label maker (if you don't)

Manila folders

Stamps and envelopes (so you're not always wasting time scrounging for postal supplies)

Post-it notes

Letter opener (to avoid paper cuts)

Stapler

Calculator

Pens and pencils

2. Put it to use

Before you start filing, neatly label your hanging folders. My suggested categories are:

Taxes

Insurance

Health Care

Banking

Retirement/Brokerage (retirement accounts are many people's brokerage accounts)

Credit Cards

Home

Auto

Legal

Estate (for a copy of your will, living will, health-care proxy, and other estate-planning documents)

To-Do

To-Be-Paid

You may also want folders labeled:

Pets

Kids

Mom and Dad

Benefits

Flexible Spending

Travel

Next, label manila file folders to put into each of the hanging folders. Suppose you have three credit cards—MasterCard, Discover Card, and Banana Republic. You'll want a manila folder for each of them labeled with the year: MasterCard 2006, Discover Card 2006, Banana Republic 2006. When the year turns to 2007, you will make new manila folders labeled "MasterCard 2007," "Discover Card 2007," and so on. Once you pay your taxes and close your personal books on 2006, you can take all the 2006 folders out of your box and move them to a file drawer in which you have hanging folders set up in a similar way. That way your bills-in-a-box filing system remains portable, and you will be able to put your fingers on any important piece of paper at any particular point in time.

You'll eventually get good at figuring out what category needs its own folder. Give yourself leeway to create the folders you think you will need.

And that's it. Now you're set to start organizing.

The Four Ds

Here are the steps you need to take. I call them the Four Ds. And remember, this is merely a big closet you're cleaning. It just happens to be a closet full of paper.

DUMP

If you clean a closet as I do, the first thing you do after you buy hangers is pull everything off the racks and toss it onto your bed or the floor. Do the same with your bills and paperwork. If it's all sitting in a pile on your kitchen table, then move it to an area that can be messy for a little while. This can take anywhere from several hours to several days, depending on how much stuff you have to plow through and how much time you have to devote to the process. One thing is certain: You don't want to have to move your workstation halfway through. Next, go through the other repositories for your bills and paperwork, and add those to the pile. Your briefcases, tote bags, desktop, pocketbooks—every one of them should be given the once-over.

DISTRIBUTE

When cleaning the aforementioned closet, you separate your clothing into piles—things you want to keep, things you want to toss, and things you're not quite sure of. With paperwork, you do the same. Take the statements or bills out of their envelopes. Open them to full size (unfolded they take up less room). Staple the pages of each month's statement together so they don't get lost. If you find a bill that needs to be paid, write a check on the spot, put it in an envelope, and stamp it so you don't have to deal with it again. Then immediately record the transaction in your checkbook register. Don't let the fact that you're spending time getting organized result in late fees on your credit card bills. Then put the paperwork into the proper folders, oldest bills first, so that when you open a folder the newest statement is right on top.

DIMINISH

In 2004, the *American Journal of Psychiatry* published results of a study that said chronic hoarders—people who seem to save things with more passion than the rest of us—have decreased activity in the parts of the brain used for decision making and problem solving. In other words, there may be a clinical reason why you can't decide what to keep and what to get rid of. That's why you need rules. With clothing, the rule is, If you haven't worn something for two years, it goes. With bills and paperwork, the rules vary depending on what you're looking at. ATM receipts need to be kept only until you receive that month's bank statement and verify that the numbers are correct. Tax returns have to be kept for years and years. Here's a list to keep you straight. Make a copy of it so that you won't have to keep leafing through the book to figure out what's what. Then tape the list to the inside top of your file box.

WHAT TO KEEP AND WHAT TO TOSS

TOSS IMMEDIATELY:

Credit card solicitations

Marketing material included in bank and credit card statements

THROW OUT AFTER ONE MONTH OR WHEN YOU RECONCILE WITH A BILL OR BANK STATEMENT:

ATM receipts

Prospectuses and other information about investments you are considering making (if you're not going to read them, toss immediately)

Receipts for purchases (assuming you're keeping them or there's no warranty)

THROW OUT AFTER ONE YEAR OR WHEN END-OF-YEAR CONSOLIDATED STATEMENTS COME IN AND YOU HAVE FILED THE TAXES FOR THAT YEAR:

Bank statements

Brokerage statements

Cell phone, cable, telephone, and Internet statements (except when deducting for work-related expenses)

Credit card bills

Pay stubs

Social Security statements

Utility bills

THROW OUT AFTER SEVEN YEARS (WHEN NO LONGER NEEDED FOR TAX PURPOSES):

Child-care records

Flexible spending account documentation

401(k) and other retirement-plan year-end statements

IRA contributions

Purchase records for investments

Records of charitable donations

Records on houses you've sold

Tax returns and backup documentation

KEEP AS LONG AS YOU HAVE THE UNDERLYING ASSET (SUCH AS A HOUSE OR A CAR):

Insurance policies

Receipts for important purchases like technology, art, antiques, rugs, jewelry (or anything else you may need a rider on your insurance policy to cover)

Receipts for renovations or other investments made in the property

Titles

Warranty papers

KEEP FOREVER IN A SAFE OR SAFE-DEPOSIT BOX; KEEP A SECOND COPY— IF POSSIBLE—IN YOUR ATTORNEY'S OFFICE OR ANOTHER SAFE LOCATION OFF-PREMISES:

Adoption papers

Appraisals

Birth certificates

Citizenship papers

Custody agreements

Deeds

Divorce papers

Financial aid documents

List of credit card numbers, bank and brokerage statements, and insurance policies, and toll-free contact information

List of important contacts (lawyer, accountant, doctor, children, parents, etc.)

Military records

Powers of attorney (medical and financial)

Stock certificates
Wills/Living wills

What should you do with the stuff you toss? Shred it! A crosscut shredder for at-home use can burn through five sheets of paper at a time. Heavier-duty machines can even cut through old credit cards. You can buy a decent machine for about $100 to $150. And if there's not too much paper to go through, you can tear it up yourself!

Voilà! You should now be able to fit your entire financial year inside one reasonably sized file box.

DUE DILIGENCE

Now that you have a "system," all that's left to do is maintain it. For that, you need three kinds of upkeep: daily, intermittent, and annual.

- **Daily upkeep.** What is the quickest way to turn a neat closet into a messy one? Toss today's dirty clothes on the floor. Every day, when the mail comes in, open up your file box, and open the bills one by one. Write checks (by hand or electronically), deduct the amount of each check from your check register (or electronically—watch as the bank does it for you), stamp the envelope, and put it directly in the mailbox to go out the next day or on the counter with your keys so you'll remember to take it with you the next time you leave the house. Do not procrastinate and say you'll pay bills later, after you've had dinner, after you've had a glass of wine. Start this task and finish it in one swift motion.

And what's plan B for the night that just doesn't work? The baby is crying, the dog poops on the floor, dinner . . . oh, heck, you can't even think about dinner. You'll be lucky if you can grab a bowl of Raisin Bran in time for the *Friends* rerun at 11. In that case, put all the bills that need to be filed in the same place—in your "To-Be-Paid" folder. Whatever you do, don't start separating them into separate folders. Don't put the insurance bill in the "Insurance" folder, the credit card bill in the "Credit cards" folder. You'll never see those bills again, and you'll get hit by late fees. Give yourself a break and deal with your bills as soon as you can, preferably tomorrow.

- **Intermittent upkeep.** Every time you open a new account, take out a new insurance policy, or do something else that requires record keeping, immediately make a new folder. Print a label, and figure out where the folder goes. The first thing that goes into the new folder is the contract you signed, so that if you ever need to refer to it, you know precisely where it is.

- **Annual upkeep.** Every year, after you've filed your taxes, remove last year's manila folders from the file box and place them in another set of hanging files in a filing cabinet or drawer. It is important to arrange both sets of files in the same way so that you'll know precisely where to find any document. You will even be able to tell another person where to find a particular document if needed.

LOOK HOW FAR YOU'VE COME!

It's a big relief to get your physical space under control. It provides a structure you need to move forward with your finances—but it's of no use unless you organize another important part of your life . . . your time. Read on for my time-tested strategies.

Why are my finances so far down on my to-do list when they're so important?

It may be precisely because they're so important that they are so far down your list. When something is critical to your life—getting an annual physical from your ob-gyn, calling a good friend who's having a tough time, presenting the results of your research to the nominating committee for an important prize—it's often tough to get yourself to participate. You fear that you'll fail. That you'll disappoint someone important to you. Or that you won't live up to your own expectations. So instead of acting, you do absolutely nothing. And of course, that's even worse. That's why I believe finances need to be an everyday (or at least an every few days) part of your life. The more time that lapses between the days you deal with your money, the more cumbersome the whole scenario seems to be. It's in your best interest to pay a little bit of attention all the time. That way you won't have to pay all of your attention even a little bit of the time.

What if I really don't want to spend time managing my money? Is there a way I can avoid it?

Here's my philosophy on money management: *Someone* has to spend at least some time each week and each month managing your money. It can be you (that's the cheapest way to handle it, certainly). But it can also not be you. If you finish this book and you are certain you are never going to spend time managing your money, then turn to page 214 and figure out how to hire someone to do it for you. You can hire people to take on any and all of your money management tasks. Daily money managers can be hired by the hour to pay your bills. Accountants can be hired to do your taxes. Financial planners can be hired to develop an investment plan for your retirement and discretionary accounts. Lawyers can be hired to put together an estate plan that makes sense. If you don't want to go quite that far—hiring a team of people to do your money managing for you—then you can automate as much as possible instead. You can put your 401(k), IRA, and savings account contributions on autopayment and do the same for bills that come to the same amount each month. You can sign up for automatic rebalancing of your retirement accounts at work. You can bank online. And you can keep your investments as simple as possible, covering your bases with a few index funds that are broadly diversified. Sure you can make your financial life complicated—as many, many people do, but it's far from necessary.

"I Don't Have Any Time"

DON'T BITCH

When I asked women around the country to put their fingers on why they aren't managing their money, some reasons climbed to the top of the pile, including this one:

My brain—like that of all moms—is overloaded with all the nonfinancial details of life such as whose play dates are allergic to which foods, who has a math test on Thursday, etc. I am not proud of it, but that's the way it is.
Kelly, freelance writer

I don't manage my investments enough because I never think I have time to do it well.
Lisa, pediatrician

I feel like I do enough and my plate is already overloaded.
Harriet, publicist

Frankly, I'm not surprised. Survey after survey shows that women don't feel there are enough hours in the day, and this overload stresses us out.

In other words, you know precisely how valuable your time is and how much of a problem it is in your life that you don't have enough of it. That's why research has shown that 75 percent of you would be willing to pay more for a product that saves you time than for one that doesn't. And why half of you would be more likely to purchase a product that saves you time over one that saves you money. That's also why if someone wastes your time, you're not going to give that someone another chance. If you go to a store and have an unsatisfactory experience—like being asked to wait in a never-ending line while the cashier chats on the phone—you probably will be among the 96 percent of women who won't be going back. It's why if given a choice between an extra day's pay and a day off—or a $5,000 raise versus more vacation time—you may actually opt for the latter.

Believe it or not, feeling starved for time is a relatively new phenomenon for women. Women today have priorities and aspirations different from their grandmothers' and even their mothers'. Our priorities are much more similar to men's than they ever were in the past. We want to go to college, then maybe to graduate school; we want to get a good job at a good salary. We want success and recognition in the working world. Then, somewhere in our early thirties, typically, our priorities as women begin to shift. We want to have babies, and many of us want to stay home to raise them. We want or need to take care of our parents. We want or need to give back to our communities.

As you do those things, you gain perspective on what you really believe—individually and deep down—are the important ingredients for a happy life. Sometimes, outside events, like the 9/11 attacks, serve to highlight and underline just how right you are. Result: Your aspirations change again.

Some women choose not to reenter the workforce. Others choose to take the slow lane. Even women who go back to work full-time months or years after one of these important life experiences tend to have rearranged their priorities. Money (though crucial for achieving many life goals) has become less important. Time, however, is critical. (Some men—particularly those thrust into the role of caretaker for a sick spouse or elderly parent—do eventually go through a similar reevaluation, but often not until much later.)

If you experience this values-based transformation, it becomes clear that finding an extra few minutes in your day could solve a range of problems. It could give you a little more energy to spend managing your money. But it might also provide the buffer you need to decompress with your spouse and keep your marriage out of trouble. It might be precisely the key to getting on the treadmill for long enough (20 to 25 minutes) to kick your heart into gear and your health up a notch. Finding an extra few minutes could enable you to do all of those incredibly valuable things.

But just as you need to figure out where your cash is actually going before you can find the money to get yourself out of debt, you need to figure out where your time is going before you can find the few minutes—or few hours—to improve your day.

You Are Starved for Time—but Why?

If I'm not mistaken—and I don't think I am—there are twenty-four hours in a day now just as there were when you were a kid and when your parents were kids. Your folks may have had stressful days at work, yet they were still able to get home at 6 p.m. to have dinner with the family, to take both Saturday and Sunday off, to get away occasionally for real vacations. Why can't you do the same?

More of us are in dual-career families
It was much easier for Dad to come home to dinner when Mom was there to spend three hours shopping, chopping, and putting it on the table. All he had to do was tuck in and eat. And it wasn't just dinner that the stay-at-home spouse was handling. It was doctor's appointments, vacation plans, parent-teacher conferences, and home maintenance. Stay-at-home moms, in our parents' generation, were the managers of family time. When both spouses work, that function becomes more difficult to maintain. And when both spouses work as long and hard as many American couples do today, it flies out the window. Dual-earner couples in the United States are the busiest in the world. The proportion of couples working over a hundred hours per week combined here is off the charts compared with England, Sweden, Germany, and most other countries.

Fewer people are expected to accomplish more

A human resources researcher once told me that when his wife began her position in a large corporation a decade ago, there were 97 people in her department. By the time she left, there were 7. And during those ten years, the combination of layoffs and attrition meant that every few months fewer people were expected to do what more people had been doing before.

You may well be able to handle the first round of consolidations without logging significantly more hours, but by the time the workforce has shrunk by a third or a half, you're arriving at your desk before the sun rises (or as soon as you put the kids on the bus) and still sitting there when it sets. In the past twenty or thirty years, research from the Bureau of Labor Statistics has shown, the average worker's annual number of hours in the office has increased by about 160 hours—four 40-hour work weeks.

The result: You put a ton of pressure on yourself to prove that you shouldn't be the next employee asked to vacate your desk. That's why, even though research shows workers really want more vacation days, many aren't taking the ones they already have. On average, employees forfeit three vacation days each year, a 50 percent jump from 2003. This is not how it works in other countries. Europeans get paid 13 months' salary for doing 12 months' work. In the United States, we get paid 12 months' salary for doing 13 months' work.

Life at home has become more intense

Your time-starvation can't be blamed solely on office life. Life at home has become more intense. Expectations of what it takes to be a good parent, a good spouse, even a good friend are higher than they used to be. If you want to be a good mom, there's pressure not to just say to your kids: "Go outside and play." You have to arrange lessons to further their development. You have to get them involved in sports. And once they're involved, you have to be at every practice—not just every game—to cheer them on. That's a lot of pressure when practice starts at 6 p.m., you're stuck in traffic, and everyone has to eat. That's why women who decide to stay home with the kids because they believe that they will be less time-strapped and less stressed find very quickly that they're mistaken.

That's precisely what Mindy, a 38-year-old stay-at-home mother of two, discovered:

> *I very stupidly thought that choosing to stay home and raise my child would be the break in life I was looking for. I didn't know it would involve harder, longer hours.*

Then, of course, there's technology. There was a time—if you're 30 or older you should remember it—when you (or at least your parents) were unreachable. If you went out for dinner, you left the phone number of the restaurant for the sitter in case of emergency. You finished what you had to finish before you left the office because you knew that what remained could wait until morning. Today, your personal life and your work life rarely shut down. Your spouse, parents, friends, colleagues, and clients know where they can contact you 24/7, and so they do. You might have once used your time in the car home during your commute to decompress. When you were at your son's basketball practice or your daughter's soccer game, you were really sitting on the sidelines, not checking the BlackBerry to see that the package made it to London.

Because of e-mail and cell phones and, of course, cell phones with e-mail capabilities, life doesn't stop to breathe the way it used to. Work, if you're in the workforce, never really has to shut down. Ditto for your life, if you run it like work (as many stay-at-home moms do today). What that means is that any time you do have can be swiped away from you in a flash if you allow that to happen.

Multitasking is the biggest time-suck of all

During the 1980s and 1990s, you, like me and so many other American women, were very likely lured into the world of multitasking. We all thought that the way to be more efficient was to do many things simultaneously. We were delusional. That's what several studies in *Neuroscience,* the *Journal of Experimental Psychology,* and other publications have concluded. They say if you stop working on a particular task and pick it up later, it takes your brain fifteen minutes to get back to the point where you left off. So if you're constantly stopping and starting because you're trying to do many things, you're losing hours a day.

Who Suffers? You Do!

Who bears the brunt of this time crunch? You do, of course. You feel guilt and anxiety about things you're unable to accomplish both at home and at work. You grind your teeth. You pull at—and sometimes out—your hair. Your blood pressure skyrockets. You rely on a huge cup of caffeine in the morning to rev you up and on a slightly smaller glass of vino in the evening to bring you down. What you really need is a break. You need a vacation. It'll be good for your soul, your family, your marriage, your health. The Framingham Heart Study revealed that women who take two vacations a year are 50 percent less likely to develop heart disease than those who vacation rarely or not at all. Men cut their risk by 30 percent.

Learn to manage your time, so you have time to manage your money.

GET RICH

My town's middle school offers sixth-graders a course in organizational skills and time management. It's offered selectively—only to kids whose fifth-grade teachers determine they *really* need it. Frankly, we all need a little help here, particularly with the latter. Every one of us could benefit from a little education in how to make the most of our time. Right now, it's a skill most people learn through osmosis. You watch your parents and teachers, and you do as they did. You pick up little tricks along the way and incorporate them into your life.

Unfortunately, there are more bad time management role models than good. That's why I finally realized that in order to conquer this time conundrum, you have to approach it in a bigger way. You have to understand that poor time management *is* an issue in your life and that there is *so much* to gain by getting a better grip on the clock. And then you need a way to make it happen.

In the interest of managing my own time and my own money, I have tried many prepackaged systems and solutions. I have tried every kind of calendar—electronic and paper—and rejected most of them in short order. I have tried allotting particular amounts of time (as time management experts often suggest) for particular tasks. It didn't take me long to send that strategy down the river as well.

In the world of time management, simpler is better. To get the most important things in your life done and still have a little time for things like money management and fun (yes, I believe in fun!), you need to know (1) what is important to you, (2) how to move those things to the top of the to-do pile (and get rid of things that are lower priority), (3) how to accomplish well what you need to accomplish, but in as little time as possible, and (4) how to prevent things from slipping through the cracks. If you learn how to do those four things, you'll eliminate time management issues from your money—and from your life.

Know What's Important

My friend Michael, who for many years has produced one of the national morning television news shows (a position in which time management is crucial because you're literally planning things down to the second) once told me: Pick five things in your life that you're going to say yes to. Then say no to everything else. On Michael's list of five yesses: his kids, his spouse, exercise, frequent travel to visit family, and work. I tried his method and found I needed a few more yes slots on my list. But once you get to your number, the concept is brilliant.

You are, essentially, giving yourself permission to turn down the sorts of things that—in the back of your mind—trigger the little voice that says, "You really should do this." These are things like dinners with people you don't really like, parties you don't really want to attend, networking events that may or may not do any real good for your career, charity fund-raisers for charities that aren't high on your list. They are things like cooking dinner for company when you've had a hard day, when ordering takeout really would be just fine. In other words, you get rid of the things you do out of guilt.

The key to doing this well, to figuring out what's really important, is honesty. You schedule way too many things in your life that you're doing not to please yourself or one of those people on your list of five, but to please someone who really isn't that important to you. If the event or the favor or the lunch or whatever happens to occur on a day when you've got nothing to do, that's one thing (although I'd argue that's when you say no so you can do something nice for yourself). But if it occurs on a day where you already have three or four other yesses penciled in, you have to keep in mind this may be the thing that pushes you over the edge.

What you'll realize as you start to say "No, I can't do that" or "No, that's not workable"—a great turn of phrase I got from a Manhattan psychologist—is that you do not have to give a reason. Very few people will ask for one, but if they do, just repeat "It's not workable." And saying no when you really want to say no feels *great*. You feel as though a big weight has been lifted off your shoulders.

What if you can't tell the difference between something that's a potential yes and a potential no? Ask yourself this question: What's the worst thing that can happen if I *don't* do this? If the question is, Should I file my taxes? The answer is: garnishment of wages and huge hassles. In other words, this is definitely a yes.

Real-Life Use: What if you *want* to say yes to a few things and no to most but are having trouble doing it? Then say no to everything. Well, not no, exactly. Just don't say yes. Instead, buy yourself a little time by saying, "I have to check my schedule." Or say, "I may have something that day. Let me get back to you." Then take a deep breath and remind yourself that you're doing this to become a better manager of the things that are really important to you. Finally, call or send an e-mail and get yourself off the hook. You may find it's easier, at least in the beginning, not to say no face-to-face. That's okay. You'll be able to eventually.

Prioritize

Let's say you decide you must or want to do something. Do you have to do it now? Even the aforementioned taxes, which definitely have to be done, don't necessarily have to be done now. If it's January 14 and you haven't filed the prior year's taxes, the answer to the "What's the worst thing that could happen if I don't do this now?" question is "Nothing much." If it's April 14, the answer is "I'll have to pay interest and penalties."

There are degrees of importance for everything—your work, your needs, the needs of your spouse or partner, even your kids. Technology—even though it has made life easier in a lot of ways—has completely boggled our perception of what's urgent. When I was growing up, we didn't answer the phone during dinner. That was family time. But the introduction of the cell phone—perhaps because it was expensive, rare, or simply new—made every phone call seem urgent. If someone was calling on the cell, the caller must be someone important and that person must *really* need to get you, so you'd better answer. Even if you're eating with your family. Even if you're at the movies with a date.

Of course, these days your cell phone number is likely available—just like your land-line number—through directory assistance. That means an incoming call may be not only mundane and far from urgent but a complete waste of your time. Recent research estimates that 80 percent of all incoming e-mail is spam or junk. Are you going to break your stride—interrupting your family dinner or turning away from an important project at work—to deal with it? That's precisely what many of us do. It's time to stop. Focus on deciding what you want to do; then work down your list of priorities rather than adhering to someone else's definition of what you should be doing with your time.

Lists are essential because they help keep you organized. They are also essential because they allow you to stop trying so hard to remember things. Once an item is on your list, your mind is free to try to deal with other challenges of the day. Lists work best if you keep one master list and one smaller daily list. Every day, move no more than ten items from your master list to your daily list, and let those be the things you try to accomplish within the next 10- to 12-hour period. Huge long-term goals belong on your master list, not on your daily list, where they'll loom so large they'll undermine your confidence. What you're trying to accomplish today to make a long-term goal feasible, however, does belong on your daily list.

Real-Life Use: How do you figure out which things go on your daily list? Begin by ranking them. The *crucial ones* get a 1, the *important ones* a 2, and the *pretty important ones* a 3. Anything that doesn't merit a 3 doesn't belong on your list for that day. After a while, you may find (as I did) that you are so good at prioritizing that you don't have to do this step anymore, but that may take a few months.

Get It Done (and Learn When That Means Having Someone Do It for You)

Once you've figured out what five or six or ten things you need to do today, you need a way to get them done not only quickly and easily but well. You won't be pleased, nor will your kids or your spouse or your boss, if you seem to be shirking.

Start by tackling the biggest challenges first. Suppose you have ten items on your list and two of the highest-ranking ones will take a half hour each and two others will take five minutes. Avoid the temptation to knock off the two short ones first. You'll need the most energy to tackle the tasks that call for the greatest focus and concentration, so do them first. You'll feel energized enough by their completion to be able to complete the shorter projects later in the day (you'll be able to squeeze in the short projects when you take a break from work- or kid-related stuff). Always attempt the most challenging tasks when your concentration is at its best. We all have a time during the day when we work best. (Mine happens to be at 5 a.m. while the kids are sleeping, before the phone starts to ring and the e-mail starts to whir.) Use your best hours to tackle the biggest challenges.

Speaking of e-mail—shut it off. And turn off the TV. Get rid of the radio. Move that stack of catalogs off your lap and out of your range of sight. And focus. In other words, stop multitasking. You may think that you are more effective when you're trying to do four different things at once. You're wrong.

Try to consolidate similar activities. If three of the items on your daily list require you to make phone calls, make them all together. Do likewise with errands. It makes no sense to drive to town twice in one day if you could make a single trip.

How do you shut off your e-mail in an era when even ignoring e-mail seems downright rude? My friend Julie Morgenstern, a professional organizer, suggests starting the flow of e-mail a little later in the day. Very little of importance happens electronically before 10 or even 11 a.m. Or you can write crafty "away" messages, then use them judiciously: "I'm on deadline. Will get back to you as soon as I finish." Or "I'm in a meeting with the A team. Back to you in a few hours." Or "I'll be unreachable after 6 p.m. and before 10 a.m. But I'll get back to you as soon as I possibly can."

You can do the same with your voice mail. And you should. When you think about it, one of the positives of voice mail technology is that it acts as a universal receiver. E-mail and voice mail are intended to receive messages meant for you when you're not available. They're not supposed to make you so nuts that you can't get anything done at all. What you're really doing by taking a step back from e-mail and voice mail is conducting a reality check on how irreplaceable you truly are. You need to see for yourself that the world isn't going to implode if you don't check e-mail every hour on the hour.

Likewise, you need to see that tasks can still get done—and get done well—when you don't do them yourself. That means learning to delegate. Women who give themselves an A for success hand off tasks they are unable to accomplish themselves. What should be delegated? Unpleasant tasks, certainly. For many people that means housecleaning, shoveling snow, hemming pants, and bathing the dog. Suppose the tasks that you find unpleasant include dog walking and sewing on buttons for your child or significant other. If you feel you should be doing those tasks yourself, letting go of them will be hard. Doubly hard if you believe—often rightly so—that you can do those things better than someone else. When the tasks are deeply personal (like writing thank-you notes after a birthday or teaching your child to ride a bike), you are likely to feel deep down that delegating would be wrong. But if things simply aren't getting done, you have two choices: Give in and delegate, or give up the ghost. Particularly when it comes to the personal stuff, you have to realize that it's better that these things get done by someone than not get done at all.

Real-Life Use: Run the numbers. Of course, economic considerations affect decisions about what to delegate. These days, you can pay someone to do nearly anything, from waiting at home for the cable guy (so you don't have to) to walking your dog. Figure out how much one hour of your time is worth. Double that figure for precious weekend hours. Then compare, but keep in mind that this is a rough calculation. If someone is charging you $15 an hour to walk your dog and you earn $25 an hour, you may conclude that paying for dog walking doesn't make good financial sense. But take into consideration that you would be able to work three extra hours because Sparky has gone out and done his business without you. All of a sudden, paying the dog-walker might seem a smart and rational thing to do.

Finally, setting deadlines may help you motivate yourself to finish tasks. You can identify a series of things you want to do—dinner with friends, movie with a spouse, a run in the park—but allow yourself to do them only if you complete the items on your daily list. The remarkable thing about having a reason to finish what you're working on is that it makes you work not only harder but smarter.

Before I had my first child, I used to routinely work until 7:30 or 8:00 at night. I would obsess over drafts of my stories and keep reporting even though I'd already covered my bases. I'd schmooze (a lot) with my colleagues. After my son was born, I was out of the office at 5:30. I didn't write fewer stories (I probably wrote more). And despite a lack of time to obsess, my drafts were cleaner. What made the difference? I wanted to go home so much that I stepped up the pace. It happened easily, unconsiously. Executive coaches see the same thing. Think about how you work on a typical day. Now think about how you work when you're on deadline. You don't procrastinate. Your time management is more effective.

So impose some deadlines—including one that gives you a half hour of downtime at the end of every day. What do you do with that extra half hour? Something restorative. You need to unwind so you'll be able to have an equally efficient day tomorrow. What transports you to a new place? What will reenergize you so that you can approach the rest of the week with renewed zeal and vigor? A good walk? A great conversation with a wonderful friend? Laughing your head off as Simon Cowell annihilates the next round of *American Idol* wannabes? Ask yourself what you need. Then give it to you.

MAP TO A MILLION: SHOP FOR GROCERIES ONLINE

Is going to the grocery store a task you'd like to delegate? I suppose you could, but you could also knock it off in a fraction of the time you now spend. There have been only a few times in my life when I've stumbled across a technological innovation (I am, quite often, late to the party) and thought: This is going to change my life. My cell phone did it. My iPod did not. Palm, nope. BlackBerry, absolutely, but not always in a good way. But it did happen—boy, did it happen—when the delivery guy from Peapod, the online grocery service in my area, rang my doorbell and carried a dozen bags of groceries into my house, through the foyer, and deposited them *in my kitchen.* Let me say that again: *He brought them into my kitchen.*

I didn't have to get up early on a Sunday morning knowing that the grocery store was first on my list. I didn't have to make six trips back and forth to the garage, not counting the one to slam the rear door on the station wagon. I didn't have to clean up the trail of dirty snow I'd dragged across the floor. All I had to do was settle down in front of the computer and order my groceries online. Heaven.

Okay, maybe I'm exaggerating slightly. But this online grocery stuff is pretty incredible. It's safe—as is all online shopping as long as you're using a secure website (you'll know you are if you see an "s" after the "http" in the browser line). And it's fast. Once you have a running list in the computer, the actual act of shopping takes about fifteen minutes—less time than you'd spend driving to the store. It also saves you money because you really do buy only the things you need; you don't toss cookies and donuts into the cart just because you're hungry. My next-door neighbors Larry and Jodie—who, granted, have two little kids who both "want" a lot of things when they're riding in the cart—estimates that online grocery shopping saves them $100 a week. Invest that and see:

$100 a week saved on grocery shopping over 1 year: *$5,200*

$100 a week saved on grocery shopping over 10 years: *$79,215*

$100 a week saved on grocery shopping over 20 years: *$255,045*

$100 a week saved on grocery shopping over 30 years: *$645,325*

Cross Your T's and Dot Your I's

Figure out ways to prevent little things from slipping through the cracks. Your lists, particularly if you maintain them well—crossing things off when you do them, updating the master once every week or so—should go a long way to helping you accomplish this. But there are other things you can do as well.

You can reduce phone tag by telling people what you want from them as soon as you get them on the line or, if you don't get them, by telling their voice mail. You can use low-tech methods such as "Do not disturb" signs to block out physical interruptions. You can make important mail and e-mail seem more important by giving out your address less often (stores that ask for it are just trying to market to you—that is, send you more junk) and by unsubscribing from e-mail lists you're not using. At the end of each day, you can spend five minutes cleaning off your desk or workspace to get it organized so you can start fresh tomorrow.

And you can slow down. I mean it. The mother of one of my friends used to tell him: "The more you have to do, the slower you need to go." She was right. It's when you're running around like mad that the really important things slip through the cracks.

Stop Procrastinating

I was driving home recently listening to Dr. Joy Browne—one of my favorites on talk radio. She fielded a call from a man who said, "My problem is that I'm a procrastinator."

"Tell me what you procrastinate about," said the brilliant Dr. Joy. "And don't say 'everything' because it's just not true."

Precisely.

Research has shown that about 20 percent of us are chronic procrastinators. We have a real problem getting things started and then getting those things done. A great many more people aren't quite chronic. They're intermittent. They procrastinate doing things they don't like doing. The problem is attending to finances is on the procrastination lists of far too many women.

Academicians who've studied procrastination—and yes, there are some who have—agree it's a strange phenomenon. You might assume that doing nothing—goofing off, in essence—would make your life more pleasurable because it gives you downtime. But in reality it raises your stress level and makes you feel like a failure.

People who don't procrastinate tend to think that all a procrastinator needs is a little discipline, a little willpower. But the need is much more deep-rooted and emotional than that. Nevertheless, it's a problem that you *can* solve. First, you need to recognize your particular procrastinating behavior.

There are two distinctly different kinds of procrastinators: uptight and laidback. *Uptight procrastinators* put things off because they feel insurmountable pressure to succeed. If you're an uptight procrastinator, fear of failure—of not doing the very best on a task—prevents you from starting a task. The fear is that if you show the world you're not the smartest, the most perfect being, the world might realize you're actually just human. You dream of accomplishing tasks in an impressive, attention-getting way, but you get mired in the details. Sometimes you take on so many tasks that you can't dive in at any point; that's how overburdened you feel.

Laidback procrastinators engage in a more passive-aggressive strategy. If you're a laidback procrastinator, you blow off the things you need to do because you don't like anyone—a spouse, a boss, a parent—to be able to tell you what to do. You may not like the work associated with your job, or you may be angry because you feel you don't get the respect you deserve. But rather than dealing with how you're feeling in an upfront way, you question or rebel against the rules by not doing what you're supposed to.

Whether you're an uptight or a laidback procrastinator, you may be able to cure yourself by means of the following strategies:

- **Manage interruptions.** People who have a problem with procrastination can't handle stopping and starting. Figure out how long it takes you to complete a financial task—fifteen minutes to pay bills online, for instance—and then set yourself up so that you won't be interrupted. Tell your kids or spouse or assistant not to bother you for twenty minutes. Explain to your kids that they can watch a whole program on the Disney Channel and then you'll be done. Or make this task something you tackle before the rest of the family wakes up.

- **Break large jobs into smaller, more manageable tasks.** First parse down the job before you into bite-size pieces. Start with pieces that take no more than five minutes to complete. Offer yourself a reward (or a system of rewards) to get the job done. What do you want in exchange for finishing each small piece. A yoga class? A walk with a friend? Try not to reward yourself with items that can be destructive like food or alcohol.

- **Determine a time for making a decision and the criteria for making it.** Share your deadline with someone else. If the person will be affected by your completing the task at hand (such as your spouse with the bills), he or she will hold you to your word.

- **Develop a clear mental picture of the completed task and how you will feel at that time.** Maintain a focus on the end result, not just on the process. Remind yourself how good you'll feel when you're finished.

- **Imagine the worst.** Confront the reality of what will happen if the job doesn't get done. What will happen if the work isn't done, the house isn't managed, the bills aren't paid? If a real crisis is brewing, by all means use that to motivate yourself. In the absence of a real crisis, don't just imagine the worst, describe it in writing and force yourself to read it. Talk to people who, six months ago, were where you are today and couldn't get back on the right path. Use their stories as inspiration for what *not* to do.

LOOK HOW FAR YOU'VE COME!

Now that your life is running a little more smoothly—you've dealt with your money fears, structured a system of family finances that *works,* and gotten your space and time organized—it's time to make some moolah! In the coming pages, I'll show you how to save more, spend less, invest wisely, and protect the nest egg you're building. Read on . . .

My problem with shopping is a four-letter word: SALE. *I can't resist a sale. If something is marked down, I don't want to buy one; I want to buy* more *than one. What's going on here? And how do I stop?*

I completely understand how difficult it is to resist a sale, because for many years I suffered from the very same problem. I could walk away from full-priced merchandise with no trouble. But the minute something that had caught my eye went on sale, it became a deal and I had to have it. I had the worst time at sample sales—special sale events (typically in New York) where fashion designers put their own merchandise on deep, deep discount. I'd come home with bags full of items I'd never, ever wear. The solution that worked for me was simple. Once a season, I scour my closet to see what I need: Black capris? A brown suit? A colorful skirt or two? Sandals in a neutral color? I decide how much I'm willing to spend on each item. Then I go to the store and shop for those things specifically. As long as an item is in my price range, I can buy it—whether it's on sale or not. If it's not on my list, it doesn't go into the dressing room. If the black capris I want are more expensive than my allotment, I ask a salesperson when they'll be marked down. Sometimes the store is willing to hold them for me until that happens. As for sample sales, clearance sales, and all other four-letter temptations, I'm better off steering clear. I know myself well enough to know where my weaknesses lie.

My spouse doesn't understand the cost of my clothes or the children's. He thinks I'm overindulgent and excessive. I think he's cheap. How do we get through this without a battle every time I go to the store?

I sympathize with you but understand where your husband is coming from. Chances are he's never shopped for clothing for the children, and, save for your birthday when he's more likely to spring for a buck or two, he's probably never bought clothing for you. You can't expect him to know how much things cost unless he's been in the position of having to buy them. My suggestion: Put him there. Offer to trade financial duties with him for two months. You take something off his plate (paying the bills, perhaps) and put him in charge of shopping for the kids, for groceries, and for the

household (I wouldn't put him in charge of buying your clothes). This should give him some insight into your challenges. If he's not willing to switch— and he may not be—then sit him down at the computer and do some virtual shopping. Ask how much he thinks is reasonable to spend on clothing and sneakers for the kids. Then surf to your favorite website and have him fill the shopping bag. Either he'll be surprised at how few items he gets for his money, or he'll do such a good job you'll be able to steal a few of his strategies to save the family a bundle.

Should I consolidate my debts on one low-interest credit card or with a low-rate home equity loan?

Paying off your debts at a lower interest rate is always better than paying them off at a higher one. But before you start transferring balances and consolidating, I'd suggest trying to work with the cards you have now. Pick up the phone, call the toll-free number on the back of your current cards, and ask for a lower interest rate. Explain that you've been offered better deals (that, in fact, you're offered them nearly every day), and tell the customer service representative that the company is going to have to do better in order to keep your business. If the person on the front lines is unable to help, ask to speak to a supervisor. (You may have to climb the ladder a few

times, in fact, before you find someone who can help.) If you still get nowhere, it's time to look at transferring your balances. But do not—do not!—cancel your old cards. The offers you receive in the mail are merely temptations. Only when you apply for a particular card will you find out if you actually qualify for a lower interest rate. When you apply for a new card, make sure to read the offer's fine print. Often the rate for the balance you transfer is different from the rate for new purchases, which is different from the rate for cash advances. The company has the ability to make all rates really low, but you may have to request that. As for that home equity loan, it's true that home equity loan rates are generally less than credit card rates, which means that using a home equity loan to pay off your credit card balance makes financial sense. The problem is that about half of all people who use home equity to consolidate credit card debts run out and charge their credit cards right back up again. A few years down the road they have a big home equity loan *and* big credit card debts. I don't want you in that position. That's why I recommend using home equity to consolidate credit card debts only if you know yourself really, really well and have absolutely no doubt you'll be able to keep your hands off the plastic. You have to remember, once you dip into home equity, you're putting your house on the line.

CHAPTER 6

"I Have Nothing to Wear . . ."

DON'T BITCH

It's Saturday afternoon and you're off to the mall. Your teenage daughter is along for the ride, as is a girlfriend who doesn't really need anything but thought a shopping trip might be fun. You park in the lot, agree to meet two hours later in front of the Sunglass Hut, and split up. Your daughter has plans to meet a half dozen friends at the makeup counter to check out the spring colors. You and your girlfriend make multiple stops—some planned, some not. You go from store to store, buying some things, discarding others. Soon the two hours are over. You're energized, not tired, and you have no idea where the time went.

What is it with women and shopping? In the eyes of many men, shopping is a chore, a bore, work. Given a choice between a trip to the mall and an afternoon snoozing on the couch, most men I know opt for the latter. For women, by contrast, shopping is much more than the act of finding things you want and making a purchase. When we have the money—but even when we don't—shopping is something we find incredibly difficult to resist. Why? Listen to these women and their rationales:

I make good money. Why shouldn't I buy the things I want?
Amanda, publishing assistant

You only live once. That's what I tell myself, and it's a pretty convincing way to rationalize an extra shopping spree, extravagant night out, or vacation. My problem is, I still don't see anything wrong with that reasoning.
Brandi, stay-at-home mom

I have nothing to wear.
Elizabeth, communications specialist

I can't resist a sale.
Kathryn, comedienne/writer

Why can't I indulge myself with a new pair of shoes? I've earned it.
Sue, dog walker

I feel like I was born to shop.
Amy, accountant

In fact, we all were born to shop. At the turn of the twentieth century, women were still fairly repressed. We were subject to strict codes of moral standards and behaviors, and these codes and standards affected everything from the language we were allowed to use (polite, of course), the company we were allowed to keep (female, save for our brothers and spouses), to the places we were allowed to spend our free time. Those places didn't include the pubs where men went to let down their hair. But they did include the old-fashioned equivalent of a mall. Shops were among the few places a woman could go without male accompaniment without fear of ruining her reputation.

Back then, women did about 80 percent of the shopping in this country. Today, we still do. Even on the Internet—mainly a male environment in its infancy—women are outshopping men.

Trouble is, all that shopping eats up a lot of your time. If you totaled up hours spent in stores, reading catalogs, watching shopping shows on TV, and surfing the net, you'd find that you spend an average of 146 hours shopping and buying each year. That's more time than you spend reading, relaxing, and cleaning the house, and it's precisely the same amount of time you likely spend cooking. Really.

You've no doubt seen the bumper stickers and refrigerator magnets that say "I shop, therefore I am." Like all long-lived jokes, this one contains more than a kernel of truth.

Have you stopped to wonder why this is? Why do you choose to head to the mall, when you could be throwing around a ball with your children or laughing over a movie at the multiplex? And when you're engaged in the act of shopping (which really has nothing to do with handing your already bloated credit card over to the twenty-something cashier), what is it that triggers you to buy?

You'll notice that with the exception of Elizabeth, who claimed (falsely, as everyone of us with more than one pair of black pants in her closet knows) to have nothing to wear, not one of the women quoted earlier mentioned any reason that had anything to do with need. In fact, most of the time when we're shopping for things other than groceries (and often in the grocery store as well), we're *not* buying things because we need them. Women are different from men that way.

Two-thirds of all of a woman's purchases are unplanned, whether they're made while careening down the aisles at Wal-Mart or browsing at Anthropologie. Typically you buy because you're looking for a pick-me-up or want to reward yourself for losing ten pounds. You buy because all of a sudden that blue sweater seems a lot more important than the money you were trying to save for a house or a car. You buy because J. Crew sent you an e-mail telling you that you can have first shot at the spring merchandise when it goes on sale—but only today. And you buy because a trip to the outlet center with your girlfriends is the group's chosen activity and you'd rather participate than watch.

Retailers and marketers understand these reasons. They segment customers into different groups whose needs—for emotional fulfillment or entertainment—they can meet. Then they spend big bucks hiring consultants, conducting focus groups, and testing, testing, testing to figure out how to make their environment (store, website, or catalog) and product seem to be the very best way to scratch your particular itch.

Mall operators everywhere in this country know that they can't be just landlords but must be *place makers*. That's why in addition to your favorite stores, malls have movies, restaurants, and even roller coasters. Mall owners know there has to be something besides shopping to get you there and encourage you to stay. The principle is the same if the shopping environment is on paper (a catalog) or onscreen (a website). Some people speculate that the reason magazines are having such a tough time making their numbers these days is that catalogs are so beautiful—and free besides—that consumers prefer to spend their time perusing them.

Unfortunately, all of this shopping comes with two price tags—the one on the item itself and the emotional one. In the last six months, you've probably made at least one purchase you regret. With credit card indebtedness at an all-time high, chances are also pretty good that you couldn't really afford this purchase.

Understanding why you shop, and the tactics retailers use to turn a just-looking journey into an outing that costs a bundle, can help you get a tighter grip on your wallet. And that can help you make better, more conscious choices about what you really want to do with your money. Those beautiful throw pillows may still wind up at the top of your list (and then on your couch). But at least you'll understand why they're there.

The Twelve Reasons You Shop (Besides Want and Need)

Let's leave need out of it. There are things that you need—no doubt about it. There are other things that you think about wanting, make a decision to buy, and then go out and purchase. That is not the sort of shopping we are talking about here. We are talking about unconscious shopping—the sort of shopping that can get you into trouble if you do too much of it. New research shows that more of us participate in this sort of shopping than we previously thought.

You've probably heard the term *compulsive shopping*. It's the name of a psychological disorder that affects between 2 and 5 percent of the population. People who shop compulsively need help, and later in this chapter I tell you where to find it. But there is a much bigger slice of the population—15 to 18 percent, according to researchers at the University of Richmond—that shops "excessively." Like compulsive shoppers, people who shop excessively spend more than they would like to spend and buy more than is good for their financial well-being, but they do it less often. Even more than that 15 to 18 percent engage in occasional "retail therapy."

Knowing what prompts you to shop can help you channel your energies into more productive pursuits. So . . . why do *you* shop?

Because you're feeling blue

Unless you've been living under a rock, you've heard shopping referred to as "retail therapy." The academic term is *compensatory consumption,* and it's not just cute terminology. There's real science to back it up. Psychiatrists and psychologists (thus the "therapy" part) have shown that shopping causes a rush of dopamine to the brain. Dopamine is, essentially, happiness juice. It's what flows when you fall in love (or when you get high on cocaine). Shopping can also get the endorphins going, just as exercise does. In other words, the act of shopping actually makes people feel better. That's why you may default to it when you're down.

Because you want to feel powerful

Taking money or a credit card and using it to buy something that you want is an exercise in superiority. As long as you have that cash or plastic in your hand, you are in control. Whatever it is you want to make happen, you can. And the salespeople working the counters (at least in stores that put a premium on service) will bend over backward to help you. In very few other life experiences are you so clearly in the driver's seat.

Because you want to be someone else

People shop to fill the gap between who they are and who they want to be. The fantasy is that if you buy the big black sunglasses, the cute little shift dress, and the triple strand of pearls, you *will be* as chic and classy and desirable as Jackie Kennedy. Other times, a purchase is not associated with a particular individual. You think, if I buy those fabulous boot-cut jeans that all the 29-year-olds are wearing, I will look (and feel) 29 again. In other words, you believe—for any number of reasons—that a purchase will make your life significantly better.

Because you just don't want to be you

Sometimes you have no huge desire to be someone else. Instead, you want to escape your own reality. You need to get outside yourself and how imperfect you feel your life has become. And a trip to the mall—a little easier to attain than a trip to, say, Bali—does the trick.

Because you deserve it

Whether you work outside the home or in it, you are working harder than ever these days. You're stressed and tired, and sometimes you feel that you deserve some gorgeous thing just because you're you. Or maybe you accomplished something important. You made it through a week without a cigarette or blasted the competition in this month's sales tallies. Of course, you deserve a reward—and you're just the person to give it to you. Academics call this behavior *self-gifting*. And they say that when we are buying something for ourselves in this fashion, we tend to spend a little more than we would spend if we were merely "shopping." That's precisely what the whole right-hand ring campaign from the diamond industry is playing into. It says: It doesn't matter if you're single, divorced, widowed, or married. It doesn't matter if you're 29 or 59. You deserve a beautiful piece of fabulous jewelry just because. (And of course millions of American women agreed, helping the diamond industry to move millions of dollars' worth in stones that were so small there was really nothing else to do with them. Brilliant!)

Because you'd rather shop than go to the movies

For women, shopping offers a day out with the girls. Getting the full experience means coming home with a purchase. This time, though, making that purchase is about more than getting the goods. It's about bonding. Finding a deal with a friend, trying things on and getting each other's opinion, buying the same thing in a different color—all of those are social experiences. When your friend comes to your house and sees the rug or sconces she helped you pick out, you both can feel good about being a helpful presence in each other's lives.

Because no one—and I mean no one—can tell you what to do

After a fight with a spouse or a partner or parent, have you ever hit the stores? If so, you are retaliating (in a passive aggressive way) by sending this person the message: Look, you can't tell me what to do. I am spending our money (in the case of a spouse) or your money (in the case of a parent who's given you access to a credit card), and you can't stop me. This tactic is easier than confronting the person face-to-face and explaining how you really feel. But the ramifications may be much longer lasting.

Because you need a friend (or at the very least, a compliment)

Shopping can make you feel catered to and special. The rest of the world may hate you. Your kids may be moody. Your spouse may have a migraine. And your boss may be blowing smoke from his ears. But you can count on the folks at the mall to smile and say "Thank you" when you hand them your credit card.

Before you object, pointing out that of course they're nice to you, that's what they're paid to be, let me say that on certain days you'll take a smile, a kind glance, a "honey" or a "dear" from anyone who's willing to give it to you. If that person happens to be on commission, you really don't care. Sometimes, if you're a regular at certain stores, the relationship goes deeper. You seek a particular salesperson out. You solicit her opinion. It's a one-sided, low-risk relationship with someone who's always happy to see you, whose job it is to acknowledge and stroke you and make you feel good about yourself and your choices. It can be very self-affirming. But it can also get very expensive.

Because you're on autopilot

You do some things because you've done them for so long that you don't remember how to do something else. Shopping can be like that. A trip to the mall becomes a daily diversion. A trip to the grocery store is a way to use up time in an otherwise empty day. In other words, sometimes you shop because you've trained yourself, just like Pavlov's dog, to do so. Your favorite store just happens to be on the drive home from work. So once a week you go in to see what's new. You're never sure what you want to have for dinner, so you shop every day rather than once a week, and inevitably you come out with items you didn't plan on buying. The Internet is tailor-made for habitual shoppers. You can check the sales on your favorite website 24/7, just as easily and quickly as you can your e-mail or your portfolio.

Because you don't want to die

I can't take credit for this one. Tennessee Williams put his finger on it when he wrote: "The human animal is a beast that dies, and he buys and buys and he buys and I think that secretly he's buying because of the hushed hope that what he's buying is life everlasting." Precisely. When you buy something that you're going to use or wear or drive, you do it with the expectation that you'll be around to do just that. It's like issuing a challenge to the Grim Reaper: "I'm going to spend $500 on this cashmere sweater. Just you try and get me." Although most reasons for shopping actually tail off as you get older, death-defying shopping is the opposite.

MAP TO A MILLION

What if you didn't buy these all-too-common feel-good items and instead put the money away to grow?

A CD: $11.99

In 10 years you'd have:	*$24*
In 20 years you'd have:	*$54*
In 30 years you'd have:	*$131*

A LIPSTICK: $14.99

In 10 years you'd have:	*$33*
In 20 years you'd have:	*$68*
In 30 years you'd have:	*$153*

A NEW PAIR OF JEANS: $49.99

In 10 years you'd have:	*$110*
In 20 years you'd have:	*$246*
In 30 years you'd have:	*$546*

A PRETTY BRA AND PANTY SET: $69.99

In 10 years you'd have: *$155*
In 20 years you'd have: *$344*
In 30 years you'd have: *$765*

A CASHMERE SWEATER: $129.99

In 10 years you'd have: *$288*
In 20 years you'd have: *$640*
In 30 years you'd have: *$1,421*

A PAIR OF HOOP EARRINGS WITH LITTLE DIAMONDS: $199.99

In 10 years you'd have: *$443*
In 20 years you'd have: *$985*
In 30 years you'd have: *$2,187*

ALL OF THEM: $476.94

In 10 years you'd have: *$1,058*
In 20 years you'd have: *$2,350*
In 30 years you'd have: *$5,216*

Remember: Money, invested, not spent, typically **doubles** in value every seven years.

Because it looked good at the time

At times, you shop simply because you can't help it. When your desire to have something overwhelms your willpower not to have it, you make an impulse purchase. And it all tends to happen in the blink of an eye. You go into the store looking for a white sweater; then you see something else, and you think, "This is cute, new, different, kind of fun." So you buy it. Done deal. Somewhere between half and two-thirds of all purchases are impulse purchases. They're the reason that stores are set up to look so appealing, that perfume is spritzed in the aisles. These attention-grabbing strategies work.

Because you can't stop

If you read back through the reasons people shop, chances are you can find yourself in almost all of them. I know I can. But it's important to understand the difference between doing all of these things occasionally and doing one or more of them so frequently that shopping becomes a problem in your life. The 2 to 5 percent of the population who are compulsive shoppers experience the emotional highs and lows of shopping to a much greater degree than does the general population. For them, the dopamine rush that shopping brings is addictive—they want more. To find out if you're part of this small group, answer these questions:

- *Do you have bags of like items in your closets that you have never used?*
- *Do you routinely lie to your spouse or partner about how much an item cost (or pay with half cash and half credit to hide the damage)?*
- *Do you feel your heart racing as you head to the cashier?*
- *Do you feel let down, disappointed, or angry with yourself for spending money after most shopping expeditions?*
- *Do you hide your purchase or your receipts?*
- *Do you feel incredibly guilty after each shopping expedition?*
- *Do you crave more?*

Here's the thing about shopping disorders: Unlike drinking addictions or drug problems or eating disorders, compulsive shopping is incredibly easy to mask. Even highly addicted shoppers present themselves as smart—they're great at getting a good deal—not to mention well-educated, well-dressed people. They're participating in an activity that, unlike some other compulsions, is completely acceptable. Shopping is a social activity. You can do it with your friends.

But even when you shop with your friends, the experience resonates differently with you. A normal, nonaddicted shopper can shop for a pick-me-up and typically gets a little lift, which may not last more than a day or so.

After the experience, a normal shopper's mood doesn't crater. But if you're addicted, your mood goes way up at the point of purchase and way down after, and then you immediately want a bigger high, a better high, a more expensive high.

There are additional differences between normal and addicted shoppers. Normal shoppers know who they are. They're generally accepting of themselves. When they shop for an outfit to wear on a special night out, they're want to make themselves look and feel a little better. Compulsive or addicted shoppers are trying to fill a huge void. They feel they are unattractive but would like to be magnificent—an impossible goal. So upon failing, they move on to another purchase and to another one after that.

Nonaddicted shoppers like to go to the mall. Addicted shoppers are driven to go. That's why one big difference between impulse shopping and compulsive shopping is frequency. Impulse shopping happens when you find yourself, occasionally, faced with a purchase that's too tough to resist. Shopping is compulsive when you shop more often than you'd like, feeling unable to stop.

If you are compulsive, if you find yourself in these descriptions, you need professional help. This is a problem to be taken as seriously as a drinking or drug problem or an eating disorder. Many therapists who treat shopping disorders treat eating disorders as well—the parallels are that dramatic. Here are some resources to get you started:

- *Debtors Anonymous (www.debtorsanonymous.org).*
- *National Foundation for Credit Counseling (www.nfcc.org).*
- *You can also search for a therapist at the website Psychology Today.org. To narrow the search, specify on the second pull-down menu that you're searching for help with an addiction. Then ask any therapists you call whether they've helped other compulsive spenders.*

GET RICH

Stop Shopping and Start Living

The good news is that understanding why you're shopping may be all it takes to keep you from the stores. I recently spent some time working with

Lisa, a teacher in North Carolina who went to the mall every day to the detriment of her credit rating and her marriage. Two weeks after I put a halt to the shopping behavior and gave her a pedometer so that she'd have another way to occupy her time, she said to me:

> You know, my husband and I are talking more than we have in years. He was so angry about all my spending that whenever I went home things would get nasty. So rather than go home and subject myself to that I'd go to the mall. It was a vicious cycle. But things in our home have gotten considerably better.

Lisa had the fortitude to put a halt to her shopping cold turkey. The fact that her shopping problem was being profiled on national televison and she didn't want to fail in that environment also gave her a huge kick in willpower. You may need other ammunition. Here are my favorite stop-shopping tactics.

Ask Yourself Five Crucial Questions

I got these from a very smart psychologist named April Benson. I've para-phrased . . . but before making any purchase, I want you to ask yourself these questions:

1. *What am I doing here?*
2. *What was the trigger that sent me here?*
3. *How do I feel?*
4. *Is the thing I'm about to reach for something I need? What happens if I don't buy it?*
5. *What happens if I do buy it?*

If the answers don't point to the difference between buying something and not buying it—if you don't feel the difference in your gut—then you need to delve a little deeper into those questions.

What am I doing here?

If you're at a store or website because you have a reason to shop—such as you're out of paper towels or your best friend is finally getting married and you need to buy a gift before everything good is gone from the registry—fine. You have a reason to be shopping, and you can clearly articulate it. But if you're shopping just because—because you're tired, or irritable, or bored, or feel like being someone else today—then it's time to do something else instead.

What was the trigger that sent me here?

Can you put your finger on it? If there is a need—the party is tomorrow and you don't want to go empty-handed—that's defensible. But if you're shopping for emotional reasons, your wallet will reward you for getting a grip on what they are.

Consider a teenager whose parents weren't getting along. Every time they had a tussle and there was tension in the house, the parents would send the girl to the mall (with a wad of cash) to get her out of the way and also to buy something to try to make her feel better. The purchase provided a short-term lift. In the moment of buying something, she became strong, rather than a victim. As an adult, whenever this woman felt the same sort of tension—when she had a bad day at work or a fight with her own spouse—she would retreat to spending mode. Anything she bought to restore her sense of self felt like a need rather than a want. Learning not to spend is learning to tell the difference.

How do I feel?

Think about what it feels like to skip a meal and then be so hungry that nothing is appealing. You wander the aisles of the grocery store, peruse the corners of your pantry, drive into (and then out of) three different drive-throughs. Nothing looks good. Eventually, you're so famished you eat a donut. Or a bag of chips. Or an order of fries. Or ice cream. Whatever you put in your mouth, though, doesn't do the trick. It doesn't taste as good as it might have if it were your first choice, if you'd found a way to get rid of the edge. That's precisely how a shopping expedition should *not* feel. It shouldn't feel frantic, or fraught, or pressured, or manic. If it does, even in the least, it's time to go home and put your feet up, watch bad cable, or take a bubble bath.

Is the thing I'm about to reach for something I need? What happens if I don't buy it?

There's a bothersome scene in *Love, Actually*, one of my favorite movies. Alan Rickman, playing a successful magazine editor, asks his assistant what she wants for Christmas. "Something along the stationery line, perhaps?" he asks. "Are you short of staplers?"

"I don't want something I need," she replies. "I want something I *want*. Something pretty."

The scene is bothersome because he's old and married and she's young and not, and he just can't help himself. She's got him and she's reeling him in one pricey heart-shaped necklace at a time. She does have one thing over most people in the universe, though. When it comes to needs and wants, she clearly knows the difference. Do you? Perhaps not.

Here's the bottom line. Wants are optional. If you don't end up with them in your possession, your health will not fail, you and your family will not go hungry, you will not end up running down the street naked. Needs are the opposite: heat, food, shelter, love. If you don't have them, something bad will happen to you: frostbite, starvation, illness, severe loneliness.

What happens if I do buy it?

Perhaps your purchase will make you happy—for a little while. But research has shown that most purchases never make us as happy as we think they will for as long as we think they will (also, *not* buying something won't make us quite as disappointed as we think it will.) And when the bills roll in, you may find yourself beating yourself up emotionally for acquiring stuff that you truly can't afford.

Help Yourself Succeed

Everyone can use a helping hand when trying to incorporate a new behavior into their lives. Here are my favorite ways to help yourself:

Do it: Teach retailers to leave you alone. A marketer who has you pegged as a habitual customer will do whatever it takes to increase the frequency of your shopping and the amount of merchandise you buy. Here's how you can turn off the come-hither tactics:

1. *Cancel the store credit card. You got it originally, I know, to save 10 or 20 percent on a particularly large purchase. Getting it made sense at the time, but now is the time to get rid of it because the coupons and catalogs and other enticing offers that come through the mail are temptations you simply don't need. Plus, store credit cards are a notoriously bad deal. Interest rates on these cards can be double those on bank cards.*

2. *Unsubscribe from retail websites. Many of them send you e-mails on a daily basis with all sorts of attempts to draw you in. They're a waste of your money and your time.*

3. *If you stay up late at night or while away the mornings shopping away your savings on QVC, switch to basic cable so that shopping channels no longer come to your set. The money you save on cable alone will add up to a bundle over time. Note: If they are part of basic cable, call your cable provider to ask if they can be blocked.*

Say it and sound smart: *"Since I switched to basic cable, my kids are watching TV less and spending so much more time outside!"*

Do it: Give yourself nonshopping options. Emotional shopping tends to veer toward its most expensive and most damaging if you do it when your resources are depleted: when you're tired; when you've had a couple of glasses of wine, a fight with your spouse, a lousy day at work; or when (for whatever reason) you're feeling that you're not looking particularly good. You buy something because you think it will make you look or feel better.

You need to give yourself other options, and I suggest exercise. Like shopping, exercise makes you feel good. Unlike shopping, exercise is good for you. It makes your body feel better, and it makes your body look better. That's why one of my favorite tactics is to give addicted shoppers a pedometer and tell them to focus on achieving ten thousand steps a day rather than focusing on the next trip to the mall. They need a different, more healthy object of obsession, and the pedometer fills that need.

I realize that exercise is not the solution for everyone. So pick something else you can do on a regular basis. Take a bath. Read (Hemingway, Jackie Collins, or the Bible—what you choose makes no difference as long as it resonates with you). Knit. Call your mother. The key is deciding—planning—in advance that when you feel like shopping you're going to do this other activity instead.

Say it and sound smart: *"Since I stopped shopping and started jogging, I've lost 8 pounds—and I'm sleeping better!"*

Do it: Break the habit. As I said before, shopping is something some people do not because they want to but because they've done it for so long they don't remember how to do something else. There's a chain of events that leads to a particular consequence, and in this case the consequence is a trip to your favorite fashion website or to the mall. If this describes you, figure out what happens to get you to the point of purchase.

If you shop on the Internet at night, what happens before? Perhaps you eat dinner, clear the table, bathe the kids, make their lunches, read them a story, tuck them into bed, then sit down and click onto the computer while simultaneously watching TV. Maybe you need to have something else to do with your hands while you watch your favorite shows? Stitchery might work, or a sudoku book, or even a jigsaw puzzle.

Perhaps each day as you leave work you pass by your favorite store on the way to the car. There's always something enticing in the window, so you go in. To break this habit, you need to bypass the store. So park in a different garage, or walk to the garage with a friend whom you've told of your desire not to shop.

Whatever your particular chain of events is, find two things you could do instead so you'll have options to fall back on. Then make sure to fall back on those options every day for three weeks. By that point, your new habit will become your default, and you'll be home free.

Say it and sound smart: *"I haven't shopped online for three weeks now. I'm getting so much more done at work, I've been out of there at 5:30!"*

Do it: Carry a shopping diary. When you're shopping for entertainment, you tend to buy because you feel guilty about *not* buying. How can you spend nothing when your friend is already toting three shopping bags? How can you spend nothing when the salesperson has given you forty-five minutes of her time? Doing something will help to take the edge off. So carry a shopping diary and write down how you're feeling and what your rationale is before you make a purchase. That activity in and of itself may create enough of a delay to get you off the shopping course. Another successful tactic: Put the items you're considering on hold. If you're still desperate to have them tomorrow, you can return to the store and buy them. Putting a little distance between yourself and the purchase will help you evaluate it more rationally.

Say it and sound smart: *"By keeping track of all my impulses to buy, I've saved $250 this month!"*

Do it: Steer clear of the dressing rooms. Despite the notoriously bad lighting, research has shown that if you actually try on the clothing you're more likely to buy it. So don't try on anything. Look. Touch. Hug the garments if you have to. Then put them back on the racks.

Say it and sound smart: *"Oh boy, is it 3 p.m. already? I'll have to do this another day."*

Do it: Take it back. In the past six months, you probably have made at least one purchase you regret. Make a pledge not to wear (or use) anything new for the first twenty-four hours you own it. And make sure to save every receipt. That way, if you buy something you don't really need or want, you can take it back. But note: Buying and returning, too, can become a compulsion for some shoppers. If you or a friend or spouse notices that you're spending a lot of your time returning things or that you seem to return everything you buy, you may need professional help (see page 128).

Say it and sound smart: *"It turned out not to be the right thing after all."*

Do it: Get your friends to help you. Your best friends should be able to help you save money as well as spend it. Tell your shopping buddies what you're trying to accomplish. Those who pooh-pooh you shouldn't be shopped with again. If your shopping partner is a spouse, your challenge becomes easier because your goals are shared goals. Attach a number to the goal you're focused on most immediately. Once you know that the trip to California is going to cost $1,800, or the bathroom renovation, $8,000, you know precisely where the finish line is. Each time you take a pass on the latest in cell phones ($350) or theater tickets ($200), you can congratulate each other for not abandoning your goal.

Say it and sound smart: *"I'm counting on you to help me with this. I really value your support."*

MAP TO A MILLION: TRADE DOWN

So you deserve a splurge. But what if you splurged in a small way rather than a dramatic one. How much money could you save over time?

Store-brand jeans:	*$39*
Designer jeans:	*$179*
Savings:	*$140*
Savings after 10 years:	*$310*
Savings after 20 years:	*$689*
Savings after 30 years:	*$1,531*
1-carat Tiffany diamond ring:	*$10,000*
1-carat Tiffany look-alike cubic zirconia ring (in real gold setting):	*$95*
Savings:	*$9,905*
Savings after 10 years:	*$21,985*
Savings after 20 years:	*$48,799*
Savings after 30 years:	*$108,318*
60-minute day spa massage:	*$85*
10-minute chair massage:	*$10*
Savings:	*$75*
Savings after 10 years:	*$166*
Savings after 20 years:	*$369*
Savings after 30 years:	*$820*

Dinner with the girls:	*$30*
Coffee with the girls:	*$3*
Savings:	*$27*
Savings after 10 years:	*$59*
Savings after 20 years:	*$133*
Savings after 30 years:	*$295*

Leave the Plastic (All of It) at Home

And carry with you only the amount of cash you're willing to spend that day. Essentially, that forces your hand. You have to think in advance: How much can I spend? What do I want to spend it on? As for everything else, you're "just looking." And that can be a very enjoyable way to spend the day.

My Debt Diet

In the next chapter, we'll talk about the importance of saving money. Saving money is the key to achieving not just your small future goals (such as the California vacation and bathroom renovation I mentioned before) but also your larger ones (college for your children and retirement for yourself). At the end of the day, if you want to stop shopping and spending, the fact that all of these other things are more important to you provides the rationale. But in order to do so, you need to rethink your relationship with your credit cards.

These days, credit cards are way too easy to get and way too easy to use. They're more expensive than ever, thanks to bank fees and interest rates that shoot skyward if you're even a few hours late with a payment. Paying off the $9,300 the average household is carrying can cost three to four times that amount in interest charges and can take decades. Simply carrying it—not paying down any of it—can cost more than $2,000 a year.

I have spent the last three years working—on television, the Internet, the phone, and in person—to get people out of debt. Here is what I've learned: Once you approach the problem as if it's a diet, getting out of debt becomes easier to wrap your head around. Life's truly great diets—the Weight Watchers and South Beaches of the world—are simple. If you cut carbs or count points, you lose weight. And you have choices. The creators of these diets don't say, no way, no how, you can never have a glass of wine or a piece of chocolate again. They say, you have to make choices. If you have chocolate today, you can't have pizza and a donut, too.

This is how my Debt Diet works. You track your money—what's coming in and what's going out. You figure out how much you need to pay your monthly fixed costs, and you make better, conscious choices about the rest. You start living on what you make, rather than on more than you make. Consider it a *live-on-what-you-makeover*. Here's what you need to do to get with the program.

Remind yourself why you're going on the diet

Getting out of debt requires you to give up something today to get something tomorrow. You have to give up the shopping today to get the free cash to put toward that bigger item—a house, vacation, car, retirement, financial security—tomorrow. You have to want tomorrow's promise more than you want the fleeting thrills of today.

The hard part is that the rush you associate with shopping . . . well, it's tough to replicate by not shopping. What you can do, however, is encourage yourself to take pride in seeing your credit card balances go down. You get the rush of opening a MasterCard or Visa bill and seeing that—hooray!—you don't owe one-third of your paycheck to the piper. You can highlight credit card bills and plaster them on the fridge just as you do your sixth-grader's report card. You get the rush of seeing the balances in your savings account, your 401(k), and your IRA go up. And you can take note of the fact that owing less money makes you feel safer, smarter, more confident, and more in control. You will feel that you own your life. You will stop fighting with your spouse about your debts. And you will—in the end—be happier.

You may even be skinnier. Not only has research shown that weight loss and debt loss often go hand in hand, but also a number of the debt dieters I've worked with have dropped a size or two. Why? In part, because one thing debtors overspend on is eating out. When you start to trim that part of your budget, it likely means you're eating at home and therefore you're eating healthier. But it's also because overspending, like overeating, is an addictive behavior. Once you figure out how to better manage one of them, it's likely you can use the same tools to help you get a grip on the other parts of your life.

Specify the endgame

If you were dieting to lose weight, you'd know precisely how much you wanted to lose and how fast you wanted to lose it. You need to be as specific about your debt. So ask yourself these questions:

How much do I owe?

At what interest rates?

By when would I like to pay it back?

Don't be unrealistic. If you can find an extra $10 a day beyond the minimum payments you're making now, you can get rid of an additional $3,650 of debt in a year. That's a reasonable goal. If you want to try for more, that's great. But be aware that it takes the average family five years to go through the credit counseling process and emerge with a clean slate. Telling yourself you're going to blow through thousands in debt in just a few months may be setting yourself up for failure.

Prioritize

There is a debt-repayment hierarchy. First, make payments on things you could lose (such as your house). Second, make payments on other things you can't easily live without (such as utilities). Third, pay down your highest-interest-rate debts.

1. ***Things you could lose.*** *Not making a mortgage payment could free up a lot of cash to pay back other debts at higher interest rates. But that strategy could cost you your house, just as it could cost your car if you don't make your car payment and your paycheck if you don't pay your student loans and taxes. That's why those payments have the highest priority.*
2. ***Other things you need.*** *You need electricity, heat, and other utilities. You also need to be able to go to the doctor, so it's not wise to let medical bills fall behind. If you are not able to pay all your bills and have to choose among them, ask yourself if the bill sitting*

on top of your stack represents a need or a want. If it's from a doctor you'll need to see again, the bill gets paid. If it's from the electric company, the bill gets paid. If it's from a credit card company that could—at worst—cut off your access to its card, the bill doesn't get paid.

3. **Highest-interest-rate debts.** *Finally, focus on the debts that are costing you the most money. Pay the highest-interest-rate debts first. Make additional payments on the credit cards that are charging you 24 percent, before you make additional payments on the credit cards that are charging you 14 percent. Make additional payments on the credit cards that are charging you 14 percent, before you make an extra mortgage payment at 6 percent. If you have lots of cards with similarly high rates and one or two are more maxed out than the rest, focus on those maxed-out cards first, because doing so will improve your credit score—and that will allow you to borrow more inexpensively in the future.*

Work on your credit score

What's a credit score and why would you want to improve it? A credit score is a numerical representation of how responsible you are financially. The higher your score is (scores range from 350 to 800), the less it will cost you to borrow money in the future. Also, you'll get lower prices on auto and homeowners insurance if you have a good score, and because employers and landlords look to credit scores to gauge your responsibility, a lower score may also make it easier to rent an apartment and get a job. To find out what your credit score is, you'll have to buy it from one of the three credit bureaus (Experian.com, Equifax.com, or TransUnion.com) or from MyFico.com, the company that originated credit scoring. If you're applying for a mortgage or car loan, the lender may be happy to share it with you for free. A score of 660 or above is good, a score of 720 or above is great. To raise your score, do the following:

- *Pay your bills on time.*
- *Focus on paying down the credit cards that are most maxed out.*

- *Try to use only about 30 percent of the credit limits that card companies have extended to you.*
- *Stop applying for more credit.*
- *Do not cancel old credit cards. If you don't want to be tempted to use old credit cards, consign them to your freezer.*

Obey the rules

You know that certain diets exclude some foods, at least for a while. The Debt Diet has nine rules to follow if you want the greatest shot at success:

1. **Make debit your plastic of choice.** *When you're using a debit card, you can't spend money you don't have.*
2. **Slim down your wallet.** *Take all but one credit card (the one with the lowest interest rate) out of your wallet. That credit card is for emergencies only. Take a piece of paper or a Post-it note and write—in big letters—*FOR EMERGENCIES ONLY *on it. The fact that you'll have to read the wrapper before making a purchase should be enough to get you to think twice. If you are one of those people who have their credit card numbers memorized, call your card company, report the card stolen, ask for a replacement, and do not memorize the new number.*
3. **Stop shopping online except for groceries.** *Shopping online for groceries stops impulse purchasing and can save you time and money. All other online shopping poses an expensive risk. Whether or not you shop for groceries online, try to limit your grocery shopping to once a week.*
4. **Stick to a shopping list.** *Whether you're buying birthday presents or burgers and buns, if an item is not on your list, you didn't think about it in advance, which means you don't really need it. So don't buy it.*
5. **Make one ATM visit per week.** *Cash is even easier to blow through than plastic. Decide how much cash you want to spend each week. Take it out on a Monday, and divvy it into seven parts. Each day, carry one-seventh of the total amount with you. If you*

spend less than your allocation on a single day, you can carry over the remainder and use it for a little splurge.

6. **Pay your bills as they come in, rather than all at once.** *If you do this, you'll have more in savings, less in debt, and you'll be happier. Why? Because if you get a big bill—say, for heating—early in the month, you'll compensate and spend less on other things throughout the rest of the month. That way you'll wind up in a much smaller hole. This is a powerful habit to adopt.*

7. **Bank online.** *If you're a believer—as I am—that time is the new money, then paying your bills online saves you a lot of each. But be sure to find a bank that will give you online banking services for free.*

8. **Track your spending.** *Knowing where your money is going— on a daily basis—is your key to succeeding at the Debt Diet (just as knowing how much food you're putting in your mouth is key to losing weight on most diets). So, for at least the first month, write down everything you spend: every dollar, every dime. Adding up the expenditures by category—food, clothing, taxis, entertainment, and so forth—will show you where you have room to cut back.*

9. **Above all: Don't beat yourself up when you falter.** *Okay, let's acknowledge up front that you are not going to be able to follow this plan to the letter. I certainly wouldn't be able to. That's why, like a good diet, where one piece of great chocolate can save you from an entire weekend of overeating, this plan allows you occa-sional splurges. Reward yourself for a job well done. If you've stockpiled a little cash by the end of the week, take yourself to the movies. If you pay a really big bill and want to do a little some-thing special for yourself at the same time, well, okay. And if you go out and make an unplanned purchase, and then wear it the same day, spill something awful on it, or simply cannot bring yourself to take it back, that'll just have to be okay, too. Don't beat yourself up. Get back on the Debt Diet tomorrow.*

LOOK HOW FAR YOU'VE COME!

In this chapter, you've really put a finger on the reason (or reasons) money is flying through your hands. Knowing how to stop spending—and as a result, start saving—means you're ready to build some significant wealth. And using the tools, strategies, and techniques from the first few chapters, you'll be able to take control of that stash as well. In other words, you're doing great! Stick with me . . .

Which is more important, saving or investing?

Both are important—critical actually—to building a secure future for you and your family. But if I had to pick only one, I'd put my money on saving every time. That's because saving is a sure thing. When you "save" money, you stockpile it. You don't spend it. It's yours and it's there. When you "invest" money, you take whatever you've saved and try to make it into more. So if you save a bundle of money and put it into stocks and bonds where it earns a modest return, you'll be much better off in the long run than if you save a so-so sum of money and earn a terrific return. Why? Your savings represent your base, and by saving more you're building on a base that's larger to begin with. Of course, in the best of all possible worlds—and in your world as soon as you complete the next two chapters—you can save a bundle *and* invest wisely. Then you can sleep at night knowing your retirement is taken care of.

I'm not a great saver, but I'd really like my kids to be. What's the best way to make that happen?

I believe that kids never really start to grasp money (from saving it to spending it to investing it to giving it away) until they have some of their own to manage. So I believe in allowances. Personally, I don't tie them to grades or chores—my children are expected to get decent grades and to do certain jobs around the house simply because they're part of the family—but I do know parents for whom this connection has worked well. The way you teach your children to save is by managing their use of their allowance. There need to be certain things that you expect them to pay for themselves. If they can't afford those things on their weekly pay, they have to save money to make it happen. As long as you are able to stick to your guns, your kids will learn how to stockpile.

I started my children at $1 a week in kindergarten and then increased it by $1 a year through elementary school. When my son entered middle school, he got a raise—not because he had done anything to deserve it, but because he was expected to pay for more things. If and when he wants something really expensive (video games, for instance) that would be tough

to come by on a $10 allowance, I offer him a way to earn additional money. From time to time, I've also offered a homespun 401(k): I match the money he saves himself so that it doesn't take him an unreasonable amount of time to amass a larger amount.

The key to this process—and to raising kids who are not only great savers but conscious managers of their own money—is avoiding the bailout. When your children buy something that proves to be a total dud (it tastes lousy, it breaks the second day, they don't like that color anymore, whatever), they have to live with their choices. You cannot give them the money back. You do not buy them something else. They made a choice, and they have to live with it. If you can't stand firm on this one, you will be bailing them out when they're twenty-five. I guarantee it.

"I'd LOVE to Start Saving, but I Don't Know How"

DON'T BITCH

This past weekend, my husband called to tell me that our cell phones were disconnected for nonpayment. Three months ago, he went to the gas station to fill up his car and the credit card was denied for nonpayment. This has happened a lot in the past year since I started my own firm and have been trying to balance family, kids, work, and self.
Joyce, entrepreneur

Has this ever happened to you? A bill goes unpaid. An important appointment is missed. You meant to do your taxes or go to the bank or make an IRA deposit or . . . whatever. It was on your list. You planned to do it. But life got in the way. Well, the organizational and time management strategies that I laid out for you in previous chapters will go a long way toward solving those problems.

But sometimes in your financial life you can (and should) take advantage of financial systems, products, and technologies that allow you (in the immortal words of infomercial king Ron Popeil) to "Set it and forget it."

Look, there are a million or more reasons you can give yourself for not doing something—anything—to ensure that you'll really save some money this time around. You can tell yourself you'll be just fine without savings, that someone will come along and take care of you. You can push it off until next month or next year as these two women did:

> *I'm still young. I'll have time to save later in life.*
> Heather, account manager

> *I'm getting a tax refund in February so I'll do it then.*
> Suzanne, restaurant hostess

Or you can simply own up to the fact that retirement is a very, very scary proposition if you don't have savings and resources to back you up. You can acknowledge these three concerns:

1. ***You fear you'll have to live in poverty during retirement.*** *Some 38 percent of women (and 53 percent of women of color) ages 30 to 55 have that fear, according to data from the Heinz Family Foundation.*
2. ***You fear that you'll have to work full-time or part-time after the age at which you'd prefer to retire.*** *Nearly half of women share that anxiety.*
3. ***You're afraid that you're not adequately able to sock money away for later life.*** *That wouldn't be surprising. More than half of all women—54 percent—say they have no money left to save for retirement after they pay their bills.*

Those are very common fears. They take many different forms. And getting past them means doing one thing and one thing only: *saving more money.*

Every year, the folks at *Real Simple* magazine conduct something they call the "Problem Detection" study. They send a team of researchers out into the field to talk in depth with real women about the problems that are plaguing their lives. Every year two problems emerge in the top three: finding black pants that fit (I'm not kidding) and saving too little while spending too much. That's certainly the story of Lee Ann's life. The nursery school teacher writes:

We purchased a fixer-upper that has been draining most of our funds.
There seem to be so many things that we want to do to the house that
I may never be able to save enough so I can stay home for a few years
and afford a baby.

You have to learn to think of life as an equation. If you need to keep more of the money you have coming in (it helps to know why you need it), there are two and only two ways to do that: (1) You can spend less of it (we talked about a host of ways to do that in Chapter 6). (2) You can save more. They are interlocking pieces of the same puzzle. You have to do one in order to do the other. Here's what I want you to do.

Five Steps to Saving More

Step 1: Eyes on the prize

Know what you're saving for and how much it's going to cost you. Let's say you want to put a down payment on a house two years from now. You'd like to aim for 10 percent. The houses you're considering cost about $300,000, so 10 percent is $30,000. The fact that you have two years between today and the time you want to make that down payment gives you 24 months—48 pay periods—to come up with the money. If you're starting from scratch, you should be saving $625 every pay period.

1. *What am I saving for?* _____
2. *How much does it cost?* _____
3. *Do I already have anything saved?* _____
4. *How much more do I need? (Line 2 – Line 3)* _____
5. *How many months (or pay periods) do I have to come up with*
   this money? _____
6. *How much do I have to save each month (or pay period) to meet*
   my goal? _____

Step 2: Know what's coming in

Whether you're trying to save $625 a paycheck or significantly more or significantly less, it helps tremendously to know how much you have coming in. To live within your means, you have to know what you're making.

That means setting up some sort of record-keeping system. I use a personal finance software program, but you could just as easily use pencil and paper. On a worksheet, record what you receive from all sources. Your paychecks, any Social Security payments, any income from real estate or investments. Subtract the taxes you owe on all of these things, and what's left is your monthly nut. Note: Taking out the taxes is a key step. People who focus on their *gross* income rather than their *net* income inevitably overspend.

Step 3: Know what's going out

On the same worksheet, what I call the Get Rich Spending Tracker (see pages 160–163), lay out your *fixed* expenses. What do you spend each month on rent or mortgage, car payment, insurance, debts (student loans, installment debt), existing credit card debts, utilities, and the like? Next, take a look at your *variable* expenses. How much did you spend the last three months (your credit card statements may be helpful in tracking this) on food, entertainment, clothing, and so forth? Save every receipt for at least a month until you start to see patterns. Perhaps you're spending more than you ever intended on birthday gifts for the dozens of parties your kids are invited to. Perhaps you didn't realize that a $5 lunch each day adds up to $1,200 a year.

Step 4: Make changes

Once you know what's coming in and what's going out, you can make the needed changes to keep yourself living within your means. For instance, you can decide to curb the amount you spend on lunches out or on gifts. You might decide to bring leftovers from dinner every other day. That will put another $600 a year into your pocket—or one month's worth of that down payment toward your house.

Here are the percentages of your take-home pay (your *net* salary) that I want you to funnel into your various expense categories:

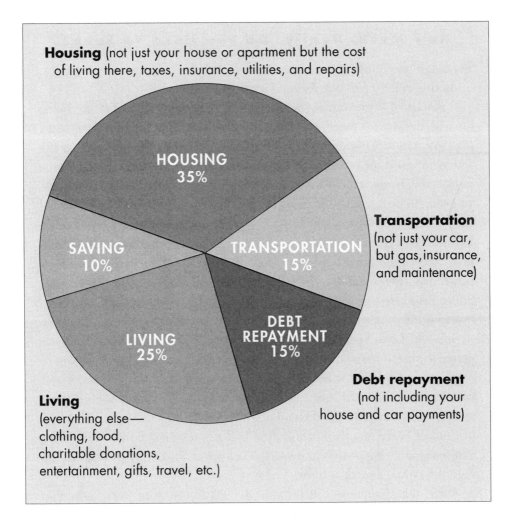

Housing (not just your house or apartment but the cost of living there, taxes, insurance, utilities, and repairs)

HOUSING
35%

Transportation
(not just your car, but gas, insurance, and maintenance)

SAVING
10%

TRANSPORTATION
15%

DEBT
REPAYMENT
15%

LIVING
25%

Debt repayment
(not including your house and car payments)

Living
(everything else—
clothing, food,
charitable donations,
entertainment, gifts, travel, etc.)

Step 5: Automate to force your own hand

Once you figure out how much you should have left, you can start to save the money you're not spending. The very best way to save—the way I do it—is by asking the bank to move some money out of checking and into savings automatically each pay period. If it helps, set up separate savings accounts for separate goals.

How Much, Really, Do You Need to Save?

To start: Something.

In the end: 10 percent. More, if possible.

I get asked "How much should I save" all the time, and I'm not being flip with my answer. Here's the thing about saving: It's a habit that you must start to get into. What we know about habits is that you have to perform the action in question repeatedly (most research says 21 times or for three weeks straight on a daily basis) in order to make it a part of your life. Do you want to be a runner? If you run every other day for six weeks, you will be. Do you want to stop smoking? If you cut out the puffing every day for 21 days, you can call yourself a nonsmoker. Do you want to be a saver? Well, save something—anything—every day or every week or every paycheck (whichever increment you find easiest to handle), and put it away for your future goals. Do this roughly two dozen times. Then you can call yourself a saver for life.

Initially, I don't put a number on "how much" because I know from experience that once you start seeing your money add up, even if you're putting aside only a few dollars at a time, you will start to feel good about your progress. You will start to feel jazzed that the $5 you've been stuffing in a jar every day is $35 at the end of every week and $150 (give or take) at the end of every month. Eventually, you'll run a calculation in your head and figure out that at this rate you'll have saved $1,825 by the end of the year. And voilà, a saver is born.

Once that happens, you've won the battle, because very soon that $1,825 is not going to be enough for you. You're going to feel inspired to try to save more. And you should. It is very hard for me to put an exact number on how much you should be saving for yourself. But I can tell you this: The research that I did for my book *The Ten Commandments of Financial Happiness* taught me that people who save 5 percent or more of their income are much happier than those who save less. So for that reason alone—I think being happy should be a line item on everyone's wish list—I encourage you to reach for that 5 percent and then exceed it.

I also can tell you that when it comes to each particular goal you're trying to reach during your lifetime, it will pay to run the same sort of calculation I ran on that $30,000 down payment I mentioned earlier in the chapter. Essentially, when you are trying to save for any goal, there are some blanks that you need to fill in (see page 147). Filling in those blanks will give you a rough calculation without factoring in any interest or return you can earn on your savings. (If you want to include interest, go to my website—www.JeanChatzky.com—and surf to the saving calculator.)

Why Savers Stay Out of Debt and Nonsavers Don't

I've given you a lot of really good reasons to start saving: You'll be happier. You'll sleep better at night. You'll avoid poverty in retirement. You'll be able to provide a better life for your children. But here's another reason, and it's really compelling: Savers stay out of debt, particularly credit card debt.

There is a huge problem with debt in America. The average household is carrying nearly $10,000 in credit card debt alone. At an interest rate of 18 percent, it costs almost $2,000 merely to pay the interest on that debt each year—which means you're paying back none of the money you borrowed. That's a big burden. And it doesn't include car loans, student loans, mortgage loans, unsecured personal loans, and all the other types of debt you've likely been offered on a silver platter over the past decade.

Suppose you didn't have that $10,000 in credit card debt. You could save the money. Instead of paying $2,000 year to simply tread water, you could put the equivalent dollars—$166 a month—into a savings or money market account. And it wouldn't take you very long to accumulate a fairly sizable emergency cushion.

Having an emergency cushion—having savings—is the key to staying out of debt. Why? Because unexpected expenses turn up all the time. Sometimes you can't classify them as emergencies; they're just the cost of living on the planet. The transmission goes. The dishwasher needs repair. Your child wants to participate in a local theater group, and the cost will be $300. If you have savings and, after careful consideration, decide to spend money on these things, you can write a check.

But what if you don't have savings but you decide these are important things to spend your money on? How are you going to pay for them? You're probably going to put them on a credit card. And even if you've been making decent headway paying down your credit card debt, the transmission or dishwasher is going to put you right back in the hole. You're going to feel that all your hard work has been for naught. And it's going to be tougher to convince yourself tomorrow that continuing to work to pay down your debt is worth your time.

How do I know about this vicious cycle? I've seen it time and time again. I've experienced it myself. These every-so-often expenses, the ones you can't plan on or budget for, are true villains in the credit card game. So even if you're working on paying down debt, I want you to save something on the side. Even if you can scrape together only $2 a day, by the end of the year you'll have more than $700. That would cover the dishwasher. It might not cover the transmission, but it would cover many car repairs.

If you're like many women, you're starting from scratch to build an emergency cushion. More than four out of ten women (and more than half of women under age 25) do not have even $500 saved for emergencies.

But let's not focus on the dismal statistics. Let's focus on this goal: building a true emergency cushion—three to six months' worth of living expenses that you could rely on in a real pinch, such as if you're laid off and if you're ill and for any reason unable to work. When I say living expenses, by the way, I don't mean your total budget for the month. I mean the bare bones, the money that you have to spend. How much do you need? The items listed here should cover it:

Rent or mortgage:	$_____
Car payment:	$_____
Cost of bare-bones transportation (for job hunting, say, but not commuting):	$_____
Food (not eating out):	$_____
Health insurance (COBRA payment):	$_____
Other insurance (home, auto, life):	$_____
Utilities:	$_____
Children's necessities:	$_____
Other:	$_____
Total:	$_____
× 3 for two-income families:	$_____
× 6 for one-income families:	$_____

The emergency-cushion money should go in a savings or money market account that pays a decent rate of interest but is completely safe and completely liquid—that is, you're guaranteed not to lose any money and you can withdraw the money whenever you need it. CDs don't work for this purpose. Although they offer the safety you need, you can't get at your money before the CD matures without paying penalties.

MAP TO A MILLION

What would happen if you took the interest you're currently paying on your $9,300 credit card debt and simply socked it away? Even if you didn't invest it but rather put it in a money market account where it could earn 4 percent, you'd have a big chunk of change very quickly:

In 1 year: $1,488   *In 5 years: $17,926*

In 2 years: $3,036   *In 10 years: $20,145*

In 3 years: $4,648   *In 20 years: $44,652*

In 4 years: $6,325   *In 30 years: $84,495*

Note: If you're among the millions of Americans struggling with debt, I want you to pick up a copy of my book *Pay It Down*. You can buy it in paperback or borrow it from your local library. It includes all of my very best tools to free you from the thumb of your creditors—including more information on my Debt Diet, a quick-start version to getting rid of a lot of debt in a little time (I modeled it after the Quick Start you find on great diets like Weight Watchers). It will show you how you can move very quickly from where you are into wealth.

So Where Do You Put Your Money?

Keep in mind that we're talking about your savings here, not your investments. *Savings* represent money you might need in the short term, as soon as tomorrow or as far away as three years from now. *Investments* are money for the long term, three years or more from now. (Chapter 8 is devoted to where to invest your money.)

When you're socking your money into savings, assess these three features of any accounts you're considering:

- *Return (or interest rate)*
- *Liquidity (whether or not you'll be able to withdraw money when you need it and at what cost)*
- *Convenience (how easy it will be to get your money when you need it—in terms of hassle and time)*

Naturally, you're not going to be able to have your cake and eat it at precisely the same time. The parking places for your savings that offer the best return might not offer the most convenience or easy liquidity. And those that offer liquidity and great convenience probably won't offer the best return. Here's how to make the call:

If the most important thing to you is getting the best interest rate on your money . . . go to bankrate.com and compare the best current rates on money market accounts and certificates of deposit (CDs) of up to one year. The numbers will give you your answer. Sometimes CD rates are better than money markets, sometimes vice versa. Often the best rates will be from banks that operate over the Internet rather than from brick-and-mortar stores. That's okay as long as you don't need everyday banking services.

If liquidity is important to you—if you want the ability to get your money at any time . . . then tying it up in a CD doesn't make a lot of sense. So knock CDs off your list, and focus on money market and high-interest-rate savings accounts. Interestingly, money market accounts don't always pay more than savings accounts. You'd think they would because of the name, but they don't. Some banks offer a high-interest-rate savings account consistently just to bring people in the door. They think of it as the cost of doing business. You should think of it as a good deal. Again, bankrate.com can point you to the best deals.

If convenience is important to you—if you want to be able to walk into the bank and deal with a person rather than operating over the Internet, by telephone, or by mail . . . then you're probably going to have to give a little bit on the return. The chances that the best savings rates in the country will be available in your town are pretty slim. Still, you can use the bankrate.com search engine to find the very best rates in your area and go with those. If the difference is 0.5 to 1.0 percent, that's fine. But if we're talking about any more than that—sometimes the best savings rates in the country are 2 to 3 percent higher than what you can find near home—my advice is to take a swing at banking online so you won't be giving up all that income. In this case, open a checking account at a bank near home. Keep your savings with the Internet bank. Then transfer a few thousand dollars at a time to pay your living expenses, if need be, and keep yourself liquid.

MAP TO A MILLION

What's the difference between putting your savings into a so-so money market account or savings account and a fantastic one? It can be 3 percentage points a year, if not more. As I write this, the average money market account is paying 3 percent, the best is paying around 4.5, and the worst is paying less than 1 percent. Let's say you are socking $200 a month into savings consistently. Over time, what's the difference between putting that money into an account earning 2 percent and putting it into an account earning 4 percent? At first, not much. But in the end, a lot of money!

$200 a month at 2 percent after one year:	*$2,422*
$200 at 4 percent after one year:	*$2,444*
Difference:	*$22*
$200 a month at 2 percent after 5 years:	*$12,609*
$200 at 4 percent after 5 years:	*$13,259*
Difference:	*$650*
$200 a month at 2 percent after 10 years:	*$26,543*
$200 at 4 percent after 10 years:	*$29,449*
Difference:	*$2,906*

$200 a month at 2 percent after 20 years:	**$58,959**
$200 at 4 percent after 20 years:	**$73,348**
Difference:	**$14,389**

So Many Options, So Little Time: How to Make Financial Choices

Recently, I ducked into Starbucks to get coffee for my commute home. I was in a rush, but not a mad one, so I tried to come up with some new, fascinating combination to put in my cup. Did I want tall or venti? Hot or iced? Whole or skim? One of nine flavoring syrups? It wasn't long before my head started to spin. The minutes were flying by. I let several people jump ahead of me in line. Finally I gave up and ordered what I typically order when I venture into the Green Machine: a nonfat latte. Nothing new about it. But I made the train.

That's what choices are like for me. I look forward to having them, to being able to pick a new restaurant or lease a new car. But when I get down to the actual decision making, all the options overwhelm me. Which is why I typically eat at places where I have the menu memorized and why—despite being drawn to the concept of a minivan—I'm pretty sure I'll drive yet another station wagon off the lot.

When it comes to knowing where to put your money—where to save it, where to invest it—you have not dozens, not hundreds, but thousands of choices. There are more than eight thousand mutual funds. There are as many money market funds. CDs, bonds, stocks—they all come in more flavors than Jell-O. Unfortunately, a bounty of new academic research makes the case that when it's your money on the line, having so many choices is not only daunting but actually can hurt you in the long run.

Take 401(k) plans, for instance. Sheena Iyengar, a professor at Columbia University, and Barry Swartz, a professor at Swarthmore College, examined the 401(k) plans of 650 different companies in 69 industries. They found that the more choices employees were offered, the fewer people participated. In plans that offered employees only two options, 75 percent of employees participated. For every additional ten options that a company put on its menu, participation declined 2 percent.

And that wasn't the only problem with offering more choices. As the number of options on the menu went up, employees became increasingly likely to go with the default option in their company plan—usually a low-risk/low-reward money market fund. Is that what you'd choose if you were making conscious, considered decisions? I hope not.

Oh, and there's one other problem that women in particular face when making financial decisions: That driving urge to be "right" that I wrote about in Chapter 1. It's hard enough to choose between exercise classes at the gym or between types of cereals in the grocery aisle. But when you get into an area where you know the choice is truly important, it's even tougher to pull the trigger. Worse, the more time you spend making a decision, the less likely you are to be satisfied with the outcome, even if more time spent means a better outcome than you would have experienced otherwise. So what can you do?

Define your objective. Before you go in search of anything, get clear on the qualities that are most important to you. If you want a money market account for your emergency cushion, for instance, knowing that you want it to give you an above-average rate of return as well as the ability to write as many checks as you want will enable you to narrow the field. You can go on the Internet and pretty much home in on the accounts that make sense. Not knowing will leave you floundering.

Observe the rule of three. Your goal should be to narrow the field until you get down to three. Start by eliminating the choices that are poor on all counts, like a savings account that pays less interest and has a very high minimum deposit. Having three, not two or four, makes the choosing simpler. One inevitably rises to the top.

Quantify the trade-offs. Next consider that there may be more than money invoved in making this decision. Let's say you winnow the choices down to three savings accounts. One of them pays slightly less in interest—say, half a percentage point less—but it's at your local bank. Do you go for it? That half a percent is meaningless until you put it into extra dollar terms. On $1,000 a year, it amounts to $5; on $10,000, to $50. Is it worth it to you to not have to go through the hassle of banking with a faraway company? Or will you be handling everything electronically anyway? If you're stuck and you can't choose, think about the person or company making you the offer. Is it a firm that has your best interest in mind (such as a company that wants you in its retirement plan to buy your loyalty) or someone who wants to exploit you (such as a salesman)? If it's the former, you might want to sign on.

Finally, find the "good enough." Swartz's research has shown there are two kinds of decision makers: "Maximizers" are people who are happy only when they feel they've found the best. "Satisficers" are people who are happy when they've found something that's good enough. The latter are much happier humans overall, and you can be that way if you put your mind to it. Once you know what you need your money to do for you—once you're focused on the endgame and understand how much it will cost you to pay for that down payment on your house or Christmas vacation in Florida—then you also know how hard you need your money to work for you in order to reach that goal. Once you find a return that's in range, you can stop looking.

GET RICH

Spend Less Than You Make

Yes, it's that simple. And yes, you can do it—no matter how strapped you feel trying to make ends meet each month.

I know, I know. You're reading this thinking that you can barely get the mortgage paid, sneakers bought, dance lessons signed up for, and (heaven forbid) a manicure or something fun to wear for yourself. Sometimes running a household feels like standing on the street corner handing out money to just about anyone who passes by.

I'm convinced, however, that anyone who *wants* to save more *will* save more with only a little extra effort. And I don't care if you start with $5, $50, or $100 a week. Whatever the amount, you've got to put your hard-earned cash to work for you in more ways than paying the bills.

Plan Your Future Spending—and Saving

Remember that I suggested you take a piece of paper or a notebook or your computer and write down everything you spend money on for a solid month?

We're going to use that information now. On the following pages is the worksheet. Make a copy of it if you want, or go to my website,

JeanChatzky.com, and print out a new one. This is a Spending Tracker. I want you to use it to fill in the blanks for the most recent month. You will then have a log showing how much you spent.

Then I want you to fill in the blanks for the coming month, indicating how much you *want* to spend on those same items. Some things—mortgage payments, car loans—will be fixed, they'll be the same from month to month. For those that are variable, over which you can exercise control, I want you to start with *small* changes—changes that you'll be able to achieve.

In Chapter 6, I talked about ways you can cut back on your spending. So I'm not going to use this space to tell you not to buy a cup of coffee when you need one to get through the morning. Or to skimp on soccer league for the kids. Nor will I tell you to skip a much-needed dinner out with girl-friends at a fancy restaurant or the family vacation. Like a too-strict diet, financial deprivation doesn't work. You'll end up resenting the fact that you feel deprived and blow a chunk of money on something else.

But just as sensible eating helps you lose pounds, sensible spending helps you save. Most people have a place or two in their lives where they're spending more than they realize and more than they want to. Little things like birthday party presents or weekday lunches add up to big expenses. When you cut back on the sneaky things that add up, you don't feel deprived; you actually feel good about doing it.

Everyone's budget is different. And I know as well as anyone that you've got plenty of bills to pay. But if you're diligent about recording and tracking your spending, I promise you'll find ways to redirect a chunk of your money straight into savings—painlessly.

So as you subtract from the other categories you've been spending on by making changes in your budget, use the column off to the side to keep a running total of how much you'll be able to save. Then we'll talk about how to get that money into savings—automatically—so that it can go to work for your future.

GET RICH SPENDING TRACKER

Expense	Month	Month	Month	Month	Estimated Savings
HOUSING					
Rent/mortgage	_____	_____	_____	_____	_____
Home equity loan	_____	_____	_____	_____	_____
Heat	_____	_____	_____	_____	_____
Water	_____	_____	_____	_____	_____
Electricity	_____	_____	_____	_____	_____
Insurance	_____	_____	_____	_____	_____
Phone	_____	_____	_____	_____	_____
Internet	_____	_____	_____	_____	_____
Cable	_____	_____	_____	_____	_____
Lawn/garden	_____	_____	_____	_____	_____
Repairs	_____	_____	_____	_____	_____
Other services	_____	_____	_____	_____	_____
% of total	_____	_____	_____	_____	_____

(Remember: Housing should represent 35%)

Expense	Month	Month	Month	Month	Estimated Savings
TRANSPORTATION					
Car payment 1	_____	_____	_____	_____	_____
Car payment 2	_____	_____	_____	_____	_____
Gasoline	_____	_____	_____	_____	_____
Insurance	_____	_____	_____	_____	_____
Repairs/upkeep	_____	_____	_____	_____	_____
Commutation	_____	_____	_____	_____	_____
Parking	_____	_____	_____	_____	_____
Other	_____	_____	_____	_____	_____
% of total	_____	_____	_____	_____	_____

(Remember: Transportation should represent 15%)

Expense	Month	Month	Month	Month	Estimated Savings
CREDIT CARDS/LOANS					
Credit card 1	____	____	____	____	____
Credit card 2	____	____	____	____	____
Credit card 3	____	____	____	____	____
Credit card 4	____	____	____	____	____
Other loan 1	____	____	____	____	____
Other loan 2	____	____	____	____	____
Other	____	____	____	____	____
% of total	____	____	____	____	____

(Remember: Debt repayment should account for 15%)

Expense	Month	Month	Month	Month	Estimated Savings
CHILD CARE					
Babysitting	____	____	____	____	____
Tuition	____	____	____	____	____
Clothing	____	____	____	____	____
Lessons	____	____	____	____	____
Toys	____	____	____	____	____
Gifts	____	____	____	____	____
Other	____	____	____	____	____
FOOD					
Groceries	____	____	____	____	____
Eating out	____	____	____	____	____
Entertaining	____	____	____	____	____
Other	____	____	____	____	____
PERSONAL					
Clothing	____	____	____	____	____
Beauty shop/barbershop	____	____	____	____	____

Expense	Month	Month	Month	Month	Estimated Savings
Dry cleaning	_____	_____	_____	_____	_____
Health club	_____	_____	_____	_____	_____
Cell phone/BlackBerry	_____	_____	_____	_____	_____
Gifts	_____	_____	_____	_____	_____
Other	_____	_____	_____	_____	_____

MEDICAL

Insurance	_____	_____	_____	_____	_____
Co-pays	_____	_____	_____	_____	_____
Prescriptions	_____	_____	_____	_____	_____
Unreimbursed medical	_____	_____	_____	_____	_____

ENTERTAINMENT

Tickets (movies/theater/concert/sports)	_____	_____	_____	_____	_____
CDs/DVDs	_____	_____	_____	_____	_____
Books/magazines	_____	_____	_____	_____	_____
Other	_____	_____	_____	_____	_____

TRAVEL

Vacation	_____	_____	_____	_____	_____
Other	_____	_____	_____	_____	_____

PETS

Food	_____	_____	_____	_____	_____
Medical care	_____	_____	_____	_____	_____
Grooming	_____	_____	_____	_____	_____
Other	_____	_____	_____	_____	_____

Expense	Month	Month	Month	Month	Estimated Savings
OTHER					
_____	_____	_____	_____	_____	_____
_____	_____	_____	_____	_____	_____
_____	_____	_____	_____	_____	_____
% of total	_____	_____	_____	_____	_____

(Remember, all these categories *combined* should account for 25%)

SAVINGS/INVESTMENTS					
401(k) contribution	_____	_____	_____	_____	_____
Other retirement contribution	_____	_____	_____	_____	_____
Monthly savings	_____	_____	_____	_____	_____
% of total	_____	_____	_____	_____	_____

(Remember, you're aiming to save 10%)

HOW MUCH MORE CAN I SAVE BY NOT SPENDING?

Expense/Item

+ _____

+ _____

+ _____

+ _____

+ _____

+ _____

+ _____

+ _____

+ _____

= _____

MAP TO A MILLION

The numbers you're coming up with may not look encouraging at first. But I want you to see how much of a difference even a few dollars can make.

Research shows that 65 percent of women say they could find an extra $20 a week to save for retirement. That pocket change—it's less than $3 a day—works out to $1,040 a year. Let's say you managed that. You put the money away. And you earned an 8 percent average annual return. How much of a difference would it make in your life if you retire at age 65?

If you start at 20, you'll have an extra $440,606

If you start at 25, you'll have an extra $291,620

If you start at 30, you'll have an extra $191,618

If you start at 35, you'll have an extra $124,496

If you start at 40, you'll have an extra $79,443

If you start at 45, you'll have an extra $49,203

If you start at 50, you'll have an extra $28,906

If you start at 55, you'll have an extra $15,282

If you start at 60, you'll have an extra $6,137

Give Your Savings a Bonus

Okay, so now you're locked and loaded. You're on the program. And you're looking to save even more. Here's one great way: Every time a little extra money comes your way, earmark all or at least part of it for savings. This is one of the best ways you can give yourself a financial boost. Where is this extra money going to come from? Here are a few ideas:

- **Your next raise.** You've already been living on the money you're making now. Pretend you didn't even get a raise, and automatically bank the difference in your savings account.

- **Your bonus.** You may have been counting on some of your bonus to cover expenses. But be sure to sock a generous percentage of it away in savings.

- **Tax refunds.** Deposit refund checks straight into savings. It's found money. Or, better yet, check with your payroll department to see if those refunds are coming because you're withholding more than you need to. If you are, withhold less and put the extra cash from each paycheck into savings so some of that money is earning interest all year.

- **Paid-off credit cards or other loans.** Your car is paid off? Fantastic. The $359 (or whatever) you were paying to the car lender should go straight into savings. A few transactions like this and your savings balance will soar!

How Do You Conquer the Urge to Splurge? Make It Automatic

What if, as you find all this money, you suddenly feel flush, and instead of saving, you find yourself spending? Now, you think, I can afford that new couch or trip to the islands.

The key to conquering the urge to splurge is to keep your money out of your hot little hands. And to do that, you need to start saving automatically. When I talk about automatic savings, I'm talking about giving your bank the power and permission to move some money every month or every payday out of your checking account, where you're likely to spend it, and into savings, where—from now on—you're going to tell yourself it's hands-off.

Once you've done that, you can forget about it. Your financial systems will be in place and working for you. You won't even have to remember to write a check.

So pick up the phone and call your bank—or better yet stop by in person—and elect to save some money (whatever you came up with on your worksheet) every month automatically.

There are some other automatic steps that I want you to take as well:

Do it: Direct-deposit. Most employers will automatically deposit your paycheck into the bank account of your choosing. You can even split it between checking and savings! All you need to do is fill out a simple form and you'll avoid long bank lines and paperwork. The bonus: Your money will show up in your account faster than if you waited for the check to clear.

Say it and sound smart: *"Of course I direct-deposit my paychecks. Do you think I want to make all those trips to the bank?"*

Do it: Open an automatic investment plan. When should you stop saving and start investing? Once your short-term needs are met. Once you have a three-to-six-month emergency cushion, then you can stop funneling money into basic savings and start putting it into stocks and mutual funds, where it can work even harder.

In the same way you invest automatically in your 401(k) through paycheck withdrawals, you can invest automatically with most mutual fund companies and brokerage firms. And many let you open an account with super low minimum investments, as little as $50 in some cases. You simply complete an automatic investing form, and the process begins. (Note: It's important for you to invest automatically in your retirement accounts before you invest automatically outside of your retirement accounts. Why? Money inside retirement plans grows tax-free until you have to pull it out and sometimes even longer than that. That allows it to add up to more. You'll read more about this in the next chapter.)

The great thing about investing this way—just like saving this way—is that you do it without even thinking about it. You won't miss an opportunity to save because you spent the money somewhere else before you got around to writing the check or making the transfer.

Also, by investing automatically, you actually take advantage of a sophisticated financial strategy called *dollar cost averaging.* The term simply means that you invest a set amount in regular installments—say, once a month. Since you buy shares of a mutual fund or stock over time, you lower your risk of investing a chunk of money right before the share price dives. Most Wall Street experts swear by this slow-and-steady approach.

Say it and sound smart: *"I invest a few hundred dollars automatically every month. I never miss it—and you wouldn't believe how fast it's adding up!"*

Do it: Automate your bill payment. Just as you can elect to have money funneled into savings automatically, you can elect to have bills paid automatically by your bank. This system means less check writing, less stamp buying, spending less time schlepping to the bank, and—most important—fewer late payments that can sabotage your credit score. It makes the most sense to automate the bills that will be for the same amount every month, so that you don't come up short: mortgage or rent, student loan (you'll get a deduction on the interest rate by electing auto-bill-pay), health club, insurance, and so forth.

Say it and sound smart: *"My credit score is up 30 points since I started paying bills automatically. I'm sure it's because I'm never late anymore."*

Do it: Bank online. If you like paying bills automatically, you'll love banking online. As you know, I do, and so do more than 50 million people. Today almost every bank offers online service. Most offer it for free. What used to take hours—paying bills, balancing your checkbook, transferring funds—now can be done online in a few minutes with just a few clicks. Record keeping is also easier. Your withdrawals and deposits show up on your electronic statement almost instantly, so you're account is always balanced. No more scrounging for ATM receipts, entering transactions in your check register, and waiting for statements to come in the mail.

Say it and sound smart: *"Getting organized online saves me time and money. How did I ever do it any other way?"*

LOOK HOW FAR YOU'VE COME!

You've covered a lot in the first seven chapters. You've figured out why you were so reluctant to handle your money, and you've blown through some of those inhibitions spectacularly. And in this chapter, you've really gotten started on the road to wealth by starting to save. This is a financial habit you're going to feel great about in the years to come. You're going to want to share it with your spouse and to pass it on to your children and grandchildren. In the next chapter you're going to learn how to make your money work as hard as—if not harder than—you do.

Should I break a 3 percent CD and take a short-term hit if rates on money market accounts have climbed to 4.4 percent, or should I wait?

The penalty for breaking—or pulling your money out of a CD before the due date—is fairly significant: It's typically all the interest on a 30-day CD, three months of interest on CDs of up to 18 months, and six months of interest on CDs of 2 years or more. That makes it easy to do the math. It's also the reason in a rising-interest-rate environment, you're often best off searching for a high-paying money market account instead. Rates won't be as high, typically, as you could get in the best CD, but they will float up every time the Federal Reserve issues a rate hike. And you'll be able to capture increases along the way. (In a falling-rate environment, CDs make more sense.)

Which are better, 529 plans or prepaid tuition plans?

First, a clarification. Prepaid tuition plans, just like state-sponsored college savings plans, *are* 529 plans—named for the part of the tax code that allows them to exist. For most people, college-saving 529s are the better option, although prepaid tuition plans can be the better deal. Let me explain. With a 529 college-savings plan, you put money away and it grows tax-free. Then you can use it to pay for college at whatever the rate/tuition is where and when your child goes to school. A prepaid tuition plan allows you to pay for college today, at today's prices, then send your child when he or she is of school age. Depending on tuition inflation at the schools you're considering, this may be a terrific deal. The problem is, most pre-

paid tuition plans limit the schools they pay for. If your child decides to go elsewhere, you get your contributions back, but you don't get growth on that money. Unless you are absolutely certain you can predict where your child (who may be in diapers now) will want to go to school at age 18, that makes a 529 college-savings program the better way to go.

How can I save for college without ruining my chances of getting financial aid?
The way the financial aid formulas work, 35 percent of any money in your child's name must be used for college each and every year, but only 5.6 percent of any money in a parent's name must be used for college. Money in retirement accounts doesn't count, however, which is one reason why I believe that you're best off contributing money first to a Roth IRA. The funds can be used to pay for college without penalties or taxes. (You're eligible for a Roth IRA even if you participate in a retirement plan at work, as long as you don't earn more than $100,000 for singles, $110,000 for heads of household, or $160,000 for married people filing jointly.) After you've exhausted your Roth capabilities, look at 529 plans. You do *not* want to open a Uniform Gift to Minors Act account. Assets in UGMA accounts are considered the child's and are counted heavily in the financial aid formulas, and the money actually becomes the child's at the age of majority. That means it doesn't have to be used for college at all. Your child might decide he prefers, say, a motorcycle to a year at MIT. And at that point, you would have no legal right to tell him how to spend the money.

"I Can Deal with My Money— It's Investing I Can't Stand"

DON'T BITCH

Let's think about all the things you can do with money.

Can you make money? Absolutely. In fact, women are doing that with such aplomb that increasing numbers are outearning their spouses.

Can you spend money? Do I really need to answer that question? But yes, women spend the vast majority of all the household income in this country. (And if you apply the strategies in Chapter 6, you will do so smarter, better, and more efficiently than ever before.)

Can you invest money? Can you? Hmmm.

For many women there's a huge disconnect between making and spending money and investing money. Think about it. You can wow your colleagues with an in-depth analysis of what's wrong with the competition's promotional strategy. You can turn a rundown beach house into a fabulous summer hideaway with a couple of vintage bedspreads and a few cans of paint. You can get three kids out the door in the morning with their teeth brushed, hair combed, and homework complete. And you can know—deep down—that you've done all of these things as well as any person on the planet.

Yet when it comes to investing, you don't trust yourself. And because you lack that trust, you rob yourself of any real shot at a prosperous financial future. Let me repeat that: By not investing, you rob yourself of a huge shot at getting rich.

What many women don't understand is this: It's best to allow your money to work as hard as you do if you're ever going to be able to reach your goals, retire, and feel financially secure. You might be a whiz at negotiating a raise, great at shopping the sales, even addicted to tracking your spending using a legal pad or a personal finance software program. But when it comes to buying a stock, bond, or mutual fund, you freeze—unable to pull the trigger.

I know the feeling. I used to be the same way. Remember the story I told you about how at age 23—not knowing what a 401(k) was despite the fact that I had been contributing to one for years—I quit my job and didn't roll the dough into an IRA? I cashed the check my former company sent me, bought clothes, and worried about the taxes later. It wasn't a lot at the time, but if I had left the money alone to grow, it would be worth a huge sum today!

Even now I probably have half a dozen women friends in the same boat: accomplished professionals and fabulous stay-at-home moms, all of whom can do just about anything, except invest. What I have to say to them and to you is this: It doesn't have to be that way!

Investing does not have to be difficult. In fact, it can be easy. I'm going to show you how to simplify the process with an investing plan that runs on automatic pilot. You'll need to check the controls only once in a while—no more than four times a year. And if you follow my advice, you'll sleep well each night, secure in the knowledge that you haven't taken any crazy risks and that your money is doing the very best it can for you. But first you need to knock down four big obstacles standing in your way.

Why Don't You Invest?

Reason 1: Investing bores you
For some women, the mere words "Wall Street" elicit a big yawn. Listen to what Roberta, an interior designer, has to say:

> I would rather listen to a scientist talk about cell mutation than an analyst discuss corporate finance. I was in an investment group for about a year thinking that would spark my interest. It didn't.

Roberta is not the only one. Sixty percent of all women say they want to spend as little time as possible managing their investments.

I hear you loud and clear. Plenty of things about investing are more than a little on the tedious side. The paperwork, for instance. It's just so easy to toss those statements into a pile and leave them unopened for months. And when you do open them, it seems as though every financial firm has its own way of presenting the numbers. If you stare at them for more than a few minutes, your eyes glaze over. The statements may as well be hieroglyphics carved into a pyramid wall. And because you don't instantaneously understand them, they register as boring. No wonder you'd rather do the dishes.

Reason 2: Numbers make your eyes glaze over

We talked about this a lot in Chapter 2, but it's another tree to cut down along the road to a portfolio of your own. If you can't get past the basic math, it's very difficult to get yourself to make even the simple decisions about how much of your money you want to invest, what percentage of your income makes sense. If I'm talking directly to you, go back to pages 42–48 and reread my strategies for starting to get over your math anxiety. As I said then, the computations involved aren't all that cumbersome. (Besides, you'll never catch *me* admonishing you for using a calculator. I say use it with abandon and get the numbers right!)

Reason 3: You don't speak the language

I spent a few years working on Wall Street (actually, on the sixty-third floor of Tower II of the World Trade Center, and to this day I can't go to downtown Manhattan without losing my bearings). Anyway, I remember during my first few weeks on that job in the equity research department of what was then Dean, Witter, Reynolds (and is now a part of Morgan Stanley) feeling as though I was in a foreign country. The terminology—P/E ratio, basis point, Excel—swam in one ear and out the other, and I would reach for the bottle of Advil long before the day came to an end.

So I understand that of course you'd prefer to abdicate from a world you don't understand. It is a completely normal, natural, and understandable reaction. And a huge number of women—47 percent compared to 30 percent of men in one recent study—feel that way. If you're like them, when it comes to investing, you feel dumb.

Julie, an elementary school principal, does. She says:

As far as investments go, I feel very stupid. All of our money is in funds or handled by a counselor and I just don't understand it. I would like to learn, but it seems like too much work to figure it all out.

So does Emily, a stay-at-home mom:

There is some mystique to finance that I can't get over. For instance, I'll leave money in one mutual fund rather than doing some research and figuring out how to diversify our investments and increase our return.

Yet neither of those women is stupid. Far from it. Julie is Ivy League educated. Emily has a graduate degree. What happened to them and to many other women is that they internalized the belief that what they have to say isn't right, isn't important, or isn't on target, particularly in areas in which they don't feel comfortable from the start—such as the world of money.

There are so many other occasions where you may know *for a fact* that you're right. You're on target. There is no doubt. Yet when you're not operating in your comfort zone, you don't always feel able to assert that rightness. This phenomenon happens not only with investing but also with medicine, legal matters, parenting, any area in which we feel a little wobbly.

The problem is, when we are convinced that we don't know enough about something and are unprepared to deal with it, it becomes a self-fulfilling prophecy. The same women who say they're unprepared to invest, don't have the confidence to invest, or are anxious about their ability to do so, are the ones who in later years express real regret about not investing sooner.

Reason 4: You're scared

When you come right down to it, you're afraid that if you invest your money, you'll lose your money. That's why you keep your money where you think it's "safe" (I'll explain why it's not in a moment) in the bank. That's why you, like Andrea, a psychotherapist, do absolutely nothing. Here's her story:

I received some money in a lawsuit two years ago, and it sat in a regular savings account for one and a half years. I was afraid of making a wrong move—of putting it in stocks when I should have put it in real estate, or putting it in real estate when I should have put it in stocks. Knowing it was a nice chunk of money, I wanted to maximize my investments, but I was paralyzed as to what I should do.

Women are particularly fearful about investing, and there's a good reason for that fear. Two-thirds of us grew up in houses where money wasn't discussed with us. Girls, parents rationalized just a few decades ago, didn't need to know about those things. It's little wonder you feel you have no role models when it comes to making financial decisions in your adult life.

Of course, there's another reason you're a fretful investor—and it's a perfectly rational one, too. Losing money is no fun. In fact, it's a horrendous experience. If you saw your tech-stock-heavy 401(k) get cut in half by the market bust a few years ago, or if someone you know bought Lucent or IBM or, more recently, Enron and lost his or her shirt, or even if you've watched your elderly parents get pinched by super low interest rates to the point where they can't make ends meet, you've got plenty of reason to be wary.

If you've been burned in the past, you have to realize that investing losses are like any other losses. You have to lament them and move forward. That means understanding why you made the mistake or had the problem, and determining what you need to do to have a better experience in the future.

Not Crossing the Investing Threshold Is Even Worse

You are probably wondering: Why? Why do I have to learn this language, cross the math hurdles, stomach the boredom, and get over my fears? Why? Because if you don't, then the only money you will have over your lifetime is money that you earn from working and any money you inherit or get as a gift. Moreover, if you don't invest, your money will actually lose value over time. Come again? That's right. If you do nothing with your money, your dollars will be worth less tomorrow (and the tomorrow after that) than they are today.

When you invest, you are taking one kind of risk—*market risk*, the risk that you could plunk your money into a stock, say, and the value of that stock could fall rather than rise. When you don't invest, you are in fact taking all sorts of other—hidden—risks with your money. And those risks, in many ways, are worse than the risks you take by investing. They include *tax risk*, the chance that taxes will eat away at your return, and *inflation risk*, the risk that inflation will eat away at your return.

Here's how it works. If you're not investing, if instead your money is sitting in a savings or even a money market account at your bank where it's earning a mere 2 or 3 percent, at the end of the day you're losing money. Taxes and inflation are eating away your entire return and sometimes more.

Let's look at the numbers. Say at age 40 you have a $100,000 nest egg. Not bad, right? But left to sit twenty years in a savings account earning 2 percent, it will amount to only $148,595 by the time you're 60. That may sound pretty good. But what if inflation is 3 percent, as it's been pretty consistently for the last decade? Then, twenty years down the road you actually will have lost 19 percent on your money.

That same nest egg at 8 percent— a reasonable assumption for the average stock market return—is worth closer to a half million, $492,680 before you factor in inflation. After you factor in inflation, it's still worth $263,508. Not as much, clearly, but you still made a tidy profit. Do you understand now *why* you have to invest?

You're Afraid? Use Your Fear to Your Advantage

I know you're afraid, afraid that you're going to lose money. As a formerly fearful investor myself, I'm here to tell you that the most successful investors use fear to their advantage. They see a best friend get divorced and her standard of living plummet. Forget about trips to Europe! She has to curb her trips to the mall. And they decide, that's not going to happen to me. They see their mother lose a spouse and have little to no idea of how to run the family finances, and they decide: Not me. I am never going to be in those shoes.

The key is positive thinking. Where investing is concerned, I need you to become a glass-half-full person instead of glass-half-empty. Instead of focusing on possible losses, think instead about all you could accomplish if you started investing a little bit today.

MAP TO A MILLION: INVEST A LITTLE BIT TODAY AND HAVE A LOT TOMORROW

What if you could find $10 a day to invest. That's $70 a week. It's the price of dinner for two in a moderate restaurant, the price of one pair of pants at Ann Taylor. In other words, it's very little. But when you put that money to work at 8 percent, when you shelter it in an account like an IRA or a 401(k) where you don't have to pay taxes until retirement, it can grow to be a bundle.

INVEST $10 A DAY = $304 A MONTH

In 10 years you'll have:	*$55,615*
In 20 years you'll have:	*$179,062*
In 30 years you'll have:	*$453,069*
In 40 years you'll have:	*$1,061,266*

If you don't invest, you won't have the money you need for a long, comfortable retirement. You won't have any extra cash to give your kids a helping hand, and you won't be able to survive the burden of an ill or dependent parent. You can decide today that you don't want to be in that situation tomorrow.

The Good News: Women Are Great Investors

When women make up their minds to put their money to work for them, they are actually better investors than men. This we know from years of work by Terrance Odean and Brad Barber, professors at UC-Davis. They looked into the discount brokerage records of thousands of investors, comparing those of men to those of women, and they found

- *Women are far less likely than men to hold a losing investment too long.*

- *Women don't wait too long to sell winning investments. Men do.*
- *Men are much more likely to put all or too many of their invest- ment eggs into one basket. Women are more likely to diversify.*
- *Men trade securities so often that the transaction costs are a drag on their investment returns. Women buy and hold on to their advantage.*

The upshot of all of that positive behavior? Women make more money on their investments than men. Let me say that again: Women investors make more money. According to the data, married men, who trade 45 percent more often than women, earn returns that are 1.4 percent less than those of married women. Single men trade 67 percent more and earn an average of 2.3 percent less a year than single women. Hallelujah!

But there's more. We women not only make fewer investing mistakes but are much more likely than men to learn from any mistakes we make. Bar- ber and Odean's research shows that women are much less likely than men to make the same mistake twice. Here's what they found:

- *When men reported buying a stock without doing any re- search, 63 percent said they did it a second time. Only 47 percent of women repeated that mistake.*
- *When men reported waiting too long to sell an investment, 61 percent of them said they did it a second time. Only 48 percent of women repeated that mistake.*
- *When men reported ignoring the tax consequences of a particular investment decision, 68 percent of them did it more than once. Only 47 percent of women repeated that behavior.*

Okay. Enough. You get the idea. Now, it's time to get started. You've got all the information you need to get over the obstacles and conquer your fears. You now realize that doing nothing with your money is far riskier than any losses you might experience. Most important, you've seen the proof that women have the makings of great investors. You're sure to be one, too.

GET RICH

Do you recall the four things—the only four things—you really need to do if you want to be wealthy?

1. *You need to make a decent living.*
2. *You need to spend less than you make.*
3. *You need to invest the money you don't spend so that it can work as hard for you as you're working for yourself.*
4. *You need to protect yourself and this financial world you've built so that a disaster—big or small—doesn't take it all away from you.*

The one we're talking about here is number 3: investing money you don't spend so that it can work as hard as, if not harder than, you do.

I know these are scary waters. But I also know that there's a lot of satisfaction in knowing that you can sit home, take a vacation, take maternity leave or a sabbatical, and your money will still be working. And you'll never have that satisfaction if you don't plunge right in. So relax. The water is less turbulent than you think, especially if you use a solid, smart investing strategy and stick with it.

Here's the six-step approach that I have followed and have been recommending for nearly a decade. It works for timid investors as well as those who are tough as nails, for people who have all the time in the world to invest as well as those who want to take the set-it-and-forget-it approach. I'm confident it will fit well into your busy life.

Step 1: Set Your Goals

Ask yourself, "What do I want my money to do for me?" Retirement in Arizona? College for three kids? A first home? A second? On the computer or the back of an envelope, separate your list into three sections. (1) Start with short-term needs, like putting away three months' salary (if you're married and part of a two-income household where someone else might be able to pick up the slack) or six months' salary (if you're single) for an emergency or getting the money together for next summer's vacation or camp bills. (2) Then list any midrange goals, like a down payment on a larger house in five years or a looming college tuition bill. (3) Long-term is next, and it's the most obvious. It all boils down to one word: retirement.

How do you know how much you'll need for retirement? There are plenty of retirement calculators on the Internet. But many people still prefer to run the calculations by hand. For that, I have long relied on a worksheet developed by a team of economists at the American Savings Education Council in Washington, D.C. The ASEC folks put their very best power-brains into a room and wouldn't let them out until they came up with a worksheet that allows you to ballpark (thus the worksheet's name) your retirement needs in under an hour. It works fabulously, and I thank ASEC for letting me reprint it.

But before you fill out the worksheet, I want you to read a little more. Setting goals sounds easy. But sometimes women need a little attitude adjusting to do this first step right. Women are likely to say, "I don't care about money. It's not important. I'd rather have independence or be able to help others." To you, wanting money—admitting you want money—may seem selfish, greedy, *unattractive.*

Baloney. The reality is, you can't have freedom, you'll never be independent, and you won't be able to help anyone—whether it's your family or your favorite charity—without the money you need to take care of yourself and meet your goals. And as for unattractive? Chances are you're imagining someone you know who showboats with the money she has. Who wears it loudly and talks about it even more so. But just because you have money does not mean you have to behave like that. Instead, money can be your quiet little security blanket. It can be the secret that allows you to sleep at night and do whatever it is you want to do in the morning. Having enough money gives you choices about how to live your life.

Once you understand that, the desire to get wealthy can be a great motivator. So use the worksheet to inspire yourself to put a price tag on your goals. How much will you need to retire the way you want to? What do you need to make on investments to pay for your kids' college? What would you need in reserve to be able to tell your intolerable boss to take a long walk off a short pier?

I keep coming back to goals because knowing what you want your money to do for you is the first step to investing success. Statistics show that women who identify their goals, then construct a financial plan to meet them, end up with a higher net worth than women who do no planning at all. Got it? Then grab a pencil.

GET A BALLPARK E$TIMATE® OF YOUR RETIREMENT NEEDS

Planning for retirement is not a one-size-fits-all exercise. The purpose of Ballpark is simply to give you a basic idea of the savings you'll need to make today for when you plan to retire.

If you are married, you and your spouse should each fill out your own Ballpark E$timate® worksheet taking your marital status into account when entering your Social Security benefit in number 2 below.

1. **How much annual income will you want in retirement?**

    (Figure at least 70% of your current annual gross income just to maintain your current standard of living; however, you may want to enter a larger number. See the tips below.)

    $_____

    TIPS TO HELP YOU SELECT A GOAL:

- *70% to 80%—You will need to pay for the basics in retirement, but you won't have to pay many medical expenses as your employer pays the Medicare Part B and D premium and provides employer-paid retiree health insurance. You're planning for a comfortable retirement without much travel. You are older and/or in your prime earning years.*
- *80% to 90%—You will need to pay your Medicare Part B and D premiums and pay for insurance to cover medical costs above Medicare, which on average covers about 55%. You plan to take some small trips, and you know that you will need to continue saving some money.*
- *100% to 120%—You will need to cover all Medicare and other health care costs. You are very young and/or your prime earning years are ahead of you. You would like a retirement lifestyle that is more than comfortable. You need to save for the possibility of long-term care.*

2. **Subtract the income you expect to receive annually from:**
   - *Social Security—If you make under $25,000, enter $8,000; between $25,000-$40,000, enter $12,000; over $40,000, enter $14,500. (For married couples—the lower earning spouse should enter either their own benefit based on their income or 50% of the higher earning spouse's benefit, whichever is higher.)*

     − $_____

   - *Traditional Employer Pension—a plan that pays a set dollar amount for life, where the dollar amount depends on salary and years of service (in today's dollars)*

     − $_____

   - *Part-time income*

     − $_____

   - *Other (reverse annuity mortgage payments, earnings on assets, etc.)*

     − $_____

   This is how much you need to make up for each retirement year:

     = $_____

Next you want a Ballpark E$timate of how much money you'll need in the bank the day you retire. For the record, we assume you'll realize a constant real rate of return of 3% after inflation and you'll begin to receive income from Social Security at age 65.

3. To determine the amount you'll need to save, multiply the amount you need to make up by the factor below.

Age you expect to retire:	Choose your factor based on life expectancy (at age 65):					
	Male, 50th percentile (age 82)	Female, 50th percentile (age 86)	Male, 75th percentile (age 89)	Female, 75th percentile (age 92)	Male, 90th percentile (age 94)	Female, 90th percentile (age 97)
55	18.78	20.53	21.71	22.79	23.46	24.40
60	16.31	18.32	19.68	20.93	21.71	22.79
65	13.45	15.77	17.35	18.79	19.68	20.93
70	10.15	12.83	14.65	16.31	17.35	18.79

$_____

4. If you expect to retire before age 65, multiply your Social Security benefit from line 2 by the factor below.

Age you expect to retire: **55**   *Your factor is:*   **8.8**

                                   60   **4.7**

+ $_____

5. Multiply your savings to date by the factor below (include money accumulated in a 401(k), IRA, or similar retirement plan).

If you plan to retire in: **10 years**   *Your factor is:*   **1.3**

                                     15 years   **1.6**

                                     20 years   **1.8**

                                     25 years   **2.1**

                                     30 years   **2.4**

                                     35 years   **2.8**

                                     40 years   **3.3**

− $_____

Total additional savings needed at retirement:

= $_____

Don't panic. We devised another formula to show you how much to save each year in order to reach your goal amount. This factors in compounding. That's where your money not only makes interest, your interest starts making interest as well, creating a snowball effect.

6. To determine the ANNUAL amount you'll need to save,
multiply the TOTAL amount by the factor below.

If you want to retire in:		*Your factor is:*	
	10 years		*.085*
	15 years		*.052*
	20 years		*.036*
	25 years		*.027*
	30 years		*.020*
	35 years		*.016*
	40 years		*.013*

= $_____

Reprinted with permission from EBRI Education and Research Fund.

Step 2: Dip a Toe in the Water

I've said it before, but here it is again: *You can't win this game if you're not in this game.* Investing too little too late is one of the most common mistakes women make. The longer you wait to get started, the more you'll lose over time.

You don't have to take my word on this. I have numbers to prove it to you.

MAP TO A MILLION: INVEST EARLY OR INVEST LATE

Here's the bottom-line difference between starting and waiting. Let's take our average investor. And let's call her Jane. Jane is 30 years old and earns $35,000 a year. If she puts 10 percent of her gross income into a stock market index fund each year for the next thirty-five years, she'll have a bundle at retirement. That's assuming she gets absolutely no raises in pay. That's not factoring in any matching dollars from her employer. Add in a 5 percent match from her employer, and watch what happens.

START AT AGE 30

Invest 10 percent of $35,000 salary a year
Retirement savings: $457,254

Invest 10 percent of $35,000 salary plus 5 percent employer match
Retirement savings: $685,881

Suppose Jane waits to start saving until age 40. That's only ten years down the road. There are things she wants to do—see the world, get a puppy, buy that all-too-trendy handbag. Besides, at 40, her salary will be $10,000 higher. If she does those things, with the money she should be investing, she'll end up with much less money than she otherwise could have had at age 65. It's a huge difference.

START AT AGE 40

Invest 10 percent of $45,000 salary a year
Retirement savings: $343,746

Invest 10 percent of $45,000 salary plus 5 percent employer match
Retirement savings: $515,619

Plenty of people say they're going to start saving and investing more, then promptly do nothing. If you're among them, this time around it's going to be different. This time you're really going to do it, because I'm going to show you the secret to making it *easy*.

Step 3: Make Investing Automatic, Too

In Chapter 7, you worked on saving and paying your bills automatically. Now you're going to use the same tactics to *invest* automatically. These days, thanks to automatic withdrawals, it's easier than ever to invest effortlessly.

One thing you need to understand is that certain investments are "tax-advantaged": You get a tax benefit for making the investment. Sometimes— as in the case of a 401(k), 403(b), Individual 401(k), Keogh and SEP-IRA for the self-employed, some Individual Retirement Accounts (IRAs), and even some 529 college savings plans—at the end of the year, you get to deduct from your income the money you're investing. As a result of that deduction, your taxes are computed on a smaller amount. That benefit can be a big deal. The other tax benefit on the table is the opportunity to allow the money you put into the account to grow without your having to pay taxes on it until you pull it out (in the case of 401(k)s, 403(b)s, and some types of IRAs) or forever (Roth IRAs).

Because these tax benefits are *so* valuable, you want to take advantage of them by putting your first investment dollars into these vehicles. Within these categories, I suggest investing in the following order:

1. *401(k)s and other tax-advantaged retirement accounts that pro-vide matching dollars. Invest enough to max out the match.*

2. *Roth IRAs, which are tax-advantaged retirement accounts that don't provide matching dollars but grow tax-free forever, don't force you to withdraw money at a certain age, and allow you to pull out money to buy your first house or for education for your kids.*

3. *All other retirement accounts for which you get a tax break, including deductible IRAs, SEP-IRAs, and Keoghs. (Nondeductible IRAs, which still allow your contribution to grow tax-deferred forever, fall last in this category.)*

4. *Tax-advantaged college savings accounts.*

5. *Tax-advantaged health savings accounts. This is an account you can open if you buy health insurance with a very high deductible. You fund the account with money that is to be used to pay for healthcare you need. If you don't use the money, it can grow, tax-deferred, for retirement.*

6. *Investment accounts that don't have tax advantages. These are your plain vanilla brokerage accounts, the ones you set up at, say, Schwab or Vanguard or Fidelity or Merrill Lynch or wherever, to buy stocks or bonds or mutual funds with the extra money you've been able to save. The reason these fall last on the list is that you've already paid taxes on the income and you'll pay taxes on whatever money these investments earn for you on a yearly basis. That doesn't mean they're not valuable—they are. But they're not as valuable as the five items that come before.*

Here is a closer look at these options and how to put them on automatic pilot.

Invest in 401(k) or 403(b) plans using automatic deductions

Here's some good news: If you work for a company with a 401(k) or 403(b) that automatically takes money out of your paycheck and puts it into your retirement savings, you already know this. You may be doing it without considering what you're doing. You may even be getting a match from your company—automatically. My father used to say, "There's no free lunch." Although he was right about almost everything, he was wrong about this. The plan match is a free lunch smorgasbord where you can—and should—eat every last morsel. Otherwise, you're leaving money on the table.

If you are already enrolled in your company's plan, excellent. If you're not, I want you to pick up the phone, call the benefits department, and ask when you can get in. When determining how much to contribute, keep the match at the top of your mind. Most companies will match half of what you contribute, up to a certain percentage. Some really generous companies match even more.

The trick is to try to grab every one of those matching dollars. So if the company will kick in up to 3 percent of your salary as long as you kick in 6 percent, that 6 percent is the first hurdle you want to cross. If you don't believe you'll be able to live without that 6 percent in your paycheck, start with 2 percent. Then skip ahead two months on your calendar and write a note reminding yourself to assess how you're doing on that take-home pay. (Remember, you're living in the world of *conscious* finance now. You are going to think about the choices you're making.) If you're doing just fine—and I promise you, you are not likely to miss 2 percent—pick up the phone, call the benefits department, and increase your contribution to 4 percent. Another two months down the road, do the same thing. If you are struggling to pay your bills when even a small amount is removed from your paycheck, then the minute you get your next raise, use it to boost your contribution. Again, call the benefits department. You probably can adjust your contributions whenever you like, though it may take a paycheck or two for the change to take effect. Within the year, you want to be at the point where all of the matching dollars—the whole free lunch—is yours.

Once you are maxing out on matching dollars, you'll want to start investing automatically in other ways, too. What I love most about investing automatically is that you rarely feel the pain. It's the old pay-yourself-first philosophy, but with the help of technology, you don't actually have to write the check. It's amazing how easy it is to get by without that $100 or whatever it might be a month if you never, ever see it.

Increase your 401(k) contributions automatically

The ability to bump up contributions automatically is a fairly new benefit that a lot of companies have put in place. It's a system that defaults you into saving a portion of your salary and then increases that portion as your wages rise over the years. If this benefit is on the menu at your company, choose it and don't look back. It offers a golden opportunity.

Automate contributions to a Roth IRA or other retirement plan

Even if you are contributing to an employer-sponsored plan like a 401(k), you can save for retirement in an IRA, even a Roth IRA (as long as your income doesn't exceed $100,000 for singles, $110,000 for heads of household, and $160,000 for married couples filing jointly). And I believe it's easiest when you make those contributions on a per paycheck or monthly basis automatic. If you have small amounts pulled from your bank account through the year, you won't have to come up with several thousand dollars at tax time. For all of the reasons I listed above, many financial experts believe that Roth IRAs are a gift from the financial gods (or at the very least from Congress). Any mutual fund or investment company will help you open one.

Invest for college automatically

If you have kids, then you've thought about investing for college. You've probably thought you should put money away for college before you put money away for retirement. You've read articles on state-sponsored college savings plans (529 plans) and prepaid tuition plans (they are another form of 529 plan); you've heard of Coverdell Education Savings Accounts and UGMA accounts, and you're tempted to open at least one such account. After all, shouldn't college—and your kids—come first?

Probably not, no matter how selfish what I'm about to tell you feels. You have to remember that there's no financial aid for retirement but there's plenty of financial aid for college. If you get to the first tuition payment and you don't have enough socked away, loans for education are available at decent rates. If you don't want your children to be responsible for those loans after they get out of school, you can offer to help with the repayment. (And if your parents—their grandparents—are volunteering to help with college, you may want to encourage them to help in this same way, by offering the kids money after they graduate to repay student loans.)

If you've socked as much money as you can into your retirement accounts, maxed out your 401(k), and made an IRA contribution, then of course you can start putting money away for college. Unless you are positive you aren't going to receive financial aid (and these days, *very* few people should feel positive about that), knock UGMA accounts—Uniform Gift to Minors Act accounts—off your short list. The money in those accounts belongs to your child and will inhibit his or her ability to qualify for aid. Instead, look at 529 plans and Coverdells. Coverdells are more flexible, they allow you to invest the money wherever you like, but you can contribute only a few thousand a year. You can put more into a 529 in any given year. And because you can't dip into both a 529 and a Coverdell to *pay* for college simultaneously, a 529 is preferable if you can swing contributions of more than a few thousand.

You can make automatic monthly payments and pay no taxes on the earnings if you use the money for college expenses, just as if you put the money into an IRA. If you choose the 529 college savings plan route, look into your state's plan first to see if you're eligible for a tax deduction or other break. If you are not (or if your state's plan isn't particularly good—go to www.savingforcollege.com for ratings), be sure to pick a low-expense plan like the one in Ohio or Utah so unnecessary fees don't eat into your gains. If you do buy a plan like this, enroll in that plan directly through your state's plan manager. Do not—I repeat *do not*—buy it through a broker. Doing so will saddle you with unnecessary and often hefty fees that are completely avoidable.

Set up an automatic investment plan that's not part of your retirement fund

You can make automatic monthly payments from checking to nearly any mutual fund or brokerage account. You'll want to do this for money that you want to grow over the medium to long term but do not want to lock up in a retirement account where you'll pay taxes and penalties for pulling it out before you turn 59 1/2. So, for instance, if you think you'll want to buy a house in five years, this is a good way to invest your down payment. Because your time horizon is short (relative to, say, retirement or college) be sure that you pick an investment that's not especially high-risk. A short-term bond fund, for instance, is better for this purpose than a stock mutual fund. The plus of this type of automatic investing: Your money will go right to work for you, and you'll have the advantage of dollar cost averaging, which is a fancy name for cutting your risks. As I explained briefly earlier, with dollar cost averaging you invest a fixed dollar amount on a regular (generally monthly) schedule regardless of share price. Over time, more shares are purchased when prices are low, and fewer shares are bought at high prices. That strategy lowers the risk of investing a large chunk of money in a single investment at the wrong time.

Step 4: Know Where to Put Your Money

So you've got the idea. Investing automatically is the way to go. But by now you're asking, "Where do I send all these automatic payments each month? There are thousands of mutual funds and investment firms to choose from. And what about individual stocks and bonds?"

Don't worry. I'm going to simplify this process, too. But first, let me go over three basic principles that no successful investor can afford to ignore.

Asset allocation

When you allocate your investment assets, you split the money in your portfolio among different asset classes, such as stocks, bonds, and cash, to get the maximum return for the risk you take.

- **Stocks:** Also called equities, stocks are shares in public companies that trade on a stock exchange. Stocks are the highest-risk, highest-reward asset and the place where you can make real gains—or lose your shirt. If you're 40 or younger, you should invest the bulk of your long-term portfolio in stocks to maximize your gains while you still have time to make up for any losses.

- **Bonds:** When you buy a bond, you're buying the debt of a company, government agency, or other entity for a defined period of time for a specified interest rate. In other words, you're becoming a lender, and the money you earn on your bond is a combination of (a) the interest you're paid for making that loan and (b) any return you get for making a smart bet by lending money at that particular time. If it becomes more expensive to borrow money in the future, you could sell that bond at a higher price. If it becomes less expensive to borrow money, the bond you purchased earlier becomes less valuable—so if you sold it before it came due, you would likely lose money. (If you hold it until the due date or maturity date, you'll get your money back plus the interest you were promised.) Bonds are less risky than stocks, but they have less potential, too.

* **Cash:** Cash-like investments such as money market funds and certificates of deposit constitute the safest asset class because they aren't subject to the risks of the markets. In low-interest-rate environments, however, cash is the lowest-returning asset.

Allocating your assets simply means deciding what percentage of each type of asset will get you closer to achieving your goals. You need to balance the risk you're taking in each asset class with the reward you need to move you forward to your own personal endgame. In general, the younger you are, the more you should have invested in stocks for long-term goals. Older investors should put a good chunk of money in bonds and cash.

What should your allocation be? Take 100 and subtract your age. That's the percentage you want in stocks.

Diversification

Diversification is what happens after you allocate your assets among stocks, bonds, and cash. You have to make sure that you have different kinds of stocks (growth, value, large-company, small-company, international, and domestic) and different kinds of bonds (high-yield, corporate, government, inflation-protected) to keep your risk of losses as low as possible. A lot of people believe that as soon as they put money into a mutual fund they are instantly diversified. But they're not. Just as there are different stocks and bonds, there are different types of mutual funds. There are stock mutual funds and bond mutual funds. And within those large categories there are large-stock funds, small-stock funds, growth-stock funds, value-stock funds, domestic-stock funds, international-stock funds . . . well, you get the idea. To be truly diversified, you need a mix of mutual funds just as you would need a mix of individual stocks and bonds. The easiest way to achieve diversification with the fewest funds is to put your money into broad funds that invest in big baskets of stocks and bonds. If at age 40 you put 50 percent of your money into a total domestic stock market index fund, 40 percent into a total bond market index fund, and 10 percent into a global stock fund for international exposure, you could argue that you have your bases covered. You could also put your money into one "target-date retirement fund" that would diversify and then re-balance on your behalf. (More on this in a moment.)

Rebalancing

The first time you allocate your assets, you'll come up with some numbers. Maybe you'll decide to put 60 percent of your money in stocks, 20 percent in bonds, and 20 percent in cash. The problem is, after you make those choices the stock market moves. If stocks go up (as we all hope they do), you could quickly end up with 70 percent of your assets in stocks by doing ab-solutely nothing. That's a far different—and riskier—allocation than you began with. Rebalancing is the strategy of selling some stocks and buying some bonds or vice-versa to bring your allocation back in line. If you have money in a couple of index funds, rebalancing is fairly easy. You pick up the phone, call the firm that manages your account, and make a few trades. Or you do it online. If you have money in a target-date fund, rebalancing is easier still because the fund manager handles it.

There's no overestimating how important rebalancing is: When the dot-com stocks took the wind out of the market a few years back, plenty of peo-ple were overloaded in technology because those stocks had run up so far and so fast. Those investors hadn't stopped to consider rebalancing. If they had, they would have lost a lot less money.

All in all, it's not brain surgery. So what's the problem? You are. Asset allo-cation, diversification, and rebalancing may be a breeze from a technical perspective. But emotions can get in your way. Even people who say they understand asset allocation and diversification also say they can't bring themselves to rebalance their portfolios. Why? Because rebalancing is counterintuitive. It means selling assets you have the greatest affinity for because they've been making you the most money and buying assets you have distaste for because they haven't been working.

The trouble is: You're human. You hear about a great stock or a great sector, so you buy it—probably after the big money has been made. You hold on to losing stocks or funds too long because selling is admitting you made a mistake in your research. So many portfolios are constantly out of balance and into flux because so many investors have such a tough time reining them in.

Put the Money There Automatically

Let's say you have an hour or two of free time. Which would you do: (a) Wash your windows? (b) Rebalance your portfolio?

Fifty percent of a thousand investors surveyed said they would wash windows (if the tasks on the list had included folding the laundry or doing dishes, I suspect the number not choosing rebalancing would have been significantly higher). Unfortunately, no matter how dirty your windows are, washing them is not the profitable choice.

Setting and then maintaining an asset allocation that helps you take the right amount of risk at the right time is one of the most important things you can do to make sure you have enough money to retire. The right mix can help you keep pace with the market in good times, and it can protect you from big losses in bad. So I recommend that you do what I do: Not only put contributions into your investments on autopilot, but put the diversification of that money on autopilot as well.

Take yourself (and your emotions) out of the rebalancing process. In the last few years, mutual fund companies have rolled out "life cycle funds," "target-date funds," and "asset allocation funds." The first two ask you what year you're planning to retire. As you approach that date, the fund company shrinks the percentage the fund has in stocks and boosts the percentage it has in bonds to reduce your risk over time. This way, if the stock market tanks a year or so before you're set to retire, you should still be okay.

Asset allocation mutual funds ensure that you maintain a steady balance of say, 60 percent stocks and 40 percent bonds (which is the balance pension funds keep and what most investors should have as they're actively saving and investing for retirement). But funds of this type do not adjust their allocation to reflect your advancing age. Instead, you switch to a fund with a different allocation as you get older.

Some 401(k) plans offer management services. You pay a small percentage of your assets, and the plan manager rebalances on your behalf. If you're operating outside of your 401(k), ask your brokerage firm what sort of services are available to keep your allocations in line. Reallocating may cost you a few bucks, but the expense is worthwhile if you're not going to tend to your portfolio yourself.

Any of these is a great solution compared to doing what most people do: nothing. Even a tiny difference in returns over the lifetime of your portfolio can make a huge difference.

Avoid These Mistakes

Automatic investments like life cycle and target-date funds help us avoid some common but costly mistakes. We've talked about waiting too long to get started—one of the biggest mistakes that investors make. But there are other traps that can jeopardize your finances as well. I want you to know about them so that you can be sure not to make them along your way to wealth:

- **Don't leave 401(k) matching dollars on the table.** I said it earlier, but it bears repeating: Not investing enough in your 401(k) to qualify for the full amount of any match your company offers leaves free money on the table. And you need every bit if you're going to retire well.

- **Don't cash out a 401(k) when you change jobs (no matter how little money you've accumulated).** More than half of all job changers do this. Problem is, when you change jobs a dozen times over the course of a career—as we do in this country— all this cashing out means little to nothing left for retirement. Roll the money into an IRA instead or into a new 401(k). Or leave it in your current employer's plan.

- **Don't put all your eggs in one basket.** Having more than 10 percent of your money in one stock is too much. I'll up that percentage to 25 percent if you're talking about company stock, but I won't do it happily. Why is this important? Enron. Rite-Aid. Lucent. And every other stock debacle of the last seventy years.

- **Don't chase hot money.** I know it's tempting to go after the latest hot stock (after it has already run up), rack up a lot of trading costs, and hold your ground hoping against hope that you'll get your investment back and make millions. It rarely works. But if you simply can't help yourself—and I know there are times when you really believe something is a sure thing—minimize your potential for losses by limiting the amount you sink into any one investment (whether it's a stock, a friend's business, gold coins, or wine futures) to 5 percent of your money. That way if your hot prospect becomes, well, tepid, you won't lose your ability to retire on time.

MAP TO A MILLION

How much will it cost you to make those mistakes? I asked the folks at Princeton's Bendheim Institute to run the numbers to figure out how much such errors cost the average investor. You might want to make sure you're sitting down for this next bit of information. Over three decades, if you make just one—one!—of the missteps listed above, you stand to have $300,000 less than you would have had if you hadn't made the error. That could be the difference between a comfortable retirement and a real struggle.

Don't Take Your Eye Off the Ball

In the movie *You've Got Mail*, Tom Hanks discovers that the woman he has fallen in love with via e-mail is Meg Ryan. She becomes completely enamored of his online persona and eventually asks in an e-mail message whether he thinks it's time for them to meet face-to-face. He knows he must win her over in person before she finds out that his big-box superstore put her charming bookshop out of business. So he stalls for time and responds that he's in the midst of a project that needs "tweaking."

I want to prepare you for the fact that your financial life will need tweaking. Even if you take my advice and go the automatic route, you'll still have to do certain things.

Do it: Open your statements. Each quarter, you need to keep track of the direction your investments are going in and where you stand. If you're computer-savvy, using personal finance software programs will help you do this tracking quickly and will prove a godsend at tax time. But whether you do it on the screen or by hand, paying attention means you'll spot any errors in your account immediately. And you'll notice if the asset allocation you've chosen is getting you to your goals in a timely fashion or if you need to rebalance your investments to take on a little more or a little less risk.

Say it and sound smart: *"I know it's time for* CSI. *Just give me a minute to look at how my investments are doing."*

Do it: Ask questions when something seems wrong. If you don't understand something on your statement—and yes, this means you should be opening and then reading your statements—call the toll-free number. This is no time to be shy. Tell the customer service rep what's on your mind. Little miscalculations and other errors will get worse with time. And you want to make sure that any transactions you made are reported accurately.

Say it and sound smart: *"It says on my statement that on April 21 I bought shares . . . I don't recall making that transaction. Can you go back into my record and tell me what you see?"*

Do it: Make changes when appropriate. Yes, this plan should set you on automatic pilot. But changes in your life will dictate changes in your retirement and other investing plans. What sort of life changes? A raise, for example. You will want to increase your contributions into your retirement and other savings accounts every time you get one. Bonuses, tax refunds, and inheritances are all a cry to rejigger as well. Anyone who has done an outstanding job of accumulating wealth will tell you how important this strategy is. Give your own savings a raise every time you get one, and put at least part of every windfall to work for you.

Say it and sound smart: *"I'm putting 75 percent of my bonus away for the future. I hope we'll have a lot more years like this one, but if this is the end of the gravy train I don't want to spend the money and regret it."*

To my mind, successful investing boils down to three things: (1) investing habitually, (2) managing your investments automatically, and (3) keeping your eye on the ball. If you do those three things, and you're diligent about them, there's no reason you shouldn't have the money you need to achieve your goals.

LOOK HOW FAR YOU'VE COME!

Even if investing has presented a roadblock to you in the past, it's now one you're ready to conquer. You know where and how to find some money. You know how to move it out of your hot little hands before you have the opportunity to spend it. You know what sort of account to open or fund. And you know what type of mutual fund to put the money in. Presto! Now all you have to do is sit back, open your statements, and watch your gains materialize.

I think I could use some financial advice. But I don't want to hire a full-time financial planner. Is there an in-between solution?

I'm a big fan of using financial advisers kind of like short-term therapists to solve particular problems. In fact, the first time I used a financial planner it was to figure out how much I could afford to spend on a house. The good news is that planners today are much more willing to be paid by the hour. Smart planners know it's good for them to get a foot in the door even if you pay them for only an hour or three of their time. That way when you need more financial assistance, their name will be the one that comes to mind. To find a planner willing to work by the hour, go to garrettplanningnetwork. com, a national network of fee-only planners who have flexible fee structures. (A plus: The network is run by a woman named Sheryl Garrett.)

I've been hearing a lot lately about reverse mortgages. Are they a good idea?

They can be, but they can also be expensive traps. Reverse mortgages are programs that essentially allow a homeowner to sell her or his house back to the bank while continuing to live there. You have to be 62 or older to qualify, and the payout you'll receive can come in the form of a lump sum, a line of credit, or a monthly payment. Interest rates on these loans are set. You don't have to shop around as you do for a traditional mortgage, but you do have to be careful about fees. More important, you need to be careful about the reasons you choose to take out a reverse mortgage. The folks at AARP note that an awful lot of people who go the reverse route do so thinking that their adult kids are desperate to inherit the family house. In many cases, those adult kids are nothing of the sort. They'd rather their parents sell the big house, trade down to something smaller, pocket some money, and be in a position of feeling more financially secure. So that's the place to start. If you or your parents think that a reverse mortgage might make sense, have a discussion about how much sense it makes to keep the house and to live in it. And if you decide a reverse is the way to go, check out the calculator on the AARP website (www.aarp.org/revmort/) to see what sort of payout you can expect.

CHAPTER 9

"I'm Too Old— It's Too Late for Me"

DON'T BITCH

You're over 40 and you haven't started saving—seriously saving—for retirement, or you haven't started facing up to your other money issues. You have more debt than you'd like or less real estate. And you can't pretend anymore that you're waiting until you grow up.

Okay. Let's acknowledge up front and out loud that this is not a great situation to find yourself in. If you had it to do all over again, you would start earlier. You would be smarter. You would spend less and save more. You would . . . you would . . .

And you know what? You are not alone. Not in the least. As I was gathering stories for this project, plenty of women responded like Alice, a social worker, who said:

> I'm too old to change my financial situation. There's not enough time before retirement to make a difference.

A mind-set like that is the reason for the following statistics:

- **Only 40 percent of women have even tried to calculate the amount of money they will need to live in retirement.**

- *Of those who have tried to calculate their retirement needs, most seem to vastly underestimate those needs. Nearly 40 percent believe they will need less than $250,000 to live on past age 65.*
- *Just 59 percent of women are actively saving for retirement.*
- *Only 36 percent of women contribute to a workplace retirement plan.*

The result: 75 percent of female baby boomers are not prepared for retirement. Women will have substantially less money to live on than men. And, on average, we will live four years longer. Unless something changes, too many of our gooses are cooked.

And we know it. That's why so many of us get back into bed and pull the financial covers over our heads. It's a strange mentality but it's common enough: The less you've saved in the past, the less likely you are to start saving now. Every time you think about starting, the thought of all the time and opportunity lost are overwhelming. You'll never catch up, you say to yourself, so why start now?

Because you can catch up and you can *win.*

A number of financial things will have to change if you're going to play this game of catch-up and win: Your savings habits will have to change. So will your investing, spending, and other habits that are preventing the wealth and life you could build. But before attempting these changes, you have to change something even more important: You have to change your mind.

Change Your Mind; Change Your Life

I am a huge fan of Ann Richards, the former governor of Texas. I admire her energy, her spirit, her *hair.* Mostly, though, I admire the lesson she preaches whenever she gets the chance. If life isn't working for you, change your own mind. Witness this interchange between Richards and interviewer Hugh Downs, who was guest-hosting on *Larry King Live.*

DOWNS: You once said that it was better to look ahead and not to look back.

RICHARDS: Oh, yes, because there is nothing you can do.

DOWNS: Well, that is true. You can't change the past.

RICHARDS: You know, I have got a friend who went to her hairdresser, and she said, "Agnes, I think my hair looks terrible." And Agnes said, "Well, change your mind," because Agnes wasn't going to do anything about her hair. So I have sort of used that as a mantra for years. You know, if something is wrong, I have changed my mind.

DOWNS: Changed your mind.

RICHARDS: Because my whole life is right here in this head and how I see things.

Ann Richards changed her mind. And you can, too. In other words, you can have a do-over starting today. You can have a mulligan, a gimme, a second chance.

"Doing it today won't make that much of a difference, will it? I'm never really going to get rich, am I?" That's what Karen, a real estate broker, wanted to know. But in fact, it will make a big difference, and it can make Karen—and you—really rich. This chapter is all about how to break out and become an exception to those depressing statistics.

We've already talked about what the first step is: *You change your mind.* You get over the feeling that it's too late to save for retirement. That attitude is simply not acceptable. Why? Because your future—and by future I mean being able to afford the things you want for you and your family after age 65—is far too important to simply throw in the towel. I won't let you get away with it.

And the truth is, it is not too late. Plenty of people in their forties, fifties, and sixties believe that. I'm constantly surprised and dazzled by the optimism and energy of some so-called late starters—the ones who don't let regrets about missed opportunity get them down. True, by starting late you've lost the advantage of years of compounding. You simply won't have thirty or forty years to watch your nest egg grow, as twenty-something savers will. But older savers have plenty of reasons to be optimistic, anyway.

Retirement isn't what it used to be

Maybe when your parents or grandparents turned 65, their worlds stopped turning. But that was then. Baby boomers are reinventing the whole notion of retirement. Now people turn 65 and keep working another five years, or turn 65 and start a new business, or turn 65 and start working to nab the dream job they've always wanted. The majority of baby boomers say they expect to keep working and earning in retirement. No, they don't plan to stick to a nine-to-five schedule. That would be too difficult (and likely too depressing). Instead, their plan is to cycle in and out of periods of work and play, work and travel, work and leisure. Part-time work in a field you love is the name of this new game.

Old age isn't what it used to be

Your parents planned a retirement of ten years, fifteen years at the most. They were surprised if they found themselves alive at age 75. They thought of their later years as an unexpected gift. We, however, can pretty much count on living into our seventies full of energy and vitality. For our parents those years were largely a time to wind down; for many of us the sixties and early seventies can be a time to gear up but in a slightly different way.

You're established in your career and enjoying your prime earning years

You've got decades of experience behind you and plenty of confidence to continue advancing. If you're in your forties, you're just hitting your peak earning years. If you're in your fifties, you're smack dab in the middle of them. So you're in a much better position to put away a big percentage of your salary toward retirement than you ever were in the past.

Your kids are older

If you are in your late forties and fifties, your kids are likely teens (they may even be out of the house). That gives you a big burst of that other precious commodity—time. If you're a stay-at-home mom, now you can go back to work and bank that extra salary. If you're a working mom, you may have the time to do extra projects or freelance work that can bring in some extra money to stash away.

Your house is paid off (or very close to it)

Chances are good that you're sitting on a pile of home equity thanks to the overheated real estate market of recent years. If you strategize properly, you should be able to convert that into a stash of money that can help you even out the bumps in your retirement planning. How can you do that? One way is by selling the large family house and trading down to something a little smaller and less expensive. If you need the big house because your kids— and their kids—come to visit, you can sell a house in a pricey school district (where taxes continue to take a huge toll even after your kids are out of school) and buy one in a cheaper neighborhood. After all, you don't need the public schools anymore. Or, if you're nearing the end of your working life, you can swap a house that's high-priced because it provides a short commute for one that's lower-priced because it doesn't. Finally, if you're determined that you're going to keep your house until the day you die, you may still be able to get considerable equity out of it by means of a reverse mortgage, which is exactly what it sounds like: an agreement by which you continue to live in the house *while* the bank pays (on a monthly basis or in a lump sum) to buy it back from you.

You're seasoned enough to handle what life throws at you

Emotional maturity is a *good* thing, not an *old* thing. It means you've lived through enough hirings, firings, career changes, and other facts of life to know that slow and steady, even at a late stage, wins the race. You won't be tempted, like twenty-somethings and thirty-somethings, to get out there and find the next Ebay. When you do start saving, an age-appropriate well-balanced portfolio will be your modus operandi. And you'll have the wisdom to protect your hard-saved cash from the next market downturn.

Knock Down Any Remaining Roadblocks

You've read far enough into this book to know that I'm a big believer that knowing and understanding your motivation and rationale for doing things a certain way (or in this case *not* doing them) is the key to change. Otherwise, I may be able to get you to start saving, but I'm going to have a bear of a time getting you to stick with the program. You need to understand why you've been avoiding financial reality. Is it plain inertia? Is it fear? (If so, I want you to go back and reread Chapters 1 and 2.)

Or is it something bigger? I want you to understand a little more about the roadblocks that have been standing in the way of women who don't start saving and investing until they are well into their thirties and forties. Here's what some of the research has shown.

You are more risk-averse than most men

Academics argue about whether this is a true statement or an out-dated stereotype. I believe it's true. A cautious nature helps make you a safe driver and keeps your kids from falling off the jungle gym, but it can cause problems in your financial life. You're not only less likely to invest but also less likely to fight for a raise or to leave your company for a higher-paying position. You're less likely to take a job that requires you to take a risk (whether that involves flying on an airplane or work-ing in a plant), and that caution can hold down your earning potential for years.

But let's say I'm wrong and the whole scared-of-risk label *is* a stereo-type. This stereotype affects women's pocketbooks. Why? Because employ-ers may automatically pay women less or offer women lower-paying positions because they are perceived as less able to handle risky situations and decisions. Not fair, you say. Life's not fair, I answer. Moving beyond the inequalities is up to you.

Forget about actually *losing money. You don't even like the* idea *of losing money.*

This may sound like a no-brainer, except that it is getting in the way of *mak-ing* money. Even when the chances of losing money are highly unlikely, you may be one of those women who can't stomach risk. This explains why you shy away from even conservative moves, such as moving your balance out of money market and saving accounts into higher-yielding but still rela-tively safe bond funds. You probably feel safer keeping money as close to home as possible. That's why you go for the savings account at the bank down the street that pays 2 percent even though an Internet bank in Utah is paying 4 percent. It's also why you let your money sit in savings earning 2 percent when you could make 8 times the return by paying down the bal-ance on your credit card that's charging 16 percent.

You make smaller investments than men

Think about the last time you walked into a casino with your significant other. He headed for the $10 tables. You? Quarter slots. That's how women tend to invest as well—in smaller pieces. And this strategy hurts us over time. We make fewer investments in and contribute less to our 401(k)s than men do. That's a particular problem for late starters, because *now* is when you have to save a bundle if you're going to make up for lost time.

You don't take risks on the job

One of the implications of being risk-averse is that women aren't likely to take jobs that seem less secure than traditional positions. You may avoid positions that pay less than you're making now but have the promise of a big bonus. Or you shy away from jobs that pay potentially lucrative commissions rather than straight salary.

No matter how many of those items ring true (and I suspect at least a couple of them do), you can get past them. You've seen them laid out in black and white. You know what's at stake. You're motivated. You want to do it. You know deep in your gut that the riskiest thing you could ever do is . . . nothing. You won't jeopardize your future that way. I'm sure of it. You just need a plan—and that's what I'm going to give you. But first I want to give you a money mantra to hold in your mind. Say it to yourself over and over if you have to . . . like Dorothy wishing herself back to Auntie Em:

It's not too late.

It's not too late.

It's not too late.

GET RICH

Save More—A Lot More

Remember when I said older savers can't rely as heavily on the magic of compounding as younger savers can? That leaves only one other strategy to pursue: To retire comfortably, you've got to sock away more money each month. No matter how strapped you feel or how impossible that task seems, you can do it. Why? It's simple: because you have to.

Before I show you how, I want you to do something easy and quite gratifying. The truth is, it is rare that anyone really starts from scratch when it comes to saving for retirement. Most people have something stashed away somewhere. Maybe you have been contributing steadily to your company's retirement plan but only 2 or 3 percent of your salary. That's not nearly enough, but it is a good start. Your money is growing tax-free and maybe you've even gotten a small company match.

In other words, sometimes we actually forget about money we've put away. So I want you to think back, maybe even go for a treasure hunt in your file cabinets. For instance, did you ever open an IRA way back when? You may have contributed for only a year or two and eventually lost track of the account. Or remember the go-go days of the late 1980s and early 1990s? Maybe you were feeling flush and decided to put a thousand dollars in a high-tech stock fund. You watched closely when it skyrocketed to $15,000, but when it plummeted back down to about $4,000, you stopped paying attention. That's still real money.

Maybe years ago you worked long enough at a big company to get vested in the pension plan. Granted, you probably weren't making much at the time so payments won't be a lot, but it's worth a call to the benefits department to see if you're due something when you turn 65.

Do you have savings bonds or shares of stock you were given as a gift? Chances are, they've appreciated.

Finally, is there a savings account, money market account, or checking account that you opened somewhere then forgot? Does it have a balance? Can you put that toward retirement?

When you've unearthed every cent that could be used to build your retirement foundation, here's what you need to do to add to it so you have what you need when you retire.

Save More

We covered a number of saving strategies in Chapter 7, but let's review the basic concepts. The key to saving more money consistently tomorrow is knowing where your money is going today. That means taking the time to track your spending consistently for a few weeks to a month until you see where you can make cuts. Slashing the amount of money you're putting toward debt repayment (in the form of high- or higher-than-necessary interest rates) can also be a gold mine. If you haven't gone through the process of calling credit card companies to ask for an interest rate reduction, trying to refinance any car loan you got from a dealer (unless it was a special promotional rate), consolidating your student loan, or refinancing your mortgage to the lowest rate possible, it's time.

There may come a point when you realize that despite doing your very best to free up hundreds if not thousands of dollars to sock away each month, you just can't. Then you may have to look at some harder choices: living somewhere less expensive, driving cheaper cars, sending your children to public instead of private schools. There are a variety of tools in your arsenal.

Earn More

One great way to save more money without compromising the life you're living today is to earn more. You can do that by negotiating your way into a higher salary using the strategies on page 48. You can do it by adding more hours or by moonlighting alongside your current job.

MAP TO A MILLION

Take a look at the difference you could make in your retirement planning if you could earn, say, another $7,000 a year throughout your late forties and fifties and put $5,000 away after taxes. Assuming the money paid an 8 percent return, you'd have the following to add to your retirement savings at age 65.

If you are starting at:	Then at 65 you'll have:
Age 45	$195,417
Age 50	$121,478
Age 55	$67,666

Pretty powerful, yes? So where are you going to get that extra seven grand? You'll need to take advantage of some of the plusses of being older I mentioned at the beginning of this chapter—being in your prime earning years and having more time to work now that your kids are grown.

If you're a one-paycheck family, the nonworking spouse can easily make $7,000 and then some working part-time. If you're both already working, volunteer for overtime or extra shifts. Or take on freelance or consulting work in your industry.

Maybe you already own your own business. Enlist your spouse or a family member to help you out at night or on weekends so you can ramp up production or take on extra clients.

Or, as many, many people are doing, you can consider working longer. Baby boomers are redefining the concept of retirement. They don't necessarily want to hit the golf course at age 65, and many expect to keep working full-time for at least five years after their retirement age. That can really pay off for late savers. A few extra years in the workforce will give your portfolio added time to grow and will cut the number of years you'll need to draw on that money. It also will give you a shot at hanging on to some valuable health-care benefits (health care is the number-one expense that retirees underestimate).

It's important to be realistic about how many years of working you'll be able to bank on. Studies show that two-thirds of today's older workers and 80 percent of baby boomers plan to work in retirement. But many overestimate their ability to keep going.

The reality is, because of failing health or difficulty finding a job at an older age, over half of Social Security beneficiaries retire at age 62, and almost 80 percent are retired by 65. What that means is that although you may think (as I do) that you'd be unhappy not working or that you can never imagine *really* retiring, you can't bank on being able to keep going. Your body may let you down. A health emergency can hit quickly and with little or no notice. That's why it's prudent to save as much as you absolutely can starting today. Working longer—though a good line item to put on the list—is not a reason to avoid saving as much as you can today for your future.

Do it: Max out your 401(k). I am a huge believer that everyone should max out 401(k) contributions if humanly possible. I can't stress it enough, though, with late starters.

Not only do you get your company's matching dollars (if offered), which are—need I say it again?—free money, but earnings on your account grow tax-free, which means they grow fast, exactly what you need. Plus it's easy to do because the money is automatically deducted from your paycheck. With a single phone call, you elect to have your contribution maxed out, and then it simply happens and continues to happen paycheck after paycheck. It may be tough at first to live on a little less money, but you will adapt. And fairly soon you'll be surprised that you ever thought you needed all that money.

And here's the best part: Over the last few years Uncle Sam has provided a great bonus for older 401(k) savers in the tax code: Workers age 50 and over can contribute $5,000 more each year than younger workers. Thanks to tax-free earnings, that boost can really add up.

Say it and sound smart: *"I talked to my benefits department to be sure I'm putting as much into my 401(k) as I can—and getting the full match."*

MAP TO A MILLION

How much can using the new older-worker contributions—the so-called catch-up provision in—mean to your retirement? If you start putting away the maximum allowed ($20,000 in 2006) and get an 8 percent (tax-deferred) return on your money, here's what you'll have by age 65:

Start saving at age:	With the catch-up bonus:	Without the catch-up bonus:
50	$543, 042	$407,281
51	$484,298	$363,223
52	$429,905	$322,429
53	$379,542	$284,656
54	$332,909	$249,682
55	$289,731	$217,298
60	$117,332	$87,999

Now, look at what you get if you work five extra years, until age 70:

Start at age:	With the bonus:	Without the bonus:
50	$915,239	$686,429
55	$543,042	$407,281
60	$289,731	$217,298

Do it: Use more generous IRAs. Late starters have other weapons in their arsenals as well. You can make larger contributions to both traditional and Roth IRAs. The numbers change each and every year (the good news is, they're headed up), but if you're older than 50, you can put more money into an IRA than the rest of the population. You also can make a contribution of the same size for a nonworking spouse. This one move can double the amount you're putting away for retirement.

Say it and sound smart: *"It isn't easy putting so much away for retirement. I'm cutting back on vacations and eating out, but I know I won't regret it down the road."*

Do it: Bulk up contributions if you work for yourself. Here's what we know about people who work for themselves. They are less likely to save for the future because they're busy plowing their profits back into the business. There are more of them than there have ever been in the past. And since women start businesses at twice the rate of men, this hits us particularly hard. If you really want all your hard work to pay off, you have to focus on tomorrow. And that means you have to pay yourself for your retirement first. My suggestions?

Either use a SEP-IRA, which lets you put away as much as 25 percent of your gross income up to a maximum of $44,000 (this was the limit when this book went to press; but thresholds generally go up each year). Or use an Individual 401(k,) which lets you save up to $44,000 a year, or $49,000 per year if you're age 50 or older. A Keogh works as well.

Say it and sound smart: *"It's tempting to put every last dollar back into my business, but I know focusing on my retirement is not selfish. It's crucial."*

Do it: Use as many of these accounts as you can—combined. As you start socking away as much as possible, you may find that you're able to do more than satisfy the maximums of one particular account. That's not only fine, it's great. At that point, you want to use more than one type of account. If you're the sort of employee who also consults, you should think about sheltering some of that self-employment income in a SEP-IRA, for instance. If you don't, think about making a nondeductible IRA contribution as a bonus. And if you've satisfied all of your tax-advantaged opportunities and you can still do more, well, as the Nike ad says: "Just do it!"

Look for low-tax or no-tax investments like stock index mutual funds or tax-free municipal bond funds for your extra savings so you can pocket as much of your return as possible. But stash, stash, stash the cash while the stashing is good.

Say it and sound smart: *"I have my IRA at the same firm that manages my 401(k) so I can see everything at once online."*

Do it: Make the most of your home. A lot of people think of their house not only as their home but also as their nest egg. That's understandable. With home values rising steadily, boomers have gotten used to the idea of counting on home equity as their main asset. And it's not such a bad idea, as long as you're making a dent—and I mean a substantial one—in your mortgage.

I have to say, though, I'm worried about all those fifty-somethings who refinanced their mortgages to take advantage of declining interest rates and started with another thirty-year loan. Sure your monthly payment is a lot lower. But the bad news is you may have twenty or more years left to pay before that loan is retired. If you were 45 when you did the deed, that means you won't be free and clear until you're 75—well into your retirement years.

And if you pulled out cash from the house in the process, I'm doubly worried. Less worried if you used the money to pay for a home improvement that will boost the value of the house so that when you go to sell it you'll see at least some of the cash come back. And less worried if you used the money to pay for college for your children—you would have borrowed the money at higher rates anyway. But if you frittered the cash away, if you can't in a sentence or two say where the money is, then I want to be sure you are pumping the brakes now. Moreover, whether you're dealing with a long-term loan or a big long-term loan, you need to make an extra effort—starting today—to get that mortgage paid. This is how you can do so:

- **You can make one extra payment a year.** This will cut a thirty-year mortgage down to a twenty-three-year mortgage.

- **You can make bimonthly mortgage payments.** This will accomplish the same thing without the pain of having to scrape together an extra mortgage payment once a year. How? Once you divide the year into weeks instead of into months, you end up with 52 of them. Making a payment every two weeks yields the equivalent of 26 biweekly payments or 13 monthlies.

- **You can come up with a sum you can swing and start adding that to your check each month.** Start at $100, $200, whatever makes sense within the context of your financial life, but make sure the bank knows this is an extra payment on the principal. (Call your lender. The bank may tell you to write a second, separate check.)

- **You can stop putting your biggest asset at risk by borrowing against your home.** Home equity loans (which are fixed-rate) and home equity lines of credit (which are variable-rate) are second mortgages. As such, they're more risky (for the bank) than first mortgages and more expensive for you. If you've taken a second mortgage, it's likely costing more in interest than your mortgage. As soon as possible, pay it down so that you don't owe a bundle when you go to sell your home.

As soon as you own your house outright, pretend that you don't and put the amount you would have spent on your mortgage payment into retirement savings each month. Finally, consider doing what many others have done to take advantage of rising home values in recent years: Trade down. That's right. Consider moving to a smaller home and stashing your profit in your retirement savings.

How can you tell if you're a candidate for downsizing? Examine the space you have now. Make a chart showing how big each of your rooms is and how frequently you use each space by the week or by the month. You'll see immediately if you have space that is underutilized.

In addition to the profits on the sale of your existing home, trading down means you'll pay less in utilities, landscaping, and other maintenance costs. You can stash the difference in upkeep each month in your retirement account.

Say it and sound smart: *"I know my house is probably my most valuable asset. I'm going to put it to work for my future."*

MAP TO A MILLION

How much could you save toward retirement by downsizing? Suppose you trade down at age 50. You've got a good fifteen years to put that money to work. Here's what you'd have with an 8 percent return in a taxable account:

Profit	At Retirement
$50,000	$129,703
$100,000	$259,406
$150,000	$389,110

If you stash the $2,500 a year you'll save in utilities, lawn care, and other maintenance by owning a smaller home, you'll have even more:

Profit	At Retirement
$50,000	$190,442
$100,000	$320,146
$150,000	$449,849

Make Your Money Last

With all this emphasis on saving *for* retirement, it's easy to lose sight of how important it is to manage your money well *during* retirement. There are two keys to making your retirement nest egg last as long as possible. The first is asset allocation (see Chapter 8). The second is keeping a lid on withdrawals.

In order to do the latter, there's a magic number you need to know: 4 percent. You need to make 4 percent your compadre, 4 percent is your friend. As long as you keep the amount of your portfolio that you withdraw each year at or below that amount, adjusted for inflation, you have a good chance of making your money last as long as you do.

One thing to remember, though, is that the balance in your retirement accounts is a moving target. If the market soars, that gives you a little bit of freedom and flexibility to do something fun or frivolous. But if you take a hit in the market during a particular year, you have to reduce the withdrawal to compensate.

And there will be no dipping in for a European vacation if it's not in the budget. There is a big difference between pulling out 4 percent and pulling out even slightly more—say, 5 percent. Imagine you have $600,000 in savings and a life expectancy of twenty-five more years. If you limit your withdrawals to 4 percent and put 60 percent of your money in stocks (with the rest in bonds or other conservative asset classes), you have an 80 percent chance of making your money last. If you withdraw 5 percent annually, you have only a 50 percent chance of making your money last that quarter decade. Ouch.

I'm not going to lie to you. Catching up is hard work. But you can do it. After all, isn't knowing you have enough to live well, no matter how long you live, worth a little extra struggle? Absolutely.

Get Help If You Need It

There are times in life when asking for help is so much smarter than struggling with a problem on your own. This is one of those times. This book will set you on the right course, but at some point you may decide you want a financial professional to hold your hand and offer you personalized advice on everything from rebalancing your retirement accounts to buying life insurance. What's stopping you from finding such a person?

You're uncomfortable with risk. Remember earlier when I talked about women being more reluctant than men to take risks with their money? Hiring someone to help you make decisions about your hard-earned savings certainly seems like a risky move. How can you know for sure that a perfect stranger is smart enough and objective enough to know what to do with your money? How do you know that this person won't push you to be more aggressive than you're comfortable being? What if you end up with a real jerk? That, you tell yourself, is a risk you can't afford.

There's the risk that you might look stupid. You're intimidated by money and all the jargon that goes with it. But rather than viewing that as the perfect reason to go to a planner, you're scared of showing how much you don't know—or, more likely, how much you *think* you don't know.

And then there's the big one. Joyce, a nutritionist, put it perfectly: "*I can't find anyone I trust.*" You figure you'll have to interview fifteen people or more before you'll find someone you click with. That's such a cumbersome job, why bother?

A lot of your reluctance is well founded. But there are plenty of professionals out there who will truly help you meet your financial goals. Also—although realizing it's getting late in the game is a good reason to seek professional help—you may want to consider hiring a planner for other reasons as well:

- **Life has thrown you a curveball, and you're in transition.** Going through a divorce or losing a spouse are probably the first transitions that come to mind. But I encourage you to think more broadly. At many stages of life your financial picture may change dramatically. You're promoted and suddenly have a heftier salary than you imagined. You start a family. You're gradually taking on more responsibility for your aging parents. Your parents pass along a sizable inheritance. Any of these changes can trigger the need for good, solid financial planning to ensure you make the moves now that will secure your future.

- **Life has gotten way too busy.** As I said earlier, my philosophy on managing your finances is simple: Someone has to do the work. That person can be you, or you can hire out. But if you are at a point in your life when you're simply too busy, it's a sign that you're taking responsibility—not shirking it—if you wave the white flag and hire someone.

- **Inertia has started to set in.** You've used the online calculators to see what you need for the future; you've diligently set your goals; you've even put a chunk of money aside. But when it comes to actually choosing savings and investment accounts, calling the toll-free numbers, and making the withdrawals, you freeze. You simply can't get started. A planner can help you jump-start that process and provide the structure, deadlines, and help you need to get going. There's nothing like having a coach in your corner.

- **You're starting your own business.** A good planner can provide the information you need on lots of things you won't have time to research yourself. Some examples: What kind of and how much insurance will you need for yourself and your business? What self-employed retirement plan is right for you? How long can you manage on a minimal salary while you give your business space to grow?

Do you recognize yourself in one of those scenarios? Then you're ready. But who among the thousands of planners out there do you turn to? The tremendous growth in the financial planning industry in the past two decades has made that question hard to answer. It seems everyone who does anything with money is calling herself a financial planner these days. Even traditional stockbrokers at big Wall Street firms prefer the more consumer-friendly sounding "financial adviser" title, although their job—selling stocks—has basically stayed the same.

Planners themselves throw around an alphabet soup of certifications and designations after their names. CFP, for instance, stands for Certified Financial Planner. If you hire a CPA/PFS, you'll get a Certified Public Accountant who is also a Personal Financial Specialist. Or you may run across a ChFC, which stands for Chartered Financial Consultant. Though you can't tell it from the title, this person is actually a specialist in insurance.

I'm going to let you in on a secret—and it's a real shortcut for picking a planner. The letters after the names are not nearly as important as the answer to one fundamental question: How does the planner get paid? You want to hire a fee-only planner if possible, not someone who earns commissions. Why? These advisers are paid a flat fee for their services. No commission means less conflict of interest. A fee-only planner won't be tempted to sell you something—an insurance policy, mutual fund, whatever—simply because she or he will make more money on this deal than on a different product. It's almost impossible for a commission-based planner to be totally objective if she or he is getting paid to sell you something.

Fee-only planners are getting paid directly by you. They get a flat fee for the plan, a fee by the hour, or a percentage of the assets you give them to manage (1 percent is typical). Their paycheck isn't tied to a particular financial product; it's tied to making you happy. And by the way, don't be fooled by terms like *fee plus commission* or *fee offset.* These types of planners are compensated by commissions, too.

So what do you do now? Start with the National Association of Personal Financial Advisors, an organization of fee-only financial planners. Go to the website (www.napfa.org), and plug in your zip code. You'll get a list of names in your area.

Next, go to the Financial Planning Association (www.fpanet.org) and do the same. This site has names of planners who are paid by commission as well as those who are fee-only. So make sure you specify what you're looking for. It's worth the trip, because the FPA database is so large.

Searching online is one way to get names. But don't forget to ask friends, family, and people whose financial skills you admire (your accountant, insurance agent, estate planning attorney) for recommendations.

Once you get a list of prospective candidates, you'll need a little face time with each of them to figure out who's right for you. Most planners will schedule a get-to-know-you session for free. Those who won't get scratched from your list immediately. Use that time wisely. Bring the following checklist of questions with you, and listen carefully to the answers:

Q: How long have you been in the business?
A: More experience is better. You want someone who has been doing this for at least five years, but you also want someone with enough energy and enthusiasm to keep up with the latest developments.

Q: Will I be working with you or meeting with an associate?
A: If the answer is an associate, that's not necessarily bad, but you'll need to make sure the two of you (you and the associate) are also compatible. Ask

the planner to call her associate in so you can get a first impression now, not after you sign up.

Q: Do you offer comprehensive planning?

A: This is a big buzzword in the business these days, but it is important. It simply means, is your planner smart about all aspects of finance, not just one specialty, such as insurance or stocks. Will she or he be able to help you plan for college, buy a house, and deal with retirement? To get a feel for how comprehensive your prospective planner is, ask if she offers advice on goal setting, budgeting, tax planning, investments, estate planning, insurance, tuition saving, and retirement planning. If she answers affirmatively, you know you're in good hands.

Q: Are you (or is your firm) registered as an investment adviser?

A: Federal and state laws require that most advisers be registered with the Securities and Exchange Commission or your state's regulatory agency. Your planner may have a good reason why she is not registered, but it's a good idea to ask, get her explanation, and see what your gut instinct is about the situation.

Q: Have you ever been cited by a professional or regulatory governing body for disciplinary reasons?

A: Surprisingly, many planners will tell you if they have been. And they may have a good explanation when they tell their side of the story. Nonetheless, my natural skepticism says move on. Why trust anyone with a less than stellar reputation?

Q: Can you provide me with references?

A: Most planners will give you the names of satisfied customers and other professionals who can vouch for them. Go ahead and call the references. Obviously the names the planner gives you are not going to give a negative review. But listen for little hints of annoyance in the conversation that can signal something that might really bother you. A friend of mine called a reference recently, and the client raved about the planner. But as she continued talking about all of her great qualities, the client let slip, more than once, that the planner was really, really hard to get on the phone. That was enough of a red flag to get my friend to move to the next name on her list.

Q: Can you show me a plan you did for someone else?

A: This will give you the best sense of how the planner thinks and how aggressive she's willing to be. This is important because a planner can easily say you can meet your goals by playing with the numbers and upping the return she expects your investments to make over the years. But is she being realistic? Another friend recently nixed her planner because he told her the $30,000 she had stashed away for her son's college tuition was more than enough to pay the bills. When my friend dug a little further, she found that the planner was using a 10 percent average annual return to meet that goal. But the 529 plan my friend was invested in wasn't earning anywhere near that much. What's more, as her child got older, the college savings plan would automatically switch to lower-risk, lower-yielding investments. Be sure the planner is using realistic calculations for returns at a level of risk with which you're comfortable.

Q: How will I pay you, and how much will it cost?

A: All the planners you interview may be fee-only, but different planners have different payment structures. Some charge a flat fee—say, $2,000 for a comprehensive plan and quarterly meetings. Recently some planners have agreed to charge hourly rates. You pay upwards of $100 or $150 an hour for as many sessions as you need to address particular needs. Or, if you want a planner who has the power to buy and sell investments for you, she'll charge a percentage of assets, usually 1 percent per year. (Sometimes these sorts of planners will impose small commissions, too. I'm fine with that as long as they represent a small piece of what you're being charged overall.) Planners who charge this way usually deal with higher-net-worth individuals and impose a minimum on the amount of money you need to do business with them.

Trust Your Gut

I am a big believer in trusting your gut once you get the answers to your questions. That means, if you find it easier to talk money with a woman, then you hire a woman. It means that if the planner in town with the very best reputation and the very best credentials rubs you the wrong way, then you walk away. And it means you do what you need to do to get the most out of this relationship.

Hiring a planner means you're delegating some tasks and taking some of the pressure off yourself. But I won't lie to you: It does not mean that you won't have to do any work. Planners can motivate and educate you to make smart decisions. But in the end, you're the one who has the final say. And you're the one who has to dig deep into your financial life to figure out exactly what is right for you. Before you begin, make sure you're willing to do the following:

- *Disclose every detail of your financial life.*
- *Question and prioritize your goals. Financial planning, with or without help, is all about meeting those goals. Push yourself to be clearheaded and determined about what you want in the future.*
- *Do what the planner tells you to—within reason of course. If you've never gotten around to writing a will or finding a guardian for your children, and the planner says this is the first priority, you've got to be willing to do it.*
- *Be honest about your risk tolerance. A good planner will never go beyond your comfort level, but you have to tell her what that is.*
- *Be realistic. If you have a weak stomach for risk but huge financial dreams, you're going to have a disconnect with your planner. You'll need to adjust one or the other—risk tolerance or goals—to make a financial plan work.*

In the end, though, it's worth it. People who use financial advisors end up with substantially more in savings and other assets than those who don't.

LOOK HOW FAR YOU'VE COME!

It's discouraging, I know, to feel you've let too much time lapse before starting to gear up financially. But now you know—it's not too late! It's *never* too late. You have tools at your disposal: catch-up provisions, your paid-off house, your ability to continue to work and earn. And now you know how to use them—and how to get help if you need it. What remains? Protecting this newly found nest egg. Read on . . .

I am getting married. Does that mean I need life insurance?

In fact, it doesn't. You need life insurance when there are other people depending on your income for their life support. That usually happens when you have children, not when you get married (unless your new spouse is going to rely on your income immediately). Or you may need life insurance if you have a parent depending on you for financial support. You don't need it if you're single with no dependents—and any life insurance salesman who tells you otherwise is giving you a line. Once you have dependents, use the worksheet later in the next chapter to figure out how much insurance you need and what sort you should buy.

I stay at home with the kids. Do we need life insurance on me?

You probably should have some. The question you should be asking yourself is, If something were to happen to you, how much would it cost your spouse to hire someone to take care of your children and do all the other things you do for the family? Next, figure out how many years a person like that would be needed. Then you can buy either a policy that will pay out a lump sum big enough to cover all those years or one that—if you invested it—would spill off enough money (invested conservatively) to pay

for the services your spouse and kids would need each year. It's a big mistake to figure that since you don't earn money you don't have real financial value. Any woman knows that is decidedly untrue.

My husband and I disagree on the issue of life support. I want it even if my condition looks catastrophic. He doesn't. Does this mean we shouldn't give each other the ability to make health-care decisions on each other's behalf? Should we give it to our parents instead?

The fact that you've discussed this with your husband makes me think that putting this ability—called a health-care proxy—in each other's hands is the right thing to do. You know his wishes. He knows yours. What you both need now is complete confidence that he'll act as you would want him to act and that you'll do the same for him. And if you're secure in your relationship, I imagine you have the confidence that you need. What you can do to cover your bases is to share your wishes with your parents as well (and have him share his wishes with someone of his choosing). Then name that person as a successor proxy. If your husband is unable to carry out your wishes, he'll have the ability to turn the power over to your number two.

CHAPTER 10

"I Don't Want to Think About It"

DON'T BITCH

Death. *Divorce. Disability.* What is it about these D-words that makes us turn our heads? That makes us feel as if we can't—here's another D-word—*deal?* It's our own sense of superstition, our own sense of impending . . . *doom.*

So what do we do instead of thinking and instead of dealing? Not a thing. Instead, we walk through our lives wearing blinders. We don't take action beforehand. We suffer the consequences after.

But here's the thing: Thinking about death or divorce or disability or other negative life events is not going to make them happen. Personally, I don't believe there's such a thing as tempting fate. Give me a ladder and I'll walk under it every single time. But even if you are a big believer in tempting fate, in superstition, let me respectfully suggest that doing nothing could quite possibly make those fate-oriented gods pretty peeved.

The bottom line is that there are some things that adults have to deal with in this life. It's part of being a grownup, and most certainly a parent. It's part of not leaving a big mess for someone else to clean up. It's your responsibility. And not thinking about or acting on that responsibility can result in some pretty dire consequences.

Here are the excuses I hear time and time again. Here are the results. And here are the often dreadful, almost always avoidable consequences.

The excuse: *"I don't want to think about unexpected bills."*
The result: You don't have an emergency cushion.
The consequences: You can't get out of debt. If you don't have an emergency cushion and something unexpected occurs—perhaps your car dies, your dog needs surgery, or you lose your job—where are you going to come up with the money to pay for the repair or the operation or daily life? You're going to put the payment on a credit card, then struggle to pay it back at 16 or 18 or 24 percent. And if you don't have a credit card, you're going to borrow from an even more uncomfortable source—a friend, a relative, a parent. Until you can pay it back, you'll walk around feeling bad about yourself, worried about your future, and worried about your family. The more your debt mounts, the more sleep you're going to lose.

The excuse: *"I don't want to think about dying."*
The results: You don't have a will, don't have guardians for your kids, don't have life insurance.
The consequences: By not writing a will, you are essentially letting your state decide who will get your stuff. If you're married, your stuff will default to your spouse. If you're not, there is a long list of relatives who will be entitled to it, generally in this order: your children, parents, siblings, grandparents, aunts and uncles, cousins. But what if you'd prefer someone else have your belongings? What if you'd prefer to give them to a cause you believe in? You're out of luck. Why? Because you didn't write a will.

If you're not married and don't have any children, not writing a will is not the smartest thing you've ever done, but it's not a tragedy. If you have kids and you don't have a will, what you've done is absolutely unconscionable. A will is the only document that allows you to name guardians for your minor children. If you and your spouse were to die together, there would likely be a lengthy and potentially very unpleasant guardianship hearing in which various people would essentially battle over your kids—or worse, in which no one would. When you bring children into this world, it is your responsibility to make sure that they are taken care of physically and emotionally if you leave it prematurely.

It is also your responsibility to make sure that they are taken care of financially. If anyone—children, a spouse, parent, or any other friend or relative—depends on your income for support and sustenance, you need life insurance. Otherwise, if you were to leave this earth, you would rob that person of a lifeline on which you've allowed him or her to depend.

The excuse: *"I don't want to think about getting sick or injured."*
The results: You don't have disability insurance, don't have health insurance, don't have a health-care proxy, and don't have a living will.
The consequences: The very same people who need life insurance—those who have others depending on their income for support—need disability insurance as well. Without it, their support vanishes. But there's another person who also should be concerned about your becoming disabled: you. If you're disabled and unable to work, who would take care of you? Who would support you? If the answer is no one, then you need to buy disability insurance to ensure your own comfortable survival.

Although there are people who don't need disability insurance (those whose spouse could provide for their needs) and don't need life insurance (most single people), everyone needs health insurance. Forty million Americans, however, don't have it. The consequences of not having health insurance are many: not being able to see a doctor of your choice; not being able to afford the specific medicines that would cure your particular problems; incurring debts, massive debts; being forced into bankruptcy. Health problems are the number-one cause of bankruptcies in this country. If you have health insurance, your chances of being able to avoid that particular court improve.

And there are other consequences of not pondering the effects of being injured or ill: You probably don't have a living will or health-care proxy—medical directives that tell doctors, hospitals, and your loved ones what kind of care you'd want if you were unable to voice your choices. Do you want life support? Feeding tubes? Pain management? It's a crapshoot unless you fill out these simple (and often free) forms.

The excuse: *"I don't want to think about getting divorced."*
The result: You don't have a prenuptial agreement.
The consequences: If you get divorced, the battle over stuff may be much more contentious than it needs to be. I'm not arguing—as some famous divorce attorneys will—that everyone needs a prenup. But you should ab-

solutely consider one if you're bringing significant assets or liabilities (like big student loans) to the marriage, if you have kids from another marriage, if you have your own or a family business, if you're anticipating a big inheritance, or if—for whatever reason—you want one.

Putting Your Protection Plan in Place

Right about now, you're probably wondering, Where are the Maps to a Million in this chapter? There are none. This chapter is the only one in the book that's not about getting rich. It's about *staying* rich. It's about preserving all the wealth you've managed to accumulate for yourself and your loved ones.

All the items I've mentioned—life, health, and disability insurance; wills; living wills and health-care proxies; prenups (and, for those who've already nupped, postnups)—help you protect yourself, without worry, so that you can enjoy the rich life you're building. As I said earlier, putting them in place is not challenging death, it's not being overly cynical, and it's not even being a glass-half-empty person. It's being practical and smart. Let me tell you how to do it, piece by piece.

A Will

What is it?

A will is a document that specifies how you want your possessions distributed in the event of your death and names guardians for minor children.

How much will it cost?

The cost depends on how complicated the will is. Many attorneys will draw up a basic estate plan—consisting of a will, bypass trust (a trust that preserves your ability and your spouses' ability to avoid estate taxes in many cases), health-care proxy, durable power of attorney for finances, and living will—for $500 to $1,000. You can do it yourself with software for a fraction of that amount.

Where do I get it?

Wills written on the back of napkins have held up in court. That's not how I recommend you go about it. My preference is for you to see an estate planning attorney—that is, a lawyer who specializes in drawing up wills. But, as I noted, that option might cost more than you want to spend. If you decide to use software, see if you can find a lawyer who—for $100 or so—will take a look at your document before you sign it. To find a list of lawyers in your area who specialize in estate planning, use the search engine at findlaw.com. Even better, ask friends or colleagues for the names of estate planning attorneys they've used and liked.

Who should be my children's guardians?

This question—the toughest one in the entire chapter if not the entire *book*—prevents many Americans from getting wills in the first place. It's incredibly hard—I know—to think about who you'd want to care for your children if something happened to you and their father. I recommend naming a single person, not a couple who could possibly—in the future—get divorced. Make a short list of the people you're considering; then use these questions to come to a final decision:

- *Does this person have the time to take care of my children?*
- *Does he or she share my values about what's important in life?*
- *Is this person young enough and in good enough health to take on this challenging task?*
- *Is the person geographically desirable, or would the person or my children be required to move?*
- *Does he or she have the resources necessary (or will I be leaving enough in life insurance and other resources so that's not an issue)?*
- *Is he or she willing to do it?*

Try your best not to be crushed if the person you decide on says—for whatever reason—no. You're better off having that information now and making another choice now than having your family struggle with it later. And do not let your fear about what the people you are *not* choosing will think of your decision get in the way of completing this process. This is a personal matter. No one but you, the father of your children, and the guardian you've selected needs to know.

A Living Will

What is it?

A living will is a document that tells a doctor or hospital what sort of action you want taken in a dire situation. Essentially, it answers the question "Do you want life support?"

How much will it cost?

Generally a living will costs very little. Often it costs nothing.

Where do I get it?

A basic estate plan comes with a will, living will, durable power of attorney for finances, and a health-care proxy. But if you don't feel like paying a lawyer, plenty of websites offer these forms—some for free, some not. Check the website of your state's bar association. Fill out the form and sign it. You don't need a lawyer. You don't even need a notary. All you need are two disinterested witnesses to put their John Hancocks on the page. Note: If you split your time between two or more states, it's a good idea to fill out the forms for each state so that you can present doctors or hospitals with a document they're familiar with. Just make sure your wishes are consistent.

A Health-Care Proxy

What is it?

A health-care proxy is a document that gives a person you choose the authority to make medical decisions on your behalf. Because many medical problems tend to be gray, not black and white, the health-care proxy is critical. In a pinch, the doctor or hospital will rely on the word of the person you've named rather than on what your living will says.

How much will it cost?

The cost will range from nothing to a few dollars for the form.

Where do I get it?

Your lawyer can prepare the document. But if you're going it alone, a terrific living will/health-care proxy combo document called "The Five Wishes Living Will" is available at agingwithdignity.org. What makes this document so great is that it asks you questions in plain English. Answer them, and you've done the job. It's effective in more than twenty states.

Whom should I name as my health-care proxy?

Generally, if you're married, you'll name your spouse. If you're not married, then name an adult child, a sibling, a parent, or some other person whom you trust to carry out your wishes. Opt for a single person (not a couple who might be inclined to disagree with each other) with the fortitude to execute your wishes despite what others might say. Naming a second, backup, proxy is a good idea, too, in case your first choice is out of the country or decides he or she can't handle the pressure. If you ever change your mind, that's okay. A health-care proxy is "revocable," which means that it can be changed at any time. You should try to gather the old documents and give the people who have them new copies, but don't worry if you can't round them all up. The one you signed most recently is the one that carries the power.

Durable Power of Attorney for Finances

What is it?

A durable power of attorney for finances is a document that gives another person the power to make financial decisions for you—including writing checks and conducting other transactions on your accounts—if you're unable to make them for yourself.

How much will it cost?

If you have a lawyer draw up the document as part of the initial package, the cost will typically range from $500 to $1,000. If you do it yourself, you can buy a form on the Internet for $15 or so.

Where do I get it?

Again, I recommend using a lawyer. But forms do abound on the Internet. Make sure you use one that is recommended by the Better Business Bureau if you go that route.

To whom should I give power of attorney?

As with a health-care proxy, most spouses give this power to each other. If you're not married and without a partner, consider whether there is anyone in your life who would be willing to handle your financial matters if you were not able to do so. Adult children, siblings, parents, and close friends are all possibilities. Note, however, that handling your finances on an ongoing basis may turn out to be considerable work. If you don't think anyone in your life is up to or willing to take that on, it's fine to give this power to an attorney or an accountant whom you've worked with for a long time and trust implicitly. Unlike a friend or family member, a professional will bill your accounts for his or her time. Make sure you understand the precise cost of this arrangement before you set it up.

Health Insurance

What is it?

A health insurance policy pays for some or all of your medical care, such as doctor visits, hospitalization, prescription drugs, and various types of therapy. There are different types of health insurance at various prices:

- *Traditional indemnity policies cover, typically, 80 percent of the cost of your health care. You pay the other 20 percent after fulfilling a deductible.*
- *HMOs (health maintenance organizations) allow you to see a specific group of doctors and go to specific hospitals and have most (if not all) of the bill paid. Sometimes there are other restrictions, such as a limited number of visits or a deductible.*
- *PPOs (preferred provider organizations) allow you to see a specific group of doctors at discounted rates. If you see a physician within the network, you pay a small fee called a co-pay. If you go outside the network for medical care, you pay higher prices.*
- *Health Savings Accounts are generally high-deductible health-care policies with tax-advantaged savings accounts attached. You buy a health insurance plan with a high*

deductible (one that will cover most of your medical ex-
penses after you hit a deductible of at least $1,050 for a sin-
gle person or $2,100 for a family). Then, you open a Health
Savings Account and fund it with pretax money up to or
equal to your deductible. You can use the money to pay for
medical expenses, but you can also invest it. Any money you
don't use for health care can be withdrawn after retirement
and used in any way you desire. But before retirement, if
you use the money for things other than medical expenses,
you'll pay taxes and a 10 percent penalty. Because the de-
ductible is so high, the premiums for these policies are sig-
nificantly less than a traditional health-care policy.

Who needs it?

Everyone needs health insurance. The statistic making the rounds is that the average family spends only $700 a year on health care. That's all well and good, until you get sick. A few weeks or even a few days in the hospital can mean the loss of your savings. Get sicker than that and you're looking at the loss of your retirement funds, even your house. You're looking at bankruptcy. That's why every American needs health insurance. If you can't afford a policy that will help you pay to go to the doctor every time you need to go, a plan with a high deductible—which will be cheaper than a plan with a lower deductible—is a good solution. It will provide you with the hospitalization coverage you need in a true crisis without breaking the bank—and simultaneously allow you to put something away for the future. If you are unemployed and temporarily without coverage, consider bridging the gap with short-term coverage. Short-term policies are relatively cheap because they exclude coverage for existing medical conditions and reimburse a smaller percentage of your costs. Go to eHealthInsurance.com to begin shopping.

How much will it cost?

Premiums vary widely depending on whether you have a company/employer sharing the bill with you or you're going it alone. Today premiums for families average more than $14,000, according to the National Coalition on Healthcare. That's why so many families are uninsured. If you're shopping on your own, you can bring the cost down—way down—by shopping around for the specific type of care you need rather than for a comprehensive policy. One thing to remember: If you're self-employed and buying your own policy, you will get a hefty tax deduction on the premium.

Where should I buy it?

If you're not getting health care through your employer, I'd recommend shopping at least two or three sources. One source should be an agent who specializes in working with individuals. Ask your life or auto insurer for a local referral, or go to www.nahu.org, the National Association of Health Underwriters, to find a person in your area. Another source can be a website specializing in the individual market. Finally, find out if any professional organization that you belong to offers group coverage for which you are eligible.

Life Insurance

What is it?

Life insurance is insurance that provides for payment of a predetermined amount of money to your beneficiary when you die. There are essentially two types of life insurance: term and cash value. For most people, term insurance is the better, more cost-effective insurance to buy, but for others cash-value coverage makes some sense. Read on.

- *Term insurance provides a death benefit, period. You buy it for a specific period—the term—which is anywhere from a single year to thirty years. You pay premiums every year to keep the policy in place. If you die before the term is up, the policy pays out. If you don't, it doesn't; it expires, and that's the end of it. Buying term insurance is the only way most people are able to buy as much insurance as they need at a price they can afford.*
- *Cash-value insurance—variations of which are called whole life, universal life, variable life, and many other things— combines insurance (a death benefit) with an investment account. The premiums are much higher than those for term insurance, but the policy builds value over time. It does not expire. If you decide not to continue paying for the policy,*

you may lose the death benefit, but there will be some cash for you to pull out. In a pinch, you can borrow against the policy. When you die, it pays your beneficiaries the predetermined death benefit plus any cash value your account has accrued.

Who needs it?

Anyone who has others depending on her or his income or services for support needs life insurance. If you stay home and take care of your children or an elderly parent, the services you provide have value, and you should think about buying a life insurance policy.

How much life insurance will I need?

Essentially, you need enough to provide for your dependents for as long as they'll remain in the family nest, plus the cost of any large expenses you want to cover—such as paying off the mortgage or paying for college. A lot of insurance agents (remember, these are people who *sell* insurance for a living and make big commissions on your premiums) use rules of thumb like eight times your income or ten times your income. I think rules of thumb work for very few people. I prefer simple worksheets instead, like this one:

CALCULATE YOUR LIFE INSURANCE NEEDS

1. *Annual living expenses for surviving spouse:* _____
2. *Number of years needed:* _____
3. *Multiply line 1 by line 2:* _____

4. *Annual child-care costs (not covered by surviving spouse's income):* _____
5. *Number of years needed:* _____
6. *Multiply line 4 by line 5:* _____

7. *Annual children's education costs (not including college; not covered by surviving spouse's income):* _____
8. *Number of years needed:* _____
9. *Multiply line 7 by line 8:* _____

10. *Other annual child-related living expenses (not covered by surviving spouse's income):* _____
11. *Number of years needed:* _____
12. *Multiply line 10 by line 11:* _____

13. *Cost of college (if desired):* _____
14. *Mortgage payoff (if desired):* _____
15. *Debt reduction:* _____
16. *Funeral costs:* _____
17. *Other:* _____
18. *Total of lines 13–17:* _____

Add lines 3, 6, 9, 12, and 18: _____

This is the amount of life insurance you should buy. Note: Each spouse should fill out the worksheet separately.

How much will it cost?

Premiums vary widely, but in general they go up with the amount of cash-value coverage you buy and down with the amount of term insurance you buy.

Where should I buy it?

Shop for term coverage on the Internet; search engines have made the market very efficient. Purchase cash-value coverage through an agent. Be sure you're talking to an agent who is recommended by a friend or colleague you trust. Also, be sure that the insurance carrier you're purchasing coverage from is rated A or better by A. M. Best (go to www.ambest.com to check company ratings). The higher the rating, the better the financial health of the insurer is.

Disability Insurance

What is it?

Disability insurance is insurance that pays out to you if you're unable to work. Usually, you'll get short-term disability coverage through your employer. Long-term disability coverage is the more pressing need. According to the Health Insurance Association of America, about one-third of people ages 30 to 65 will be forced out of work for three months or more by a disability at some point during their lives. Even if your employer does provide you with a long-term disability policy, the coverage may not be enough. You want coverage that provides about 60 percent of your total salary and benefits, and you want to be sure that the policy lasts until you are age 65 or 67, when Social Security will kick in at an acceptable rate.

Here are three other things to look for in any disability policy you're considering:

- **Own-occupation coverage.** This essentially says the policy will pay if you're unable to work in your *chosen* field. Let's say that you are a nurse. If you don't have own-occupation coverage and your disability would not prevent you from operating, say, a cash register at a restaurant, your insurer could make the argument that you're able to work and could deny your claim.

- **Inflation protection.** The value of the dollar shrinks every year. Be sure that twenty years from now the policy will pay out enough for you to live on.

- **A 90-day waiting period before your benefits kick in.** A relatively long waiting period will lower your premiums. Waiting only 30 days will cause the price of your policy to go way up.

Who needs it?
If you do not have another source of income—say, from a spouse—that could cover your needs and the needs of your family if you're unable to work, you need disability insurance. Singles, who do not typically need life insurance, absolutely need disability insurance.

Where do I buy it?
If your employer offers a group disability policy, sign up immediately. Disability insurance is costly—which is one reason so few people buy it—but it's

much less expensive if you buy it through your employer. The group policy may not provide the coverage for 60 percent of your income that you're looking for. You can cover the rest with a "gap" policy purchased from your life insurance company or through a life insurance agent.

A Prenuptial Agreement

What is it?

A prenup is a contract between spouses that states how assets and debts are to be divided if the marriage ends. Every state has rules on how assets need to be disseminated if a marriage ends. A properly drawn prenup (or post-nup, a similar contract drawn up after marriage) allows you to make your own rules. You can stipulate, for instance, that certain assets be set aside for children from prior marriages or that a family cottage stays in the original family.

Prenups and postnups don't come into effect only in divorce; they also come into effect at death. Laws in every state spell out how much a spouse gets at death. If you don't want your spouse to get the full allotment (perhaps there's a child with special needs to be cared for), or if you want your spouse to get more than that allotment, simply writing your wishes into your will does *not* guarantee that your wishes will be carried out. Prenups and postnups are more effective because they're legal contracts in which your spouse waives a right to a piece of your estate.

How much will it cost?

Generally, prenups start at between $1,000 and $1,500 and go up from there. Each spouse needs a separate lawyer, which can add to legal fees. But keep in mind that in this day and age—when nearly half of all marriages end in divorce—a prenup can save you big money in legal fees. If you decide the terms of your divorce before you wed, there's little or nothing to haggle over later.

To keep the cost down, include provisions only for assets and liabilities. It's trendy right now to throw everything but the kitchen sink into prenups. Couples use them to specify everything—from who will walk the dog, and how much weight gain (if any) will be tolerated, to whether or not they'll have kids. At the very least, these clauses are nuisances for courts: You would be laughed out of the room for asking a judge to weigh in on whether you should be a size 10 or 14. At their worst, they may be at odds with public policy and can cause your entire prenuptial contract to be questioned. Keep in mind that anything that's not strictly related to property may not be enforceable in court.

Who needs one?

Traditional customers are people embarking on their second marriages who have children, retirement accounts, homes, or closely held businesses they want to protect. Today, anyone marrying for the first time with any of the above-mentioned items should consider a prenup as well. And it's not just current assets you need to worry about. You need to consider those coming down the pike—things like inheritances and future earnings. In some states, future earnings prospects are considered property when you divorce, so you want to protect them when you marry. We now live in a world where everyone has prospects. If you're a waitress, you hope to own a restaurant. If you're a teacher, you want to be principal. If those aspirations materialize, they should be protected. Also, understand that just as a marriage gives you some of the assets of your spouse, it can saddle you with the liabilities. If you're marrying someone with big credit card, student loan, or other unsecured debts, a prenup can let you off the hook.

Where do I get one?

Consult a lawyer who specializes in writing prenuptial agreements. In order for prenups (and postnups) to be enforceable, they must be fair and reasonable and entered into mutually at the time of creation. All assets must be disclosed. The agreement should be signed before the hall is rented, the band hired, and the invitations sent out. For that reason, it's best if they're signed more than thirty days before you get married; otherwise, a judge may decide one party coerced the other into signing by threatening to cancel the wedding unless it was done. That's not to say that any prenup signed within the month before the wedding won't hold up in court. The sooner you get it signed, however, the better off you are. Whether you're entering into this agreement as the wealthier or the poorer spouse, you shouldn't do it unless you can see a benefit. The wealthier spouse will lose less than he or she would have lost without the agreement; the poorer spouse will gain more than if he or she never married. The poorer spouse has to realize that if his or her betrothed is insisting on a prenup, the choice is not between an agreement and no-agreement; it's between agreement and no-marriage.

LOOK HOW FAR YOU'VE COME!

In the chapters leading up to this one, we cleared away your resistance to talking about money, earning more money, and amassing more money—in other words, your resistance to getting rich. I know, you never thought of yourself as having your guard up against wealth, but in fact you did. Now that it's down and the money is starting to pour in, you need to make sure it's not fleeting. You need to do that for yourself, for your loved ones, for your future. And the way you do that is with all of the protective mechanisms we talked about in this chapter—with a will and the rest of a basic estate plan, with the right insurance policies, with a prenuptial or postnuptial agreement where it's called for. These are things, I know, that you don't like to think about on a regular basis. But if you are an adult (and perhaps a parent) walking this planet, *not* thinking about them is wholly irresponsible. The good news is, you can think about them once, put the correct tools and measures into place, and go on with your life. Then, once a year—perhaps on your birthday—go back and consider whether anything has changed and any revisions are needed. Does the guardian you chose for your child no longer make sense? Has your income skyrocketed to the point where you need more life insurance? Calling your attorney or insurance agent will be easier the second (or third) time around. I promise.

LET'S REFLECT . . .

Whether you've worked your way through this book by reading page by page or skipped around looking for the chapters and sections that are most meaningful to you, it's important—right now—to take a deep breath and look at all the progress you've made. You've addressed the fears and excuses that stood in the way of dealing with your money. You've put into place some automatic mechanisms to get you started saving and investing. You've started to research ways to protect the new assets you're stockpiling. And you're headed directly to a richer life!

I applaud you for taking the steps to bring your finances under control. No longer will you find yourself wandering through your life, spending a little here, borrowing a little there, making unconscious choices. From now on, managing your finances is part of your greater master plan and you are clearly in charge.

You own your money. And because of that, you own your life.

Map to a Million

Woven through the book you'll find many examples of the different strategies you can employ in your life to spend a *little* less, earn and save a *little* more, invest a *little* smarter, and as a result stockpile a *whole lot* for your future life and future dreams. How much *is* a whole lot? A million dollars: $1,000,000.

Now, I know, becoming a millionaire may sound impossible. *Millionaire* may strike you as a term that's meant for other people, not you. But that's just not true. I'll show you in the pages that follow how a regular Jane—not a super earner or someone with megabucks in the bank, but a woman who's simply willing to put a little time and mental energy toward getting on her financial feet—can get to that million dollars.

How long you are willing to give yourself to achieve that goal directly shapes how much money you have to sock away each year in order to get there. If you have thirty years to stockpile your million—as many people aiming toward retirement do—then you have to come up with only $675 a month, or $8,100 a year. If you are getting matching dollars from an employer's 401(k) or other similar retirement plan, you don't even have to come up with all of that money yourself. If you want to reach your goal in half the time, I can show you how that works as well. But whether or not there's an employer match in the picture, you're going to have to be more aggressive in your saving (and perhaps in your earning as well). Whatever timetable you're look-ing at, if you put your mind to it, it can be done. Of that, I am positive.

THE MILLIONAIRE MATH

The Thirty-Year Millionaire

If—starting today—you can find $675 a month to invest, tax-deferred, at 8 percent, thirty years from today you'll have your million dollars. Here's where 401(k) plans are so useful. If you are in a 401(k) plan that matches, you may have to come up with much less money yourself.

If your plan matches: 100 percent
You need to save and contribute: $328.50 a month

If your plan matches: 50 percent
You need to save and contribute: $450 a month

If your plan matches: 25 percent
You need to save and contribute: $540 a month

The Twenty-Five-Year Millionaire

If—starting today—you can find $1,050 a month to invest, tax-deferred, at 8 percent, twenty-five years from today you'll have your million dollars. Again, watch a 401(k) plan with a match work its magic.

If your plan matches: 100 percent
You need to save and contribute: $525 a month

If your plan matches: 50 percent
You need to save and contribute: $700 a month

If your plan matches: 25 percent
You need to save and contribute: $840 a month

The Twenty-Year Millionaire

If—starting today—you can find $1,700 a month to invest, tax-deferred, at 8 percent, twenty years from today you'll have your million dollars. With a 401(k) match, you need even less.

If your plan matches: 100 percent
You need to save and contribute: $850 a month

If your plan matches: 50 percent
You need to save and contribute: $1,133 a month

If your plan matches: 25 percent
You need to save and contribute the maximum: $1,250 a month
  in the plan and invest another $140 outside your plan

The Fifteen-Year Millionaire

If you want to get to your million in fifteen years, you'll need to find $2,900 a month to invest at 8 percent, tax-deferred. If you are in a 401(k) plan that matches, you can contribute up to $15,000 a year, or $1,250 a month. You should save and contribute the maximum you're able. Then . . .

If your plan matches 100 percent, you'll need to invest an extra
  $400 outside your plan—or $1,650 total each month—to meet
  your goal.

If your plan matches 50 percent, you'll need to invest another
  $1,025 outside your plan—or $2,275 total each month—to
  meet your goal.

If your plan matches 25 percent, you'll need to invest another
  $1,338 outside your plan—or $2,588 total each month—to
  meet your goal.

HOW AND WHERE CAN YOU COME UP WITH THAT MONEY?

Spend Less

You may need a cell phone with call waiting, caller id, and voice mail—but you don't need a landline with those features as well. Drop the latter (or cut back to very basic service). **Save $40 a month.**

Reduce your homeowners and auto insurance costs by raising your deductible from $250 to $1,000 on each. You can expect a break of 25 percent on homeowners and 40 percent on auto insurance. **Save $35 a month.**

Decide your future is worth one less night out each week. Instead, stay home, cook something, and catch up on great TiVo. Or invite your pals over for potluck and a mean game of Boggle. **Save $100 a month.**

Make every effort to be energy efficient. *At home:* Invest in a programmable thermostat, and use it to spend less on heat when you sleep. Insulate where appropriate (including the hot water pipes), and plug holes and cracks in windows and doors. *In your car:* Make sure the tires are fully inflated, the oil is changed every three thousand miles, and filters are checked at the same time. Drive the speed limit. Try to carpool. **Save $100 a month.**

Grocery-shop with a list. If you go to the store with no idea of what you need to buy (or even want to buy) or, worse, if you go to the store hungry, you'll end up spending twice what you planned. Instead, once a week sit down and do your best to decide what you need to buy and then stick to your list. Your wallet (and your thighs) will thank you.

Save $120 a month.

Pay off your car, and don't replace it with a new one. Take good enough care of the old vehicle so that it'll roll toward the six-figure mile marker without a hitch. Alternate scenario: Your lease is up. Instead of trading up for a Mercedes, trade down for a reasonable Subaru or Honda (maybe even a hybrid), and save yourself a decent chunk of change.

Save $200 a month.

Get rid of the health-club membership you haven't used in six months.
Save $80 a month.

Bundle your cable and Internet services, or go to a basic package.
Save $40 a month.

Take on a household chore you haven't done for a while. Whether it's wash-ing the car, bathing the dog, handwashing (rather than dry cleaning) your sweaters, find something you delegated and reclaim it.
Save $80 a month.

Stop shopping. Okay, I acknowledge you may not be able to stop shopping completely. There are gifts to buy and necessities to pick up. But you and I both know we spend a lot of our disposable income on items that are disposable as well. Track your spending for a month to figure out where that money is going, and put it into your savings instead.
Save $100 a month.

Trim the takeout tally. We all spend too much money on food on the fly. So buy coffee instead of cappuccino, a less-expensive sandwich instead of sushi. Bring lunch from home every once in a while, and keep a stash of (good) frozen pizzas in the freezer instead of dialing for delivery.
Save $75 a month.

Sign up for a flexible spending account. Pay for $2,000 in health care, child care, or elder care, and transportation with pretax dollars.
Save $45 a month.

Stop procrastinating. Certain things cost more when you purchase them at or close to the time you need them—shipping, vacations (airline tickets and hotel rooms), air conditioners and heaters, patio furniture, holiday decora-tions . . . you get the idea. If you do some advance planning, you can save a bundle.
Save $50 a month.

Pay Less Interest

You've probably already refinanced your mortgage. But did you know you can refinance your car loan as well? Your credit union and the Internet are the two places to start shopping for rates. Note: Unlike a mortgage refi, this is easy. You can do it within a day and at pretty much no cost. Refinance two car loans.   ***Save $60 a month.***

Once you've done some work on your credit score, it's time to lower the interest rates you're paying on your credit cards. Play the credit card game: Take lenders up on some of those bottom-of-the-barrel balance transfer rates you've been offered, and really make some headway on your debts. If you've got $10,000 in credit card debt (as most people do) and you're paying it off at 24 percent a year, it's costing you $2,400 annually just to pay the interest. Wipe that slate clean.   ***Save $200 a month.***

Do a little work on your student loans. If you haven't consolidated your student loans (I hope you did so when rates were at their lowest point in forty years), go ahead and call a lender or two. There may still be some money available to you. Signing up for direct deposit on those loans can cut your interest rate by one-quarter of 1 percent. And making your payments on time can knock another 1 to 2 percentage points off the rate in a few years' time. And, while I'm not likely to suggest you stretch out the term of a mortgage or a car loan, you *may* want to think about stretching out the terms of a student loan to lower your monthly payment and save more. Why? You're paying very little interest on this money. Conversely, you may be making a bundle on the money you're investing—particularly if you sock it into your 401(k) and get matching dollars.   ***Save $200 a month.***

Drop pre-paid mortgage insurance (PMI). If you've already paid down your house, or (as is more likely) if the value has grown in the real estate boom, you may be able to get rid of mortgage insurance. If you have paid in equity 22 percent in your home, it's up to the lender to let you know you're off the hook. Otherwise, it's up to you to realize you're at the 20 percent mark (that's the amount of your home you have to own to qualify) and ask for the release. The savings can be significant.   ***Save $50 a month.***

Earn More

When was the last time you got a raise? If it's been a while, you're probably underpaid. That means it's time to ready your ammunition and ask for one. If you work for yourself and bill your clients, it's time to raise your rates. Simply write a letter explaining that the cost of doing business has gone up, that you haven't increased your prices in, say, three years, and that starting a month from now you'll be raising them by 10 percent. Thank your customers for their business and mail the letter. Nothing will happen— except you'll see the size of your paycheck go up.   *Earn $250 a month.*

Earn more on your savings. You know the $10,000 you have sitting in a checking account earning—well—nothing? Move it to a savings account at an interest rate of 4 percent.   *Earn $33 a month.*

Work one extra hour per day—seven hours per week—at a rate of $10 per day. If you aren't working now, that means taking on a job that's truly part-time or moonlighting. If you are working, it means perhaps putting in a little overtime.   *Earn $304 per month.*

Bank your tax refund, or change your withholding and bank the extra earnings. The average American gets a tax refund of about $2,400 annually.   *Earn $200 a month.*

Sell things you're not using anymore. Everyone has junk sitting around the house. Or, if not junk, good stuff your kids have outgrown, you're not wearing or using, stuff that's simply not to your taste anymore. There's a market for this stuff. It's called eBay. Or if you'd rather not go electronic, then have a really big garage sale.   *Earn $100 a month.*

Choose Wealth

If you get to this point and you're still not hitting your targets, then it's time to take a serious look at your life. It may be outsized for your income. You may be living in a home that's more expensive than you can afford (if you want to save for your future). You may be driving cars that are too costly (or just driving too many cars), or vacationing too often and too luxuriously, or spending more than you can really afford on gadgets or clothing or furniture or eating out or entertainment or the kids. You may have put your children into a pricey private school thinking you could afford it, and you may now realize that you can pay the property taxes in your good neighborhood or you can pay the private school tuition but you can't do both. The choice is up to you, and my suggestion is that you choose wealth.

Making any one big change—trading a large house for a small one, moving to a neighborhood where property taxes are significantly lower, switching from private to public schools, switching to a more lucrative career, eliminating full-time day care or a babysitter, getting rid of a car (and car payment)—can yield $500, $600, $700 a month or more. You just have to remember that these are lifestyle decisions. It's smart, if you can, to try a test run. Stop driving the car a month before you unload it. Take a break from day care or your sitter before you quit. Add fifteen minutes to your commute each day for a month. Do all of these things to be sure you'll be able to stomach them. Then go ahead and make an actual big change.

Save $500 a month or more.

Total Potential Savings: $2,962

Add all the items I've suggested together and you come up with more than enough money to hit your million, no matter which schedule you choose. And remember, you are back in control of your money now—this is all a choice. The thing to keep in mind is that earning money, just like spending money, reflects a personal thought process. Do what feels right to you in order to make it work.

PUT THE MONEY WHERE YOU CAN'T TOUCH IT

The final key to your quest for a million is putting all this money where you can't get your hands on it. That means having it funneled out of your paycheck automatically and putting it into your retirement plan. You want to make sure that you grab as many matching dollars as possible. That means maxing out your ability to put money into your 401(k)—particularly when matching dollars are available.

After you exhaust your ability to contribute to a 401(k), then put money into the following accounts in the following order. You may not be eligible for them all, but take advantage of the ones you are able to put money in:

Roth IRA

SEP-IRA, Keogh, or Roth 401(k) for the self-employed

Tax-deductible IRA

Nondeductible traditional IRA

529 college saving plan

Health savings account

Here's what happens to your money when it's put away to grow tax-free:

SAVING AND INVESTING $675 MONTHLY: THE THIRTY-YEAR MILLIONAIRE

In 5 years you'll have $49,596

In 10 years you'll have $123,488

In 15 years you'll have $233,575

In 20 years you'll have $397,588

In 25 years you'll have $641,942

In 30 years you'll have $1,005,992

SAVING AND INVESTING $1,050 MONTHLY: THE TWENTY-FIVE-YEAR MILLIONAIRE

In 5 years you'll have $77,150

In 10 years you'll have $192,093

In 15 years you'll have $363,340

In 20 years you'll have $618,417

In 25 years you'll have $998,557

In 30 years you'll have $1,564,877

SAVING AND INVESTING $1,700 MONTHLY:
THE TWENTY-YEAR MILLIONAIRE

In 5 years you'll have $124,910

In 10 years you'll have $311,008

In 15 years you'll have $588,264

In 20 years you'll have $1,001,334

In 25 years you'll have $1,616,744

In 30 years you'll have $2,533,611

SAVING AND INVESTING $2,900 MONTHLY:
THE FIFTEEN-YEAR MILLIONAIRE

In 5 years you'll have $213,082

In 10 years you'll have $530,543

In 15 years you'll have $1,003,510

In 20 years you'll have $1,708,159

In 25 years you'll have $2,757,976

In 30 years you'll have $4,322,042

APR (annual percentage rate): The annual cost of borrowing money expressed in percentage terms. It includes not only interest but the fees you pay when you borrow the money. That is why APRs and yields on the same loan are different. APRs tend to be higher.

asset allocation: Distributing your investments across different asset classes (stocks, bonds, cash, real estate) as a way to lower your overall risk.

assets: Your belongings and investments, or the things you own.

basis point: One one-hundredth of a percentage point. Often used in describing investment costs—for example: The expenses on this mutual fund are only 25 basis points. That means one-quarter of 1 percentage point.

beneficiary: The person whom you select to receive an asset if you die. You need to name beneficiaries for life insurance policies, retirement accounts, trusts, and annuities because these are assets that cannot be bequeathed in your will. It may be mandatory to name a spouse as a beneficiary. Check with your benefits officer or life insurance agent.

bond: An investment in the debt of a corporation, government, or municipality. Bonds work like this: You loan money (the principal) to the seller of the bond. For that loan, the seller (the corporation, government, or municipality) pays you interest at a rate you've agreed upon for a certain number of months or years (the term). Once the term ends, you get your principal back. As long as you hold your bond to the end of its term, you are guaranteed to get both your interest and principal. This is why bonds are less risky than stocks. If you need to get out before the term is up, however, you may get less or more than you originally paid for the bond because of fluctuations in the market.

bond fund: A mutual fund that invests in bonds. It is very difficult for individual investors with less than, say, $50,000 to invest to put together a diversified portfolio of bonds on their own. Bond mutual funds are a more appropriate choice for most people. You can pick bond mutual funds that are very low-risk (short- and ultra-short-term bond funds) or those that have moderate to high risk (high-yield bond funds). Or you can pick a total bond market index fund, which will cover all your bases at once.

broker (brokerage firm): A person or company licensed to sell investments, including stocks, bonds, and mutual funds. You can open an IRA at your brokerage firm.

capital gain: The money you make when you sell an investment—such as stock, a mutual fund, or real estate—for more than you paid for it. A capital gain is taxed differently than the money you make on the job, which is called "earned income."

cash-value life insurance: A life insurance policy with an investment account attached. There are many forms of cash-value life insurance, including whole life, universal life, variable life, and second-to-die life. All of these forms are more expensive than term insurance, which, once it terminates, has no value to the policyholder.

CD (certificate of deposit): A bank investment that pays you a specific rate of interest for locking up your money for a particular period of time—generally 3 months, 6 months, 12 months, 2 years, 5 years, or 10 years. The longer you are willing to let the bank hold your money, the higher your interest rates are likely to be. If you take your money out before the CD comes due, you face a penalty and lose some of your interest.

Consumer Price Index (CPI): A cost-of-living index used by the government to measure inflation.

credit report: A snapshot of your past credit behavior. The word *snapshot* is deceiving because your credit report can actually go on for pages and pages. Although items on your credit report can be seven to ten years old (depending on what they are), the most important period of time is the most recent twenty-four months. That's what lenders look at most closely when trying to determine whether or not you're a good credit risk.

credit score: A numerical representation of your credit report. Credit scores range from 350 to 800. Anything over 660 is a good credit score. Anything over 720 is a great credit score.

defined benefit plan: A pension plan that pays regular sums of money to retired employees, generally for life.

defined contribution plan: A 401(k) or 403(b). Employers sponsor defined contribution plans, but they do not own them. Each employee owns—and contributes to—her or his own account. Employers may match dollars if they choose. At retirement, employees can begin withdrawing money from their defined contribution plans at age 59 1/2 and must begin withdrawing money at age 70 1/2. While the money is in the account, employees have discretion over how it is invested.

diversification: Spreading out the risk in your portfolio (or investments) by investing in a variety of stocks, bonds, cashlike investments, real estate, or other investments; often referred to—even by people on Wall Street—as not putting all your eggs in one basket. Once your asset allocation plan is complete—for example, you know what percentage you want in stocks and what percentage in bonds—then you must diversify within those categories by putting money into different kinds of stocks and bonds. Certain mutual funds offer instant diversification.

durable power of attorney for finances: A document by which you give another person the right to make financial decisions—including writing checks and trading stocks—on your behalf if you become unable to do so for yourself.

durable power of attorney for health care: A document by which you give another person the right to make health-related decisions on your behalf if you are incapacitated and unable to do so for yourself. Also called a *health-care proxy.*

earnings per share (EPS): The amount of money a company earns per publicly traded share of stock.

equity: Your ownership stake in an investment, business, or piece of property. In the case of a home, your equity is the value of the house minus your mortgage.

estate plan: A legal strategy for passing on your assets (and, these days, ideals) to your heirs. A basic estate plan includes a will, living will, health-care proxy (durable power of attorney for health care), and durable power of attorney for finances.

executor: The person you select to settle your estate.

Federal Reserve: The U.S. central bank. It has the power to manipulate short-term interest rates. For years, the Federal Reserve was run by Fed chairman Alan Greenspan. His successor, named in 2005, is Ben Bernanke. (These are names you'll hear at cocktail parties. It's good to know them.) The stock market reacts to interest rate hikes or reductions orchestrated by the Fed. When rates go up, the market tends to go down because money has become more expensive not only for you and me to borrow but for big corporations to borrow. When rates go down, the effect is generally the opposite (although interest rate moves have the opposite effect on some types of companies—banks, for instance).

financial planner (financial adviser): An individual who will help you manage your investments. Comprehensive financial advisers will also help you make decisions about insurance, taxes, college planning, retirement planning, and all other aspects of your financial life. Financial planners are compensated in various ways: by commission (when they purchase investments on your behalf), by the hour, by the plan, or by a percentage of the assets you've given them to manage for you. Fee-only financial planners do not work on commission for putting you into particular investments; therefore they tend to be more objective about which investments are best for you. For that reason, I prefer them. Commission-based planners have to consider which investments are best for you and that may conflict with which put the fattest commissions in their own pockets.

fixed rate: An interest rate on a debt or an investment that doesn't vary no matter what direction interest rates or the market moves. A 30-year fixed-rate mortgage offers this sort of stability; your payments are the same in year 30 as they are in year 1. Some credit cards also offer fixed rates. Home equity loans are fixed, but home equity lines of credit are not (they are variable, which means the interest rates move).

401(k) plan: An employer-sponsored retirement savings plan. Employees contribute their own money—through direct paycheck withdrawals—to the plan. Their contribution is often matched to some degree by the employer. The money grows tax-deferred until retirement, at which point it can be withdrawn. Unlike an IRA, a 401(k) can be borrowed from.

403(b) plan: Similar to a 401(k) plan for educational institutions and not-for-profit employers.

457 plan: Similar to a 401(k) plan for government employees.

fraction: A piece of the whole represented as a quotient—for example, ½ or ⅓. The top number of the fraction is called the *numerator,* the bottom number the *denominator.*

gross income: Income before taxes are taken out.

health-care proxy: A document by which you give another person the right to make health-related decisions on your behalf if you are incapacitated and unable to do so for yourself. Also called a *durable power of attorney for health care.*

hedge fund: A pool of money that is invested in order to make a profit in any market. Managers of hedge funds use very risky strategies in order to accomplish their goals. The minimums tend to be quite high (six figures or more). These funds are appropriate only for wealthy individuals. If you have read so much about people profiting from hedge funds that you're determined to get a piece of this action, look for a mutual fund that invests in hedge funds (a "fund of funds"), and invest a small percentage of your overall portfolio—10 percent, max.

home equity line of credit: A form of second mortgage—a line of credit that is secured by the value of your home. You get a set amount of money, then draw it down when you need to use it. Home equity lines are better than home equity loans for projects (or college) for which you don't need the money in one lump sum. The drawback is that the rates on home equity lines, unlike home equity loan rates, are variable, which means that payback could cost you more than anticipated. The interest on both home equity loans and lines of credit is generally tax-deductible, just like mortgage interest.

home equity loan: A loan that is secured (just like your first mortgage) by the value of your home. Home equity loans are fixed-rate loans. Also called a *second mortgage*.

I-bond: A bond that is indexed to keep pace with inflation. If you are worried that inflation is going to shoot up and eat away too much of your overall investment returns, I-bonds provide a way to minimize this risk.

income: The money you have coming in. You can derive income from your work. Your salary, commissions, and bonuses are all forms of income. Some investments (bonds, stocks with dividends, annuities) also provide income.

index fund: A mutual fund—or pool of investments, stocks, or bonds—that invests in order to mirror the returns of a particular market index (a group of stocks or bonds that is tracked on a daily basis). The most popular index is the S&P 500, a group of 500 large-company stocks. Other indexes include the Russell 2000 (2,000 small-company stocks) and the Wilshire 5000 (considered a total-market index). There are bond market index funds as well as international stock market index funds. Indexing is so popular that there are index funds for just about every purpose. One benefit of index funds is that because they include a *predetermined* basket of stocks or bonds, there's very little human involvement. Because there's no need to pay a fund manager a ton of money in order to maximize performance, fees and expenses tend to be quite low.

inflation: The overall increase in prices of goods and services as measured by the government. Inflation has averaged 3.8 percent a year since the 1980s but has been lower than that for the past few years.

interest: The amount of money you earn on a savings or investment vehicle, usually expressed in percentage terms. It is helpful to know how often the interest is calculated. If you're earning it, more frequently is preferable. If you're paying it, less is.

interest rate: Generally, the prime rate, or cost of funds rate, set by the Federal Reserve Open Market Committee.

IRA (Individual Retirement Account): A retirement account in which the money grows tax-deferred until you retire. You can set up an IRA with most banks and brokerage firms and then invest the money you put into the account as you choose. The limits on the amount of money you can put into an IRA go up slightly each year. *See also* rollover IRA; Roth IRA; spousal IRA.

large cap: Stocks (or companies) with a market capitalization (the total value of a company's outstanding shares) of $5 billion or more.

level premium (life insurance): A term-life insurance policy for which the premiums are the same over the life span of the policy, generally up to twenty or thirty years.

leverage: A means of investing that lets you put up a small amount of money in exchange for controlling a much larger asset. In real estate investing, you can use a small down payment (or even no down payment these days) to finance the purchase of an expensive home. Investors also use leverage to purchase other sorts of assets when they don't have (or don't want to put up) much of their own money. If your assumption is correct—that the asset you're investing in will be worth more tomorrow than it is today—using leverage is a smart thing to do. That's why leveraging is not considered all that risky when you are buying a home, because the real estate market has been fairly consistent long-term. But if you're wrong and an asset tanks, leveraging can magnify your losses.

liabilities: Your debts, or the money you owe.

living trust: A revocable trust that you fund during your lifetime (or enable your will to fund at your death). Any assets placed into a living trust do not have to go through probate. For some people in some states (or for people who own property in more than one state), probate can be an expensive and tedious process, so avoiding it is an advantage. Also, when a will is probated, it becomes public. If you have a living trust, the minutiae of what you're leaving to whom is more likely to remain under wraps. That said, living trusts can cost thousands of dollars, and they're often sold heavy-handedly to people (particularly seniors) who really don't need them.

living will: A document that tells a doctor, hospital, or other medical institution whether or not you want life support.

load: The sales charge on the purchase of a mutual fund.

market capitalization: The total value of a company's outstanding shares.

medical directive: A blanket term for living wills and health-care proxies.

mid cap: Stocks (or companies) with a market capitalization of between $1 billion and $5 billion.

money market account: A bank account that offers a return that's generally a little better than a plain vanilla savings account. Some money market accounts are a little less liquid than savings or checking accounts with limited check-writing privileges. Others have higher minimum-balance requirements. Money market accounts provide the same FDIC insurance as bank accounts for deposits of up to $100,000. To find the best money market account rates, search online at bankrate.com.

money market fund: Mutual funds that invest in very short-term, very safe investments and seek to maintain a value of $1 a share at all times. Money market funds don't offer a lot of upside as far as return (for the last few years returns have been in the low single digits), but they do offer a lot of safety, which makes them a good parking place for your emergency cushion and for money you haven't quite decided where to invest. Unlike money market accounts, money market funds do not receive FDIC protection.

mutual fund: Pools of different kinds of assets (there are stock mutual funds, bond mutual funds, and funds that mix both in different variations) that are sold—like stocks—by the share. Mutual funds offer the ability to buy multiple stocks and bonds with a single transaction, which makes them more diversified and generally less risky (although there are some high-risk categories of mutual funds) than buying stocks or bonds one at a time.

net income: Income after taxes and Social Security. Also called *take-home pay*.

net worth: Your value (on paper), measured as all of your assets minus all of your liabilities.

online banking: Using the Internet to pay bills, check account balances, and conduct other banking actions. It is so much cheaper for banks to have you bank this way instead of using their tellers and drive-through windows that many offer online banking and bill paying for free—which can save you nearly $100 in stamps in a year!

price/earnings ratio (P/E): The current price of a stock divided by its most recent earnings. One way to gauge how much investors are willing to pay for a particular stock is to compare its P/E to the P/Es of other stocks in its category. If most pharmaceutical companies, for instance, are trading at a P/E of 15 and you're looking at a company with a P/E of 20, that's a sign that the company is expensive. If you're looking at one with a P/E of 10, that's a sign the company is undervalued. Note: The price-earnings ratio is only one indication of the value of a stock. Before you purchase any individual stock, you should do considerable research.

prospectus: An offering document designed to sell shares of stocks or mutual funds to the public. Prospectuses contain information about a company or mutual fund: who is running or managing it, what its goals and objectives are, and the underlying risks of this particular investment. Always read the prospectus before you invest in a stock or a mutual fund.

rollover IRA: An Individual Retirement Account opened when you change jobs or retire and funded with assets being moved from a 401(k) or other employer-based retirement plan. The benefit of rolling over is that you can move money directly from a 401(k) into an IRA without facing taxes and penalties, and enable your money to continue to grow tax-deferred until retirement.

Roth IRA: An Individual Retirement Account funded with money on which you've already paid taxes. The money grows tax-free. When you withdraw it at retirement, no additional taxes are owed. Roth IRAs are more flexible than traditional IRAs in that you can withdraw contributions at any time. After the money has been in the account for five years, you can withdraw earnings to pay for education or your first house.

small cap: Stocks (or companies) with a market capitalization of $250 million to $1 billion. A company with a market capitaliztion of less than $250 million is called a "microcap."

spousal IRA: An Individual Retirement Account established for a spouse who doesn't have income of his or her own. Contributions into this account have the same limits each year as those for the spouse in the workforce.

stock: A share of ownership in a company that is publicly traded. You make money in stocks if the price goes up during the time you own your shares. You may also make money if the stocks you buy pay a quarterly dividend, as many utility stocks do.

stock fund: A mutual fund comprised mostly of stocks. Note: Some stock funds own bonds as well as other investments in order to hedge their bets. That's one reason it's important to read the prospectus to know what you're getting before you buy it.

term-life insurance: A life insurance policy that consists solely of a death benefit. You buy the policy for a particular period of time. When that period—the term—ends, you no longer have the coverage and no longer have to pay the premiums.

variable rate: An interest rate on a credit card, home equity line, or other loan that is not fixed but fluctuates with changes, most often, in the prime rate. Rates may also vary with other indexes like the LIBOR or COFI, so read the fine print to be sure you know what you're getting.

will: A legal document that transfers ownership of your property and assets to your heirs. A will is the only document that can be used to name guardians for minor children.

$$$$$$$ ACKNOWLEDGMENTS $$$$$$$

With every book, I gain a greater understanding of how fortunate I am to be surrounded by incredible friends and colleagues who have my back at all times. Specifically: Thank you to my agent, Richard Pine; my publicist, Heidi Krupp; and my attorney, Rich Heller, who help point me in the right directions and regularly work miracles on my behalf. Thank you to Heather Jackson of Crown, who took this book and made it better, and to the rest of the Crown team—Steve Ross, Kristin Kiser, Philip Patrick, Tina Constable, Tara Gilbride, and Donna Passannante—who went above and beyond to make it a success. Thank you to Richard Liebner, George Hiltzik, and the rest of the team at NS Bienstock. Thank you to Wally Konrad and Amanda Gengler, who bailed me out of more than one jam. Thank you to the members of my own personal Money Group: Diane Adler, Jan Fisher, Margie Alley, Debi Fried, and Elaine Sherman. Thank you to my *Today* show family—Jim Bell, Amy Rosenblum, Patricia Luchsinger, Marc Victor, Robin Sherman, Paul Manson, Betsy Alexander, Jackie Levin, Matt Lauer, Al Roker, and Ann Curry—for being so supportive of all I do. And to my new friends at Harpo—Oprah Winfrey, Ellen Rakatien, Katy Davis, Candi Carter, Bridgette Theriault, and Harriet Seitler—for embracing my mission and making it your own. Thank you to the many people in my life—some personal, some professional—who keep me focused, on track, and (oh, yeah) happy. Your fingerprints may not be all over this book, but it would not be the same (or finished) without you: Eliot Kaplan, Lisa Greene, Susan Walker, Anna Callendar, Ryan D'Agostino, Rob Densen, Bob Safian, Roberta Socolof, Rochelle Schaeffer, Craig Matters, Andy Denemark, Dan Dunaief, Eric Schurenberg, Gary Greenwald, Kaja Gam, Ken Skalski, Kelly Kramer, and Jeff Bieber. Finally, to my family, Eric Sherman and Gabrielle Roventini, Dave Sherman and Ali Kettlewell, Rosa and Bernie Meyers, and Steve and Ilene Miller, and, of course, to my children, Jake and Julia, with love; I am so very proud of the incredible people you've become.

Jean Chatzky, award-winning journalist, bestselling author, and motivational speaker, has created a global platform that is making significant strides to help millions of men and women battle an epidemic with a devastating impact—debt. She is the financial editor for NBC's *Today* show; a contributing editor for *Money* and *Travel + Leisure* magazines; a columnist for *The New York Daily News;* and is a featured money coach on Oprah's "Debt Diet" series, which became one of the most highly watched series on *The Oprah Winfrey Show* this season. She hosts a nationally syndicated daily radio program, *Talking Money with Jean Chatzky,* and is the author of four books, including *The Ten Commandments of Financial Happiness.* Her last book, *Pay It Down: From Debt to Wealth on $10 a Day,* is a *New York Times* and *BusinessWeek* bestseller. Hundreds of thousands of people receive free daily money tips and advice from Jean in her daily e-mail newsletter, available at JeanChatzky.com.

Jean has been recognized as an exceptional journalist. She received the Clarion Award for magazine columns from the Association of Women in Communications, has been twice nominated for National Magazine Awards, and was named one of the best magazine columnists by the *Chicago Tribune.*

In addition to her professional work, Jean is on the March of Dimes advisory council, lends her support and expertise to women's services groups, and is on the board of the Nora Magid Mentorship Prize at the University of Pennsylvania, which helps journalism students get a head-start in the field. She is also on the communications committee for the University of Pennsylvania.

Jean lives with her family in Westchester County, New York.